Yours in Jesus
C H Spurgeon

MINISTER OF NEW PARK STREET CHAPEL, SOUTHWARK

"THE MODERN WHITFIELD."

SERMONS

OF THE

REV. C. H. SPURGEON,

OF LONDON;

WITH AN

INTRODUCTION AND SKETCH OF HIS LIFE,

BY E. L. MAGOON.

NEW YORK:
SHELDON, BLAKEMAN AND COMPANY.
CHICAGO: S. C. GREGGS AND COMPANY.
RICHMOND: WORTHAM AND COTRELL.
BURLINGTON, IOWA: H. H. HAWLEY.
1856.

LITHOTYPED BY THE AMERICAN STEREOTYPE COMPANY,
28 PHŒNIX BUILDING, BOSTON.

PRINTED BY D. S. FORD AND CO.

CONTENTS.

INTRODUCTION.

In perusing the present volume of Sermons, the reader will nowhere find their author rising in a chilling fog of lugubrious cant, or simpering out inane formalism after the following mode: "Dearly beloved brethren, and my esteemed and respected friends: Permit me to invite your serious and solemn attention to that portion of celestial truth which you will find recorded in the one hundred and seventy-seventh verse of the sixty-ninth chapter of Saint Ichabod's sixteenth epistle to the Simpletons." On the contrary, he comes directly before the people, impelled by something acutely felt, and which needs to be speedily uttered, so that he may, as soon as possible, pass on to a yet fresher and wider space, wherein he may think more and speak better to the accumulating crowds, who always press towards frank hearts and free lips. Without doubt, in this instance, we have to do with one who uses his own observing and reflecting powers, while he reverently seeks divine aid, and is as original in his conceptions as he is untrammeled in their utterance. Let us glance at the biography of our preacher, the scene of his preaching, and the chief elements of his power.

Rev. C. H. Spurgeon was born at Kelvedon, in Essex, on the 19th of June, 1834. His father and grandfather are both living, and are Independent ministers. It is further stated in the London "Patriot," that the subject of this sketch received his early education at Colchester, and also passed a year in the Agricultural College at Maidstone, where he added to his previous knowledge some insight into natural science. Thus equipped, he began the business of life as usher in a school at Newmarket; whence he removed to Cambridge, where he held a similar appointment in a day school, employing the ampler leisure thus secured in improving his own mind. While at Newmarket,he began to address the Sunday-school children, and that in such a style as attracted grown-up hearers. At Cambridge the practice was continued, with the addition of Sunday evening sermons in the surrounding villages. The Baptist church, at Waterbeach, called this young Timothy to be their pastor. He accepted the invitation; and, while the chapel was crowded, the church was doubled under his ministry. On the week-days, eleven villages shared the advantage of his sermons, which, in one year, amounted to as many as there are days in the year. In January, 1854, Mr. Spurgeon was invited to undertake the pastorate of the Baptist church in New Park street. Not content with discharging the duties of that office, he preaches in many other places during the week.

New Park street Chapel stands on the Surrey side of the Thames, near Southwark Bridge, a locality which the untravelled hereabouts will better understand by being told that it almost exactly corresponds with the Brooklyn end of Catherine Ferry. It was on this spot that the great expositor Gill, and the hymnologist Rippon, preached and sung to successive generations long before the advent of the present popular preacher and his immense auditory. The edifice now occupied is a plain and substantial one, with a portico of eight debased Ionic columns, in pairs, carrying a heavy romanesque story, and otherwise nearly as uncouth as modern church architecture in general, and "dissenting" chapels in particular. But, like its huge neighbor, Barclay and Perkins' brewery, it has the merit of great size, and certainly should be regarded as of much more salutary use.

As in almost all the great cities of Europe and America, the old and empty churches of London are at the east end, while all the thrift is "progressing" towards the west. But stiff.

formality remains inflexible to the last gasp in its ancient seats, where once a week a few pedestrians, in threadbare dignity, and a still smaller few powdered and puffing aristocrats, mounted in coaches of tarnished splendor, fantastically embellished by flunkeys in livery, scatter their pomposity in solitary quadrangles, on whose cushioned seats, in high-backed exclusiveness, they drowsily "assist" obsequious parsons, whose "livings," on Sundays at least, are in the midst of a most sparse population. But, before the first cobweb is brushed from private velvet by the pew unlockers of antiquated churches, the vast area of compact seats in this chapel at New Park street is besieged by eager and oft-recurring crowds. Says a visitor: "Proceed thither, as the writer did on Sabbath evening, the 23d of September, and you will find all the avenues to the chapel thronged with people, although it may be half an hour before the time for the commencement of the service. If you should chance to be admitted by the side door, you will find the building already three-parts filled, and feel some compassion for those who are waiting for admission, but are certain not to get in. At twenty minutes past six the front doors are opened, and a rush commences; but it is speedily over, for the chapel is full; not only the seats, but every inch of standing room being occupied, and the gates have to be closed, with several hundred people outside. Mr. Spurgeon then ascends the pulpit, and reads the hymn which is to be sung, prefacing it, if the circumstances admit, with some striking remark, which at once arrests the attention of his audience. The special Sunday evening alluded to here, he began: 'We will sing a battle hymn to-night, friends, to stir our spirits,' and then went on:

'Am I a soldier of the cross,
A follower of the Lamb;
And shall I fear to own his cause,
Or blush to speak his name?'
'Sure I must fight if I would reign,' &c.

"The hymn concluded, which was sung by the entire audience,

and with proper spirit; although, as might be expected, with little scientific ability, the occupant of the pulpit read the following passages of Holy Writ, and gave utterance to the accompanying popular exposition."

The singing may not have been performed with the exquisitely insipid elegance which characterizes the majority of our quartette choirs, whose extraordinary "execution" is a poor compensation for the death of all the vital power and moral profit of sacred song. Good singing is more divine than poor preaching, and the former is expressed only in the sympathetic tones of an entire congregation, however diversified; just as the latter is sure to drizzle down from pulpit heights with most stultifying effect, when the whole soul of the speaker, if he has one, is forced to employ only a few feeble muscles about the front teeth, instead of a simultaneous utterance through the whole body, mind, and heart. What do those thousands of earnest, honest, and eager worshippers care for incomprehensible demi-semiquavers of operatic fancies at one end of the sanctuary? They feel that, when secular days with their exhausting toils are past, Heaven vouchsafes to them, creatures of an immortality, as well as unto beasts of the field and birds of the air, the privilege of making melodious the blessed day of rest; and they come before the Lord with singing, that they may breathe forth their own notes of gladness — inartificial it may be, but sincere nevertheless.

The preliminary exposition is not less profound, nor lacking in practicalness, because of its popular form. We have perused many specimens of such, and can easily conceive the sublime aspect presented by that sea of upturned faces, and the thrilling interest with which each rousing or subduing sentence is heard, as it stings the obdurate with aphoristic pungency, or, with melting pathos, soothes gentler souls. In such circumstances, there is no disposition to scan fine combinations of words, nor does the aroused listener pause to estimate the relative value of more material grandeurs. Chaste architecture and choice melody are by no means incompatible with efficient ministrations at God's altar; but there is great danger lest the ambition which covets adventitious attractions around evangelical worship, should gradually become content to see the blandishments of art exhibited, rather than cause the naked truth to be enforced. And especially is such danger imminent in this country, where monumental falsehood abounds in the edifices we dedicate to the true God. In storehouses for traffic and the vehicles of commerce we are original, and in the van of nations, because our endeavors are really earnest in that direction; but in church-building, especially in large towns, we are merely imitative, and earth groans under absurd abortions, being burdened. Every petty organization professing primitive humility, has its special symbol of structural pride, usually built in the "Ionic style," with classical colonnades, surmounted by feudal towers, and blank walls relieved with inextricable labyrinths of suggestive arcades and long-drawn aisles. The chief aspiration appears to aim at an immense perspective back of the pulpit, where fresco daubs are tortured into unmitigated mendacity, at least sixty yards long in appearance, and which seems designed to illustrate the correctness of outline and justness of tone which characterize the learned length of much modern preaching. Worse still, if it be possible, is the vitiating influence of our ignorant and ridiculous attempts at "Gothic" building. Buttresses of painted brick, foliated spaces of dirty plaster, canopies of crumbling stucco, and white-pine turrets grinning on the exterior; and pillars, arches, groinings inside, without the shadow of one true foliation or accurate moulding, from sham pavements to embossed roofs, all shams as well, painted to imitate stones the most solid and woods the most rare, are not only tolerated, but ignorantly admired, by our upper circles; so that you often meet entire churches, of the first importance, covered all over, without and within, with nothing but structural falsehoods, an aggregate of base and degrading ecclesiological lies. We have no space in this connection to treat the miserable influence of perverted and prostituted architecture as it deserves, but will only add the following suggestion. Go through the entire Christian world, and you will find that the moral power of any given congregation will be nearly in an inverse ratio to the amount of counterfeited art in the place of their assembling; and that the stupidity of their preacher will bear an exact proportion to the soft thickness and florid ostentation of the pulpit decorations.

Having thus briefly glanced at Mr. Spurgeon's biography, and the scene of his stated labors, let us proceed to notice more particularly the elements of his professional influence. If we mistake not, he is pre-eminently intelligent, independent, and honest in purpose, as a servant of Jesus Christ; and, so long as he remains such, no degree of success, however great, ought to be regarded as being either wonderful or dangerous.

In the first place, Mr. Spurgeon is an intelligent man. His personal influence implies this, and his published works prove it. Fools abound, it is true; but it is hard to find a whole community of them, even in London or New York. Religious people may not always acquire the most ponderous erudition; but such knowledge as they do possess, is of a sort the least likely to be imposed upon by a charlatan. The heart of a humble disciple of Jesus is more sagacious than the head of any unsanctified philosopher; it will sooner revolt from plausible imbecility, and most tenaciously cleave to the supreme excellence it adores. Heaven vouchsafed the effulgence of lofty science for the guidance which benighted Magi required; but the more ethereal wisdom of lowly shepherds at the same time poured light upon their unfaltering feet, and recognized angelic tidings from the sublimest skies.

Mr. Spurgeon began the assiduous study of books at an early period, and evidently has ever since been a comprehensive reader of whatever he deems of practical use. But he did not heap books so high about his boyhood as to exclude nature from a loving and ennobling view. Every realm of elegance and grandeur has been laid under contribution to enlarge and embellish his intellect. Hence the richness and variety of illustration which so much enhance the beauty and force of his public discourse. In body and mind, he appears redolent of health; and this has resulted mainly from habitual intercourse with natural charms. His studies at Colchester, and in the Agricultural College at Maidstone, doubtless did much to feed his ardent love of learning, and, especially, to enlarge his knowledge of natural science. As usher in the school at Newmarket, and afterwards, while acquitting himself of like functions at Cambridge, he accumulated no small amount of literary treasure; but his best acquisitions were secured in the early and accurate knowledge of human nature, which, through juvenile discipline in diversified life, Providence caused him to possess. He was no pet of indulgent fortune, familiarized with golden spoons, and fondled in the lap of effeminate ease. Nor was he cautiously secluded in the hot-house of supercilious pedantry, to eat and sleep out a regular course of *hic, hæc, hoc,* with the plus excellence of sines and cosines, under the auspices of some erudite ignoramus, whose potency for turning the world upside down himself, and whose aptness to teach others how such work is done, consists mainly in a diminutive quantity of antique roots in a perfumed head, a pair of green spectacles on a pimpled nose, and two lily hands buried near dyspeptic bowels. Nor was our "candidate for holy orders" blessed with the three years of consummate sermonizing, which usually succeeds the seven years of classical perfectness. Instead of all this, the young athlete was dashing at every barrier to liberal culture, exploring every source of sound wisdom, and fitting to each faculty and limb the rugged but flexible armor best suited to the varied necessities of a practical life.

Before he left Cambridge, while the dignitaries of the university and town were enjoying their lettered content, Mr. Spurgeon was wont frequently to address Sunday-schools, in season and out of season — to visit the neighboring villages, where descending day, as well as opening morn, found him still busy in refreshing the weary and spiritually destitute. Young as this Timothy was when the Baptist church at Waterbeach called him to the pastorate, he not only statedly met the claims of his own particular flock, but eleven other communities shared in his weekly ministrations, amongst whom he is said to have preached as many extra sermons as there are days in the year. Such an alumnus, we think, graduates with pretty high honors, and goes forth to his life-battle limited to the efficacy of no puny pocket-pistol of one barrel, loaded and discharged only by routine, and of too small a calibre to either kick or hit hard. Turks inscribe the choicest sentences of the Koran upon their swords, that the most important maxims of their religion may be illustrated in the closest alliance with effective blows. What right have you to boast of your sheepskin diploma, and claim precedence in the ranks of honor on account of college privileges, if your parent or patron, who paid dearly for the same, can say of the result only as Aaron once lamented with vain regret, — "I cast gold into the fire, and there came out this calf?" All honor to the generous founders and accomplished teachers of colleges; but let no one, in or out of them, claim respect any further than, with his own brains and heart, he proves himself to be respectable. How much *can do* stands in your boots? If any, go ahead; but if none, then shut up. True education does not resemble the passive process of a medicinal bath — something soaked in; it is mind educed — led forth. The candidate for the sacred ministry, or who is destined to any other sphere of professional life, that does not early form the habit, and persistingly exercise the right, of making books, schools, professors, and all their appliances his own, by an overmastering subordination to self-development, will never be of more utility than a milliner's show-block, bearing a constant change of fashions outside, and nothing original within; useful only while invested by the industry of others, and even at the best but a simple blockhead still.

Read some of Mr. Spurgeon's statements touching his early education, which at once assert the source of its greatest worth, and exemplify the beauty of its blessed influence. Says he: "When I hear sweet syllables fall from many lips, keeping measure and time, then I feel elevated, and, forgetting for a time every being terrestrial, I soar aloft towards heaven." He represents himself as having "delighted in the musty old folios which many of his brethren have upon their library shelves," and, "as for new books, he leaves them to others." To the Bible, he ascribes the discipline of his mental faculties, as well as his knowledge of divine truth. Once, he declares, he put all his knowledge together in glorious confusion; but now he has a shelf in his head for everything, and, whatever he reads or hears, he knows where to stow it away. "Ever since I have known Christ, I have put Christ in the centre as my sun, and each secular science revolves around it as a planet, while the minor sciences are satellites to their planets." He can learn everything now; and, from his own experience, he exhorts thus: "O young man! build thy studio on Calvary! There raise thine observatory, and scan, by faith, the lofty things of nature! Take thee a hermit's cell in the garden of Gethsemane, and lave thy brow with the waters of Siloa!" In one of his sermons, he remarks that "the man of one book is often more intelligent than the man of fifty." In recommending pointed preaching, he makes a remark, which illustrates his own habit of wide wandering for material, connected with the power of sudden and concentrated use. "It is not the sheet lightning, seen in all places, that takes effect; but it is the forked flash that smites the temple, or scorches the tree." Another remark sets forth the spontaneity of this rare preacher's thoughts, and the graceful freshness with which they emanate from his heart and lips. "There is much virtue which is like the juice of the grape, which has to be squeezed before you get it; not like the generous drop of the honeycomb, distilling willingly and freely."

It is justly remarked, by an English critic, that the "manly tone of Mr. Spurgeon's mind might be illustrated from the admirable thoughts which he expresses on the connection between the diffusion of the gospel and the increase of civil liberty. His graphic skill in delineating character, might be demonstrated from his life-like pictures of the prejudiced Jew and the scoffing Greek of modern times; his unsparing fidelity, from the sarcastic severity with which he rebukes the neglect of the Bible by modern professors; his powers of personification and dramatic presentation, from the scene which he paints between the dying Christian and death, or between Christ and justice, and the justified sinner; his refined skill in the treatment of a delicate subject, in the veiled yet impressive description of the trial of Joseph; the use that he can make of a single metaphor, by his powerful comparison of the sinner to 'Mazeppa, bound on the wild horse of his lust, galloping on with hell's wolves behind him,' till stopped and liberated by a Mighty Hand." It is indeed well for the church and world that, "somehow, God does choose the last men; he does not care for the diamond, but he picks up the pebble-stones; for he is able, out of stones, to raise up children unto Abraham." Many other instances might be given, which indicate the most diversified and delicate observation. "Bright-eyed cheerfulness and airy-footed love," are among his fine phrases. Winter is described as not killing the flowers, but as "coating them with the ermine of its snows." Again, the sun is not quenched, but is behind the clouds, "brewing up summer; and, when he cometh forth again, he will have made those clouds fit to drop in April showers, all of them mothers of the sweet May flowers." Saul is depicted as "bespattered with the blood of Stephen." God "puts our prayers, like rose-leaves, between the pages of his book of remembrance; and, when the volume is opened at last, there shall be a precious fragrance springing up therefrom." "There is one thing," the sinner is told, "that doth outstrip the telegraph: 'Before they call, I will answer;

and, while they are yet speaking, I will hear.'" The memory infected by the fall is described as "suffering the glorious timbers from the forest of Lebanon to swim down the stream of oblivion; but she stopped all the drift that floateth from the foul city of Sodom." It is in no feeble diction that the preacher speaks of the lightning "splitting the clouds and rending the heavens"; of "the Mighty Hand wherein the callow comets are brooded by the sun;" and of the very spheres stopping their music while God speaks with his wondrous deep bass voice." Sometimes he attains a still more impressive grandeur, as when he exclaims: "Did you ever walk the centuries, and mark the rise and fall of various empires of unbelief"? or, when supposing the extinction of Christianity by infidels, he would "hang the world in mourning, and make the sea the chief mourner, with its dirge of howling winds, and its wild death-march of disordered waves."

But no single passage will better indicate the nature and spirit of Mr. Spurgeon's education, than the following extract from his sermon on "The People's Christ." It is not reprinted entire in the present volume, since it has been so much mutilated by the fragments thence derived to redeem the poverty of our introduction. The preacher affirms that "Jesus Christ was one of the people in his doctrine. His gospel never was the philosopher's gospel, for it is not abstruse enough. It will not consent to be buried in hard words and technical phrases: it is so simple, that he who can spell over, 'He that believeth and is baptized shall be saved,' may have a saving knowledge of it. Hence, worldly-wise men scorn the science of truth, and sneeringly say, 'why, even a blacksmith can preach now-a-days, and men who were at the plough-tail may turn preachers'; while priestcraft demands, 'What right have they to do any such thing, unauthorized by us'? O! sad case that gospel truth should be slighted because of its plainness, and that my Master should be despised because he will not be exclusive — will not be monopolized by men of talent and erudition. Jesus is the ignorant man's Christ as much as the learned man's Christ; for he hath chosen 'the base things of the world, and the things that are despised.' Ah! much as I love true science and real education, I mourn and grieve that our ministers are so much diluting the Word of God with philosophy, desiring to be intellectual preachers, delivering model sermons, well fitted for a room full of college students and professors of theology, but of no use to the masses, being destitute of simplicity, warmth, earnestness, or even solid gospel matter. I fear our college training is but a poor gain to our churches, since it often serves to wean the young man's sympathies from the people, and wed them to *the few*, the intellectual, and wealthy of the church. It is good to be a fellow-citizen in the republic of letters, but better far to be an able minister of the kingdom of heaven. It is good to be able, like some great minds, to attract the mighty; but the more useful man will still be he, who, like Whitfield, uses 'market language'; for it is a sad fact that high places and the gospel seldom well agree; and, moreover, be it known, that the doctrine of Christ is the doctrine of the people. It was not meant to be the gospel of a caste, a clique, or any one class of the community. The covenant of grace is not ordered for men of one peculiar grade, but some of all sorts are included. A few there were of rich, that followed Jesus in his own day, as there are now. Mary, and Martha, and Lazarus were well to do, and there was the wife of Herod's steward, with some more of the nobility. These, however, were but a few: his congregation were made up of the lower orders, — the masses, the multitude. 'The common people heard him gladly'; and his doctrine was one which did not allow of distinction, but put all men as sinners naturally, on an equality in the sight of God. One is your father, 'one is your master, even Christ, and all ye are brethren.' These were words which he taught to his disciples, while, in his own person, he was the mirror of humility, and proved himself the friend of earth's poor sons, and the lover of mankind. O ye purse proud! O ye who cannot touch the poor, even with your white gloves! Ah! ye with your mitres and your croziers! Ah! ye with your cathedrals and splendid ornaments! This is the man whom ye call Master — the people's Christ — one of the people! And yet ye look down with scorn upon the people — ye despise them. What are they in your opinion? *The common herd — the multitude.* Out on ye! Call yourselves no more the ministers of Christ. How can ye be, unless, descending from your pomp and your dignity, ye come amongst the poor, and visit them — ye come amongst our teeming population, and preach to them the gospel of Christ Jesus. We believe you to be the descendants of the fishermen? Ah! no, until ye doff your grandeur, and, like the fishermen, come out — the people's men — and preach to the people, speak to the people, instead of lolling on your splendid seats, and making yourselves rich at the expense of your pluralities! Christ's ministers should be the friends of manhood at large, remembering that their Master was the people's Christ. Rejoice, O rejoice, ye multitudes! Rejoice! rejoice! for Christ was one of the people."

Sometimes Mr. Spurgeon indulges in more copious allusions to classical incidents, which indicate the riches of mental stores at his command; but these are always employed in the same self-obvious subordination to the cause he pleads. Take the following example, from a beautiful sermon on the words: "And so He giveth his beloved sleep." It opens thus: "The sleep of the body is the gift of God. So said Homer of old, when he described it as descending from the clouds, and resting on the tents of the warriors around old Troy. And so sang Virgil, when he spoke of Palinurus falling asleep upon the prow of the ship. Sleep is the gift of God. We think that we lay our heads upon our pillows, and compose our bodies in a peaceful posture, and that, therefore, we naturally and necessarily sleep. But it is not so. Sleep is the gift of God; and not a man would close his eyes, did not God put his fingers on his eyelids — did not the Almighty send a soft and balmy influence over his frame, which lulled his thoughts into quiescence, making him enter into that blissful state of rest which we call sleep. True, there be some drugs and narcotics whereby men can poison themselves well nigh to death, and then call it sleep; but the sleep of the healthy body is the gift of God. He bestows it; he rocks the cradle for us every night; he draws the curtain of darkness; he bids the sun shut up his burning eyes; and then he comes and says: 'Sleep, sleep, my child! I give thee sleep.' Have you not known what it is, at times, to lay upon your bed and strive to slumber? And, as it is said of Darius, so might it be said of you: 'The king sent for his musicians, but his sleep went from him.' You have attempted it, but you could not do it; it is beyond your power to procure a healthy repose. You imagine, if you fix your mind upon a certain subject until it shall engross your attention, you will then sleep; but you find yourself unable to do so. Ten thousand things drive through your brain, as if the whole earth were agitated before you. You see all things you ever beheld, dancing in a wild phantasmagoria before your eyes. You close your eyes, but still you see; and there be things in your ear, and head, and brain, which will not let you sleep. It is God alone who alike seals up the sea-boy's eyes upon the giddy mast, and gives the monarch rest; for, with all appliances and means to boot, *he* could not rest without the aid of God. It is God who steeps the mind in Lethe, and bids us slumber, that our bodies may be refreshed, so that, for to-morrow's toil, we may rise recruited and strengthened. O, my friends, how thankful should we be for sleep! Sleep is the best physician that I know of. Sleep hath healed more pains of wearied bones than the most eminent physicians upon earth. It is the best medicine; the choicest thing of all the names which are written in the lists of pharmacy. There is nothing like to sleep! What a mercy it is that it belongs alike to all. God does not make sleep the boon of the rich man; he does not give it merely to the noble, or the rich, so that they can keep it a peculiar luxury for themselves; but he bestows it upon all. Yes, if there be a difference, the sleep of the laboring man is sweet, whether he eat little or much."

The best education is well stated by our preacher, when he says, that "nothing makes a man have a big heart like a great trial." And his own preparatory study is still further indicated, in a discourse on the immutability of God. "He who often thinks of God, will have a larger mind than he who simply plods around this narrow globe. He may be a naturalist, boasting of his ability to dissect a beetle, anatomize a fly, or arrange insects or animals in classes, with well nigh unutterable names; he may be a geologist, able to discourse of the megatherium and the plesiosaurus, and all kinds of extinct animals; he may imagine that his science, whatever it is, ennobles and enlarges his mind. I dare say it does; but, after all, the most excellent study for expanding the soul is the science of Christ and him crucified, and the knowledge of the Godhead in the glorious Trinity." Again, he says: "Talk of decrees? I will tell you of a decree — 'He that believeth not shall be damned.'"

The reader will probably regard the foregoing remarks as striking exponents of the natural intelligence possessed by Mr. Spurgeon, sufficiently illustrative of the early and varied culture he has acquired. We proceed, secondly, to array the proofs of what, in our judgment, is still more auspicious of professional success — his independence.

A preacher is not divinely called and elevated to be a facile weathercock, turned by the wind; but, like a tower of strength in scenes of danger, not less luminous than resolute, he is to turn the winds. It is fortunate for the interests of commerce, that the pharos-keeper is usually compelled, by the circumstances of his position, to trim his light alone, and pour its effulgence in his own undictated style. If all interested parties, on sea and shore, could but have their individual say as to the best mode of doing the business, a great cloud of impertinent advisers would soon extinguish both the light-master and his lamps. This is analogous to the effect produced on those theological students, whose tide of self-relying talent may never flood above the low water-mark of docile mediocrity. They go before their class, and its professor of homiletics, and submit a sermon for criticism. The most original thoughts will be the first condemned; on the same principle that, when several neighboring brethren preach at the same association, the dullest will be the most heartily congratulated by the rest, because he has least disturbed their stolid pride. Those who prefer to go on stilts, do not like the firm and forward tread of more intent travellers; but exhibit their nearest approach to manly energy in spasmodic denunciations of those who will not move as artificially as themselves.

Mr. Spurgeon exercises great influence in London, because he made his advent therein fresh from the quiet fields of accurate observation and independent thought. He seems to be more than willing to serve anybody, in any reasonable way, without the slightest air of assumption in his manner; but there does not happen to be cash or coercion enough in the great metropolis to create a particular track, in which alone he shall walk and talk. In a discourse on 1 John, v. 4, he says: "A very kind friend has told me, that, while I was preaching in Exeter Hall, I ought to pay deference to the varied opinions of my hearers; that, albeit I may be a Calvinist and a Baptist, I should recollect that there are a variety of creeds here. Now, if I were to preach nothing but what would please the whole lot of you, what on earth should I do? I preach what I believe to be true; and if the omission of a single truth that I believe would make me king of England throughout eternity, I would not leave it out. Those who do not like what I say, have the option of leaving it. They come here, I suppose, to please themselves; and, if the truth does not please them, they can leave it. I will never be afraid that an honest British audience will turn away from the man who does not stick, and stutter, and stammer, in speaking the truth. Well, now, about this great birth. I am going to say, perhaps, a harsh thing; but I heard it said by Mr. Jay first of all. Some say a new birth takes place in infant baptism; but I remember that venerable patriarch saying, 'Popery is a *lie*, Puseyism is a *lie*, baptismal regeneration is a *lie*.' So it is. It is a lie so palbable, that I can scarcely imagine the preachers of it have any brains in their heads at all. It is so absurd, upon the very face of it, that a man who believes it, puts himself below the range of a common-sense man. Believe that every child, by a drop of water, is born again! Then that man that you see in the ring, as a prize-fighter, is born again, because those sanctified drops once fell upon his infant forehead! Another man swears; behold him drunk, and reeling about the streets. He is born again! A pretty born again that is! I think he wants to be born again another time."

Perhaps nowhere on earth is reverence for wealth and the worship of rank so intense and all-pervading as throughout the realms of British mind. To strike boldly at that popular passion requires no small courage on the part of one who is dependent on voluntary support. But this deep cash-feeling, so especially influential in metropolitan society, is made to wince keenly under Mr. Spurgeon's sarcasm. "In England a sovereign will not speak to a shilling, a shilling will not notice a sixpence, and a sixpence will sneer at a penny." In a vivid dialogue respecting the cruelties practised on Jesus, the interlocutor, personated by the preacher, exclaims: "Why did you say, 'Crucify him'? 'Because Rabbi Simeon gave me a shekel to help the clamor.' So the multitude were much won by the money and influence of the priests; but they were glad to hear Christ, after all." And the last paragraph of the sermon on "The People's Christ," is as follows: "Ye proud ones! I have a word for you. Ye delicate ones, whose footsteps must not touch the ground. Ye who look down in scorn upon your fellow mortals—proud worms, despising your fellow-worms, because ye are somewhat more showily dressed! What think ye of this? The man of the people is to save you, if you are saved at all; the Christ of the crowd, the Christ of the mass, the Christ of the people—he is to be your Saviour! Thou must stoop, proud man! thou must bow, proud lady! thou must lay aside thy pomp, or else thou wilt ne'er be saved; for the Saviour of the people must be thy Saviour. But to the poor trembling sinner, whose pride is gone, I repeat the comforting assurance. Wouldst thou shun sin? Wouldst thou avoid the curse? My Master tells me to say this morning—'Come unto me, all ye that are weary and heavy laden, and I will give you rest.' I remember the saying of a good old saint. Some one was talking about the mercy and love of Jesus, and concluded by saying, 'Ah! is it not astonishing?' She said, 'No, not at all.' But they said it was. 'Why,' she said, 'it is just like him; it is just like him!' You say, can you believe such a thing of a person? 'Oh! yes,' it may be said, 'that is just his nature.' So you, perhaps, cannot believe that Christ would save you, guilty creature as you are. I tell you, it is just like him. He saved Saul—he saved me—he may save you. Yea, what is more, he *will* save you, for 'whosoever cometh unto him, he will in no wise cast out.'"

True independence of character is not stubbornness. Sound and useful oaks can bend to the softest zephyr, as well as resist the fiercest tornado; but rotten and hollow ones are most insensible to kindly influences, and the stiffest always. Mr. Spurgeon finds no difficulty in enjoying the amenities of social life, even to the utmost extent compatible with innocent hilarity. For instance, some five hundred of his friends chartered the good ship "Mars," and went down to "Rosherville," another "Staten Island," where they had a right nice time. The young pastor was called out for a speech, and he gave them a jolly account of a recent preaching tour in Scotland. A limpid current of genial humor always emanates from and flows fast by the granite foundation of superior character. The staid sons of the Doric North at first seemed to him to be all made of Wenham ice. "They could not understand my hot, fiery speeches at all, having been accustomed to hear dry disquisitions from learned Scottish divines. I knew that you must often enter the heart by ridicule. Tender hearts may be entered by pathos, but hard hearts must be touched by something telling and singular; so I thought I would make some of my singularities prominent, and say one or two of those things that you all know I do say now and then. I tried to provoke them to a smile, but they would not laugh, perhaps conceiving it to be a sin. I tried again, however, and I actually made one of them smile. Then I thought my triumph had begun. There came a shaking among the dry bones, and the dust came upon them. That dust, my hearers, was tobacco dust — snuff; for they passed their snuff-boxes round, and in a small wooden spoon they spooned the snuff to their noses. The Scotch are by far too 'cannie' to waste any of their snuff, so they use spoons for it instead of their fingers (laughter). As I progressed, I found the people began to be more moved; more snuff was taken; and I took it as a sign of their being really interested, when they began to pass their boxes every five minutes. At last, I saw that not only could they smile, but they could weep. When I began to tell them something about our Lord Jesus Christ, of him crucified, I found their hearts were moved, and their souls touched. I had only said those other things that I might by some means gain access to their hearts, and very gratified was I to find that some good had followed from what I said. Many persons know that on my road home I was exposed to a very imminent danger. I crossed the river Clyde in a ferry. The man who had the management of the boat had taken 'a wee drap o' the cratur,' and was not able to manage it at all; and had put twenty-six persons into a boat that had ought to have contained far less. I have been informed by one or two ladies that a report was current that I was thrown into the water and fished up by the hair of my head. Now, that was not so. We were simply in danger; but, by a little management and expostulation, which was resented by oaths and curses, we came safe to land—thanks to that God who, both on sea and land, cares for his people! I had engaged to preach at Bradford, in Yorkshire. I made first a journey to Lake Windermere, round which I sailed, and greatly enjoyed the beauties of its scenery. I went to Bradford; and on Sabbath morning I found that they had engaged the Music Hall, which holds, they say, a thousand persons more than Exeter Hall. Instead of being able to contain the crowds who came on the Sunday, about as many had to go away as were accommodated. In the evening, the streets presented a solid blockade of living men and women. The place was crammed to excess, and I had scarcely room to walk about to deliver what I had to say to the people. At the end of the day, I was delighted to find that not only had they been instructed, but they had given £144 towards the Sabbath-schools connected with the place at which I was engaged. From that place I went to Stockton-on-Tees, and there again preached the Word of God to a very numerous congregation. I journeyed on still further, to Edinburgh, and in Queen-street Hall, notwithstanding the most pouring rains, more crowds were assembled. There I was very much delighted, after the sermon, to meet with an officer of one of her majesty's regiments, who stepped up to me, and, taking me by the hand, said, 'For twenty years I have served her majesty, but never, until I first stepped into Dr. Wardlaw's chapel, at Glasgow, had I heard the Word of God to my profit. But now I am enlisted in the army of the King of kings. The Lord God of hosts bless you!—the King of kings be with you!—the God of Jacob help you everywhere!' I blessed the man, and I retired to rest, conscious that, if I had done nothing else, yet, perhaps, one of the heroes of the Crimea, who had not turned his back in the day of battle, was yet found to be numbered among the soldiers of the King of kings.

On the second Sabbath I preached again in Glasgow. In the morning I preached at Dr. Frazer's Independent chapel. There I found there was a necessity for a much larger chapel to hold all the people. They crowded everywhere; but I was still prepared to preach to them at Dr. King's chapel, the United Presbyterian. I found more people still. It held about 2500; and the editor of one of the papers told me that 20,000 persons went away, unable to obtain admission. Once more I received the help of my mighty Master, and there I preached his truth. Very much surprised was I to find, one morning, great bills sticking all about Glasgow, with these two announcements, in the largest type: 'The Rev. C. H. Spurgeon—the huge common sewer.' I wondered how I could be a 'huge common sewer;' and I could not understand the matter, till I found that in a certain paper there were two articles, one upon me, and the other upon the river Thames; and one, therefore, was called 'The Rev. C. H. Spurgeon,' and the other 'The huge common sewer.' (Laughter.) Whether I am a huge sewer or not, I cannot tell; all I know is, that it made the paper sell, and I suppose that is all the gentlemen of the press very often require. On the Thursday, on coming away, about a hundred persons came to meet me at the mansion of Mr. Anderson. There I bade them all farewell, with many expressions of regret that I should have to go away at all, under the promise that I would come once a year, backed up with Paddy's announcement, that once a year should be made every six months. (Laughter.) I have promised to go and see them once a year. They are a noble nation, and have treated me better than I deserve—surely it was for my Master's sake; and I hope when I shall go there again God Almighty will bless the services, and render them very effectual to the good of that people. I don't know how it is—I have never sought the applause of men—I speak to you now as I never spoke to any people in the world; I feel I am among my own family, and I have no reason to use reserve with you; I speak with you as I would not speak with the common people of the world—I know not how it is that I should be known. I suppose it is because the people of New Park-street are so good, that people think that I must be as good as they are. However, if God has given me any favor in the eyes of the people, it is for me to use that favor; not to be exalted above measure concerning it, but to thank God for it, and go on using it. No man can say worse things of me than have been said. No man can hurt my feelings by anything they say against me. They have said all that they ever can; and I shall always say, 'Borrowed, my lord,' after everything that may be said in future. One very good minister of the gospel tells me I never was converted; what I am now I shall be to the day of my death. I am extremely obliged to him for his charity; I love him very much for the information. However, I believe if I am not converted there is yet hope for me still, and I will try if I cannot find that hope in the blood of Jesus Christ. At the same time, no more good things can be said of me than have been said. While I am extremely obliged to my friends for all they say that is good concerning me, I would rather that they should leave me alone. I do not want anything good said of me at all. I have been puffed off as being a Whitfield, the greatest preacher of the age, which certainly I am not, and never professed to be. I am a great deal more like anything else you like to mention than that. But if people persist in saying so many bad things of me, I suppose my friends must be allowed the liberty of saying the good things; and I will mix them together, and drink both bitter and sweet, so that there will be no taste at all. Now, my friends, I have spoken to you for a few minutes, not by way of instruction, but simply of amusement. Some people object to anybody's laughing who calls himself a Christian. There is no commandment in the Bible which says 'Thou shalt not laugh.' There is no commandment which says 'Thou shalt not eat thy dinner.' Therefore I eat my dinner; therefore I laugh; therefore I come down to Rosherville Gardens to spend a happy day with a select company; and I am happy to find myself in your midst, and to enjoy myself to-day. The time is now up, and I must conclude, hoping to see you soon again at the pier-head. (Laughter and applause.)"

We have thus presented as much testimony as our space will permit, by which a judgment may be formed of Mr Spurgeon's intellectual endowments and personal independence. It remains to speak of his apparent honesty of purpose, as the crowning guarantee of professional success. It is in this latter trait, we think, that a proper solution may be found of the problem of this preacher's extraordinary influence. The able editor of the *Glasgow Examiner* says of him, that "His preaching is altogether peculiar, and not very easily described. Probably the following may convey to the reader some idea of it. Some preachers owe much to their *personnel*, or presence in the pulpit. Before they open their mouths, there is something about them which causes a sort of awe and respect to creep over the audience. The appearance of this preacher may be said to be interesting, rather than commanding. He is quite a youth, and his countenance boyish. He is under, rather than over, the middle size, and has few or none of the physical advantages of the orator in his appearance. But what he lacks in appearance, he has in reality. Soon as he commences to speak, tones of richest melody are heard. A voice, full, sweet, and musical, falls on every ear, and awakens agreeable emotions in every soul in which there is a sympathy for sounds. That most excellent of voices is under perfect control, and can whisper or thunder at the wish of its possessor. And there is poetry in every feature, and every movement, as well as music in the voice. The countenance speaks—the entire form sympathizes. The action is in complete unison with the sentiments, and the eye *listens* scarcely less than the ear to the sweetly flowing oratory. But, among the thirty thousand English preachers, and the three thousand Scotch ones, there are many sweet voices, as well as this, and many who have studied the art of speaking with the greatest assiduity, and yet they fail to attract an audience. Mr. Spurgeon is more than a 'voice crying'; he has rare powers of observation, recollection, assimilation, and creation. His field of observation is wide and varied. He seems to have opened his eyes to *nature* in all its varieties, to *science* in all its discoveries, and to *literature* in all its departments. Everything which the eye of man can look upon, or the ear hear, seems to have made an indelible impression on his mental powers. The impression is not only distinctly made, but ineradically maintained. Every mountain, every valley, every book, every sentence, which has once come in his way, becomes forever fixed in his recollection. And not only fixed, but becomes the material on which marvellous powers of assimilation vigorously operate. Out of the forms of beauty which his eyes see, other still lovelier forms are created. The loveliest natural landscape is adorned with additional beauty, by the aid of a refined and chastened fancy. The thoughts that have come floating down from the long bygone ages are placed in the crucible of his mind, and, purged of the objectionable, come out bearing his own image and superscription. There is evidently in him great power of *assimilative* genius, and occasional indications of even a higher order of genius — even that which creates fresh and new forms of beauty, which bear the distinct mark of his own mind.

"These higher qualities are evidently greatly aided by a close study of the graces of speaking. The natural had been aided by study — the gifts of the orator by the graces. Despite an occasional neglect of all the laws of logic and ratiocination, there are evidently a thorough knowledge and appreciation of both. The *negligée* sometimes forms a pleasing contrast with the precise. The bow, drawn at a venture, may send the arrow more direct to the mark than the bow drawn according to the strictest rules."

The same writer elsewhere adds: "There are, in the published discourses of our author, sentences and sentiments which might have been spared; but there are, also, strong redeeming qualities. There are vigorous thought, sound doctrine, and earnest appeal; and, considering the extreme youth of the preacher, and his great popularity, the small amount of the objectionable is probably the most peculiar feature of them. Parties anxious to find fault, can be at no loss to find out what they reckon blemishes in his matter and manner; but it might be difficult for them to say any one thing, for or against him, but what has been already said. The English press has gone the entire length, in both its praise and its censure. He has been denounced as mean in stature, inexpressive in countenance, and contemptible in intellect. On the same day, his *personnel* has been extolled as attractive, his intellectual power tremendous, and his oratory overwhelming. He has heard voices innumerable denouncing him, and voices innumerable admiring him. Many a pen has been dipped in gall by jealous rivals, and many a pen in honey by generous critics. All this has been said, and all this written, and Mr. Spurgeon still lives, and lives in the affection of thousands. The crowds which congregated on Sabbath last to hear him in this city, were not greater than the crowds that every Sabbath flock to his meeting-house in London. He heeds not his accusers; he has no time to receive the gratulations of his friends, but preaches on; and, as he preaches, the printing-press takes up the subject, and gives it a circulation much wider than human voice can reach."

In the address at Rosherville, quoted from above, Mr. Spurgeon referred to his labors at Glasgow in an ingenuous way, which clearly indicates an honesty of purpose, of sufficient depth and momentum to overcome all minor considerations, and which urges him right onward in resolute attempts to do good. "In the evening, I went to Dr. Wardlaw's chapel. I dared not recollect what classic words had once been spoken there, or what sweet, musical tones had once been heard from the lips of that eminent minister. Though a child, I mounted that pulpit; but with the greatest difficulty possible, from the simple reason that crowds of people blocked the way. I believe I was several minutes forcing my way to the pulpit. It was a glorious sight to see the masses moving down the streets to the place of worship; but, at the same time, who could prevent a feeling of deep solemnity? I then preached to them, and I believe them to have been pretty well pleased. For myself, I felt that I had the presence of my God, and I rejoiced when, in those sweet Scotch psalms, they extolled the name of the blessed God. However, I found afterwards that I had not got on quite as well as I had thought; for, in the *Christian News*, I discovered that I had thrown out platitudes and old anti-Arminianisms in the evening, at Dr. Wardlaw's—had disgusted an audience of Dr. Patterson's, and had altogether shown myself to be a great buffoon, and everything else that was worthless. I pocketed the information for my own benefit, and was pleased to find that, the week after, I was simply called a spoiled boy, of mediocre abilities, who had gained celebrity by great puffing and blustering, and who, like an early gooseberry, or an overgrown cucumber, would go back to the nihility from whence he sprung, 'unwept, unhonored, and unsung.' I thought it would be a great sparing of catgut and of lungs, if I should die altogether unsung. I had been abused from so many other quarters, that, whatever the *Christian News* (styled by me the *Unchristian News*) might say, I did not feel at all hurt by it; but just pardoned the insult, and went about my work, preaching my Master's gospel as before."

The arrangement of Mr. Spurgeon's sermons is simple and textual. The outline forms a natural contour of the theme, and is scarcely less striking than the facts, arguments, and illustrations employed to elucidate and enforce its leading truths. As he uses no notes, he is sometimes quite episodical in the course of his demonstrations; but he never diverges so far as to be unable, in a moment, to recover his position, with enhanced interest and ease. There is about him that frank, open-heartiness of manner, which hesitates not to express the most startling opinions, and which, combined with his intense sympathy with the masses, gives its possessor a sublime fascination over the popular heart. Twelve thousand listen to him at one time in the open field; and yet, with all this success, there seems to be but little or nothing about him of self-conceit. "Recollect," he says, "who I am, and what I am — a child, having little education, little learning, ability, or talent." "Without the SPIRIT OF GOD, I feel I am utterly unable to speak to you. I have not those gifts and talents which qualify men to speak; I need an afflatus from on high; otherwise, I stand like other men, and have nought to say. May that be given me, for without it I am dumb!" Give him the polite and the noble — give him influence and understanding, and he should fail; but give him his own praying people, "meeting in such multitudes to pray to God for a blessing," and he will "overcome hell itself."

This introduction has already become extended beyond the limits at first designed. But we wish to present our friend in the light of his own true character, and that can be understood only by comparing the diversified expressions of his earnest and unsophisticated spirit. A few of these we have gleaned from occasional discourses not embraced in the present collection, as we wish the reader to meet with fresh pleasure and profit on each succeeding page. Moreover, we have presented herewith criticisms from eminent pens in the service of almost every evangelical creed, and cannot better close our summary of opinions and facts, than by appending the following extract from an English correspondent to the *Independent*, of this city. He lately wrote thus:

"Great orators, whether pulpit, platform, or senatorial, make many friends and many foes. This being inevitable, we are at no loss to account for the applause and comtumely which have been profusely heaped upon the young minister, the Rev. C. H. Spurgeon, whose appearance and labors in the metropolis have excited in all religious circles, and even beyond them, attention and surprise, and in some instances, unbounded admiration. Scarcely more than a youth in years, comparitively untutored, and without a name, he enters the greatest city in the world, and, almost simultaneously, commands audiences larger than have usually listened to her most favored preachers. Almost daily has he occupied pulpits in various parts of town and country, and everywhere been greeted by overflowing congregations.

"As might be expected, many who have listened to him have gone away to speak ill of his name, while others, and by far the greater number, have been instructed by his arguments, melted by his appeals, and stimulated by his earnestness. There have been seen among his hearers ministers of mark, of nearly every section of the Christian church; laymen, well known in all circles as the supporters of the benevolent and evangelical institutions of the day; citizens of renown, from the chief magistrate down to the parish beadle; and Holyoake, the editor of the Infidel serial, *The Reasoner*, has, by his own confession, been among his hearers. That the man who causes such a *furore* must possess some power not commonly found in men of his profession, will only be doubted by his prejudiced detractors. Whether that power be physical, intellectual, or moral, or a happy blending of them all, is, perhaps, a question not yet ripe for decision.

"It cannot be disputed that Mr. Spurgeon is, in various respects, an extraordinary man. Never, since the days of George Whitfield and Edward Irving, has any minister of religion acquired so great a reputation as this Baptist preacher in so short a time. Here is a mere youth — a perfect stripling, only twenty-one years of age — incomparably the most popular preacher of the day. There is no man in Great Britain who could draw such immense audiences; and none who, in his happiest efforts, can so completely enthral the attention, and delight the minds of his hearers. While the enlargement of his chapel in New Park-street was taking place, Mr. Spurgeon preached in Exeter Hall; but this spacious building soon proved far too small to hold the crowds who thronged to hear the youthful Boanerges. It was no unusual sight, on a Sunday evening, to see placards put up outside the building, announcing that the hall was full, and that no more could be admitted. Since the enlargement of his chapel, which is now capable of holding 1800 people, it has been found necessary for the police to be present at every service, and the pew-holders are admitted, by ticket, through a side-door. This accomplished, at ten minutes prior to the commencement of the service, the front doors are opened, and a rush commences; but it is speedily over, for the chapel is full — not only the seats, but every inch of standing-room being occupied; and the gates have to be closed, with an immense crowd of disappointed expectant hearers outside.

"Although some of Mr. Spurgeon's vilifiers speak of his irreverence and witticisms, your correspondent, when he listened to the youthful evangelist, was especially impressed with the stillness and solemnity pervading the entire service. Some of his appeals to the conscience, some of his remonstrances with the careless, constituted specimens of a very high order of oratorical power. When pronouncing the doom of those who live and die in a state of impenitence, he makes hundreds of his congregation quail and quake in their seats. He places their awful destiny in such vivid colors before their eyes, that they almost imagine they are already in the regions of darkness and despair. In his preface to a volume of sermons just published, he tells us that such has been the impression produced by some of his sermons, that he has ascertained upwards of twenty cases of conversion as the result of one discourse, to say nothing of those instances of a saving change wrought on his hearers, which will be unknown, until the world to come has made its important and unexpected revelation.

"When this able and eloquent preacher first made his appearance in the horizon of the religious world, and dazzled the masses in London by his brilliancy, many feared that he either might get intoxicated by the large draughts of popularity which he had daily to drink, or that he would not be able, owing to the want of variety, to sustain the reputation he had so suddenly acquired. Neither result has happened. Whatever may be his defect, either as a man, or as a preacher of the gospel, it is due to him to state that he has not been spoiled by popular applause. Constitutionally, he has no small amount of self-esteem; but, so far from its growing with his daily extending fame, he appears to be more humble and more subdued than when he first burst on our astonished gaze. And, with regard to the fear that his excellence as a preacher would not be sustained, the event has proved the groundlessness of such an apprehension. There is no falling off whatever. On the contrary, he is, in not a few respects, improving with the lapse of time. His striking originality can be seen to greater advantage than at first. There is no sameness in his sermons. The variety of his matter — not, of course, as regards his doctrines, but as relates to his expositions, illustrations, and applications of divine truth — is as great as ever.

"Mr. Spurgeon has been thought, by many, to entertain and advocate the crude views of the *hyper*-Calvinists. He may, at times, lay himself open to such a charge; but, we verily believe, he has in truth little sympathy with those of the class referred to — his offer of a free gospel, and appeals to the sinner, being sufficient evidence in the matter with all who know anything of the preachers of the Dr. Crisp school. It cannot be doubted that he holds Calvinistic views of Christianity, and proclaims this doctrine strongly and boldly, thus presenting himself and his preaching as a conspicuous mark for controversial censure. But there is a courageous and transparent consistency characterizing the man and his mission, that ought, most assuredly, to neutralize all unfair and bitter criticism.

"It must be evident to all who have read Mr. Spurgeon's sermons, that he is no superficial thinker. He has long been a diligent and earnest seeker after truth, and is theoretically and experimentally acquainted with much of the deep spirituality of divine truth. He must have studied profoundly Leighton's writings and Wesley's hymns; for he has much of the experience of Wesley, and a high degree of the spirituality of Leighton. Some have said that William Jay, of Bath, and Robert Hall, of Bristol, are the models on which he has sought to mould his style of address; but he needs the logical acumen of the one, and the polished elegance of diction which characterized the other. He has, however, their better qualities of thorough devotion to the service of the gospel, and a power and pathos far transcending theirs. But he is too originally constituted to be an imitator, and is more likely to found a style of his own, than to imitate that of another. True, he has much of Rowland Hill's quaintness of illustration, and not unfrequently provokes a smile by some startling expression, or figure; but the general seriousness and earnestness of his tone and manner forbid any feeling of levity; and if, occasionally, his humor excites a passing smile, the depth of his pathos more frequently draws tears from the greater part of his congregation."

Brother, all hail! This last drop of ink hastens into words, which may perchance meet your eye, amidst the dust and exhausting strife incident to that great arena of your spiritual gladiatorship. Well, let them assure you of fraternal sympathy at ten thousand altars in far-off climes. When the prospective issue of your glowing thoughts was here announced, orders for the same were promptly returned from every section of our republic; and soon you will be read, as your continued usefulness is fervently desired, in homes of affluence and cabins of industry, spread under the care of our common Father, from the Eastern Atlantic to the great Pacific of the West. May Grace still bind thee in humble allegiance to the cross, and render thee yet more radiant, for the benefit of a dark and perishing world. ELM.

NEW-YORK, June 2, 1856.

SERMON I.

SOVEREIGNTY AND SALVATION.

"Look unto me, and be ye saved, all the ends of the earth: for I *am* God, and *there* is none else." — ISAIAH xlv. 22.

SIX years ago to-day, as near as possible at this very hour of the day, I was "in the gall of bitterness and in the bonds of iniquity," but had yet, by divine grace, been led to feel the bitterness of that bondage, and to cry out by reason of the soreness of its slavery. Seeking rest, and finding none, I stepped within the house of God, and sat there, afraid to look upward, lest I should be utterly cut off, and lest his fierce wrath should consume me. The minister rose in his pulpit, and, as I have done this morning, read this text, "Look unto me, and be ye saved, all the ends of the earth: for I am God, and there is none else." I looked that moment; the grace of faith was vouchsafed to me in the self-same instant; and now I think I can say with truth,

"Ere since by faith I saw the stream
His flowing wounds supply,
Redeeming love has been my theme,
And shall be till I die."

1*

I shall never forget that day, while memory holds its place; nor can I help repeating this text whenever I remember that hour when first I knew the Lord. How strangely gracious! How wonderfully and marvellously kind, that he who heard these words so little time ago for his own soul's profit, should now address you this morning as his hearers from the same text, in the full and confident hope that some poor sinner within these walls may hear the glad tidings of salvation for himself also, and may to-day, on this 6th of January, be "turned from darkness to light, and from the power of Satan unto God!"

If it were within the range of human capacity to conceive a time when God dwelt alone, without his creatures, we should then have one of the grandest and most stupendous ideas of God. There was a season when as yet the sun had never run his race, nor commenced flinging his golden rays across space, to gladden the earth. There was an era when no stars sparkled in the firmament, for there was no sea of azure in which they might float. There was a time when all that we now behold of God's great universe was yet unborn, slumbering within the mind of God, as yet uncreate and non-existent; yet there was God, and he was "over all blessed for ever;" though no seraphs hymned his praises, though no strong-winged cherubs flashed like lightning to do his high behests, though he was without a retinue, yet he sat as a king on his throne, the mighty God, for ever to be worshipped —the Dread Supreme, in solemn silence dwelling by himself in vast immensity, making of the placid clouds his canopy, and the light from his own countenance forming the brightness of his glory. God was, and

God is. From the beginning God was God; ere worlds had beginning, he was "from everlasting to everlasting." Now, when it pleased him to create his creatures, does it not strike you how infinitely those creatures must have been below himself? If you are potters, and you fashion upon the wheel a vessel, shall that piece of clay arrogate to itself equality with you? Nay, at what a distance will it be from you, because you have been in part its creator. So when the Almighty formed his creatures, was it not consummate impudence, that they should venture for a moment to compare themselves with him? Yet that arch traitor, that leader of rebels, Satan, sought to climb to the high throne of God, soon to find his aim too high, and hell itself not low enough wherein to escape divine vengeance. He knows that God is "God alone." Since the world was created, man has imitated Satan; the creature of a day, the ephemera of an hour, has sought to match itself with the Eternal. Hence it has ever been one of the objects of the great Jehovah, to teach mankind that he is God, and beside him there is none else. This is the lesson he has been teaching the world since it went astray from him. He has been busying himself in breaking down the high places, in exalting the valleys, in casting down imaginations and lofty looks, that all the world might

> "Know that the Lord is God alone,
> He can create, and he destroy."

This morning we shall attempt to show you, in the first place, *how God has been teaching this great lesson to the world*—that he is God, and beside him there is none else; and then, secondly, *the special way in which he designs to teach it in the matter of salvation*—"Look unto *me*, and be ye saved: *for* I am God, and there is none else."

I. First, then, HOW HAS GOD BEEN TEACHING THIS LESSON TO MANKIND?

We reply, he has taught it, first of all, *to false Gods, and to the idolaters who have bowed before them.* Man, in his wickedness and sin, has set up a block of wood and stone to be his maker, and has bowed before it. He hath fashioned for himself out of a goodly tree an image made unto the likeness of mortal man, or of the fishes of the sea, or of creeping things of the earth, and he has prostrated his body, and his soul too, before that creature of his own hands, calling it god, while it had neither eyes to see, nor hands to handle, nor ears to hear! But how hath God poured contempt on the ancient gods of the heathen? Where are they now? Are they so much as known? Where are those false deities before whom the multitudes of Nineveh prostrated themselves? Ask the moles and the bats, whose companions they are; or ask the mounds beneath which they are buried; or go where the idle gazer walketh through the museum—see them there as curiosities, and smile to think that men should ever bow before such gods as these. And where are the gods of Persia? Where are they? The fires are quenched, and the fire-worshipper hath almost ceased out of the earth. Where are the gods of Greece—those gods adorned with poetry, and hymned in the most sublime odes? Where are they? They are gone. Who talks of them now, but as things that vere of yore? Jupiter—doth any one bow before him? and who is he that adores Saturn? They are passed away, and they are forgotten. And where are the gods of Rome? Doth Janus now command the temple? or do the vestal virgins now feed their perpetual fires? Are there any now that bow before these gods? No, they have lost their thrones. And where are the gods of the South Sea Islands—those bloody demons before whom wretched creatures prostrated their bodies? They have well nigh become extinct. Ask the inhabitants of China and Polynesia where are the gods before which they bowed? Ask, and echo says ask, and ask again. They are cast down from their thrones; they are hurled from their pedestals; their chariots are broken, their sceptres are burnt in the fire, their glories are departed; God hath gotten unto himself the victory over false gods, and taught their worshippers that he is God, and that beside him there is none else. Are their gods still worshipped, or idols before which the nations bow themselves? Wait but a little while, and ye shall see them fall. Cruel Juggernaut, whose car still crushes in its motion the foolish ones who throw themselves before it, shall yet be the object of derision; and the most noted idols, such as Budha, and Brahma, and Vishnu, shall yet stoop themselves to the earth, and men shall tread them down as mire in the streets; for God will teach all men that he is God, and that there is none else.

Mark ye, yet again, how God has taught this truth *to empires*. Empires have risen up, and have been the gods of the era; their kings and princes have taken to themselves high titles, and have been worshipped by the multitude. But ask the empires whether there is any beside God? Do you not think you hear the boasting soliloquy of Babylon—"I sit as a queen, and am no widow; I shall see no sorrow; I am god, and there is none beside me?" And think ye not now, if ye walk over ruined Babylon, that ye will meet aught save the solemn spirit of the Bible, standing like a prophet gray with age, and telling you that there is one God, and that beside him there is none else? Go ye to Babylon, covered with its sand, the sand of its own ruins; stand ye on the mounds of Nineveh, and let the voice come up — "There is one God, and empires sink before him; there is only one Potentate, and the princes and kings of the earth, with their dynasties and thrones, are shaken by the trampling of his foot." Go, seat yourselves in the temples of Greece; mark ye there what proud words Alexander once did speak; but now, where is he, and where his empire too? Sit on the ruined arches of the bridge of Carthage, or walk ye through the desolated theatres of Rome, and ye will hear a voice in the wild wind amid those ruins — "I am God, and there is none else." "O city, thou didst call thyself eternal; I have made thee melt away like dew. Thou saidst 'I sit on seven hills, and I shall last forever;' I have made thee crumble, and thou art now a miserable and contemptible place, compared with what thou wast. Thou wast once stone, thou madest thyself; I have made thee stone again, and brought thee low." O! how has God taught monarchies and empires that have set themselves up like new kingdoms of heaven, that he is God, and that there is none else!

Again: how has he taught this great truth *to monarchs!* There are some who have been most proud that have had to learn it in a way more hard than others. Take, for instance, Nebuchadnezzar. His crown is on his head, his purple robe is over his shoulders; he walks through proud Babylon, and says, "Is not this great Babylon which I have builded?" Do you see that creature in the field there? It is a man. "A man?" say you; its hair has grown like eagle's feathers, and its nails like bird's claws; it walketh on all-fours, and eateth grass, like an ox; it is driven out from men. That is the monarch who said —"Is not this great Babylon that I have builded?" And now he is restored to Babylon's palace, that he may "bless the Most High who is able to abase those that walk in pride." Remember another monarch. Look at Herod. He sits in the midst of his people, and he speaks. Hear ye the impious shout? "It is the voice of God," they cry, "and not the voice of man." The proud monarch gives not God the glory; he affects the God, and seems to shake the spheres, imagining himself divine. There is a worm that creepeth into his body, and yet another, and another; and ere that sun has set, he is eaten up of worms. Ah! monarch! thou thoughtest of being a God, and worms have eaten thee! Thou hast thought of being more than man; and what art thou? Less than man, for worms consume thee, and thou art the prey of corruption. Thus God humbleth the proud; thus he abaseth the mighty. We might give you instances from modern history; but the death of a king is all-sufficient to teach this one lesson, if men would but learn it. When kings die, and in funeral pomp are carried to the grave, we are taught the lesson —"I am God, and beside me there is none else." When we hear of revolutions, and the shaking of empires — when we see old dynasties tremble, and gray-haired monarchs driven from their thrones, then it is that Jehovah seems to put his foot upon land and sea, and with his hand uplifted cries — "Hear! ye inhabitants of the earth! Ye are but as grasshoppers; 'I am God, and beside me there is none else.'"

Again: our God has had much to do to teach this lesson *to the wise men of this world;* for as rank, pomp, and power, have set themselves up in the place of God, so has wisdom; and one of the greatest enemies of Deity has always been the wisdom of man. The wisdom of man will not see God. Professing themselves to be wise, wise men have become fools. But have ye not noticed, in reading history, how God has abased the pride of wisdom? In ages long gone by, he sent mighty minds into the world, who devised systems of philosophy. "These systems," they said, "will last forever." Their pupils thought them infallible, and therefore wrote their sayings on enduring parchment, saying, "This book will last forever; succeeding generations of men will read it, and to the last man that book shall be handed down, as the epitome of wisdom." "Ah! but," said God, "that book of yours shall be seen to be folly, ere another hundred years have rolled away." And so the mighty thoughts of Socrates, and the wisdom of Solon, are utterly forgotten now; and could we hear them speak, the veriest child in our school would laugh to think that he understandeth more of philosophy than they. But when man has found the vanity of one system, his eyes have sparkled at another; if Aristotle will not suffice, here is Bacon; now I shall know everything; and he sets to work, and says that this new philosophy is to last forever. He lays his stones with fair colors, and he thinks that every truth he piles up is a precious imperishable truth. But, alas! another century comes, and it is found to be "wood, hay, and stubble." A new sect of philosophers rise up, who refute their predecessors. So too we have wise men in this day—wise secularists, and so on, who fancy they have obtained the truth; but within another fifty years—and mark that word—this hair shall not be silvered over with gray, until the last of that race shall have perished, and that man shall be thought a fool that was ever connected with such a race. Systems of infidelity pass away like a dew-drop before the sun; for God says, "I am God, and beside me there is none else." This Bible is the stone that shall break in powder philosophy; this is the mighty battering-ram that shall dash all systems of philosophy in pieces; this is the stone that a woman may yet hurl upon the head of every Abimelech, and he shall utterly be destroyed. O Church of God! fear not; thou shalt do wonders; wise men shall be confounded, and thou shalt know, and they too, that he is God, and that beside him there is none else.

"Surely," says one, "*the church of God* does not need to be taught this." Yes, we answer, she does; for of all beings, those whom God has made the objects of his grace are perhaps the most apt to forget this cardinal truth, that he is God, and that beside him there is none else. How did the church in Canaan forget it, when they bowed before other gods, and therefore he brought against them mighty kings and princes, and afflicted them sore. How did Israel forget it; and he carried them away captive into Babylon. And what Israel did, in Canaan and in Babylon, that we do now. We too, too often, forget that he is God, and beside him there is none else. Doth not the Christian know what I mean, when I tell him this great fact? For hath he not done it himself? In certain times prosperity has come upon him; soft gales have blown his bark along, just where his wild will wished to steer; and he has said within himself: "Now I have peace, now I have happiness, now the object I wished for is within my grasp, now I will say, Sit down, my soul, and take thy rest; eat, drink, and be merry; these things will well content me; make thou these thy god, be thou blessed and happy." But have we not seen our God dash the goblet to the earth, spill the sweet wine, and instead thereof fill it with gall? and as he has given it to us, he has said—"Drink it, drink it: you have thought to find a god on earth, but drain the cup and know its bitterness." When we have drunk it, nauseous the draught was, and we have cried, "Ah! God, I will drink no more from these things; thou art God, and beside thee there is none else." And ah! how often, too, have we devised schemes for the future, without asking God's permission! Men have said, like those foolish ones whom James mentioned, "We will do such-and-such things on the morrow; we will buy and sell and get gain," whereas they knew not what was to be on the morrow, for long ere the morrow came they were unable to buy and sell; death had claimed them, and a small span of earth held all their frame. God teaches his people every day, by sickness, by affliction, by depression of spirits, by the forsakings of God, by the loss of the Spirit for a season, by the lackings of the joys of his countenance, that he is God, and that beside him there is none else. And we must not forget that there are some special servants of God raised up to do great works, who in a peculiar manner have to learn this lesson. Let a man, for instance, be called to the great work of preaching the gospel. He is successful; God helps him; thousands wait at his feet, and multitudes hang upon his lips; as truly as that man is a man, he will have a tendency to be exalted above measure, and too much will he begin to look to himself, and too little to his God. Let men speak who know, and what they know let them speak; and they will say, "It is true, it is most true." If God gives us a special mission, we generally begin to take some honor and glory to ourselves. But in the review of the eminent saints of God, have you never observed how God has made them feel that he was God, and beside him there was none else? Poor Paul might have thought himself a god, and been puffed up above measure, by reason of the greatness of his revelation, had there not been a thorn in the flesh. But Paul could feel that he was not a god, for he had a thorn in the flesh, and gods *could not* have thorns in the flesh. Sometimes God teaches the minister, by denying him help on special occasions. We come up into our pulpits, and say, "Oh! I wish I could have a good day to-day!" We begin to labor; we have been just as earnest in prayer, and just as indefatigable; but it is like a blind horse turning round a mill, or like Samson with Delilah: we shake our vain limbs with vast surprise, "make feeble fight," and win no victories. We are made to see that the Lord is God, and that beside him there is none else. Very frequently God teaches this to the minister, by leading him to see his own sinful nature. He will have such an insight into his own wicked and abominable heart, that he will feel as he comes up the pulpit stairs that he does not deserve so much as to sit in his pew, much less to preach to his fellows. Although we feel always joy in the declaration of God's Word, yet we have known what it is to totter on the pulpit steps, under a sense that the chief of sinners should scarcely be allowed to preach to others. Ah! beloved, I do not think *he* will be very successful as a minister who is not taken into the depths and blackness of his own soul, and made to exclaim, "Unto me, who am *less than the least of all saints*, is this grace given, that I should preach among the Gentiles the unsearchable riches of Christ." There is another antidote which God applies in the case of ministers. If he does not deal with them personally, he raises up a host of enemies, that it may be seen that he is God, and God alone. An esteemed friend sent me, yesterday, a valuable old MS. of one of George Whitfield's hymns which was sung on Kennington Common. It is a splendid hymn, thoroughly Whitfieldian all through. It showed that his reliance was wholly on the Lord, and that God was within him. What! will a man subject himself to the calumnies of the multitude, will he toil and work day after day unnecessarily, will he stand up Sabbath after Sabbath and preach the gospel and have his name maligned and slandered, if he has not the grace of God in him? For myself, I can say, that were it not that the love of Christ constrained me, this hour might be the last that I should preach, so far as the ease of the thing is concerned. "Necessity is laid upon us; yea, woe is unto us if we preach not the gospel." But that opposition through which God carries his servants, leads them to see at once that he is God, and that there is none else.

If every one applauded, if all were gratified, we should think ourselves God; but, when they hiss and hoot, we turn to our God, and cry,

> "If on my face, for thy dear name,
> Shame and reproach should be,
> I 'll hail reproach and welcome shame
> If thou 'lt remember me."

II. This brings us to the second portion of our discourse. Salvation is God's greatest work; and, therefore, in his greatest work, he specially teaches us this lesson, That he is God, and that beside him there is none else. Our text tells us *how he teaches it.* He says, "Look unto me, and be ye saved, all the ends of the earth." He shows us that he is God, and that beside him there is none else, in three ways. First, by the person to whom he directs us: "Look unto *me*, and be ye saved." Secondly, by the means he tells us to use to obtain mercy: "Look," simply, "Look." And thirdly, by the persons whom he calls to "look:" "Look unto me, and be ye saved, *all the ends of the earth.*"

1. First, *to whom does God tell us to look for salvation?* O, does it not lower the pride of man, when we hear the Lord say, "Look unto *me*, and be ye saved, all the ends of the earth?" It is not, "Look to your priest, and be ye saved:" if you did, there would be another god, and beside him there would be some one else. It is not "Look to yourself:" if so, then there would be a being who might arrogate some of the praise of salvation. But it is "Look unto me." How frequently you who are coming to Christ look to yourselves. "O!" you say, "I do not repent enough." That is looking to yourself. "I do not believe enough."

That is looking to yourself. "I am too unworthy." That is looking to yourself. "I cannot discover," says another, "that I have any righteousness." It is quite right to say that you have not any righteousness; but it is quite wrong to look for any. It is, "Look unto *me*." God will have you turn your eye off yourself and look unto him. The hardest thing in the world is to turn a man's eye off himself; as long as he lives, he always has a predilection to turn his eyes inside, and look at himself; whereas God says, "Look unto *me*." From the cross of Calvary, where the bleeding hands of Jesus drop mercy; from the garden of Gethsemane, where the bleeding pores of the Saviour sweat pardons, the cry comes, "Look unto me, and be ye saved, all the ends of the earth." From Calvary's summit, where Jesus cries, "It is finished," I hear a shout, "Look, and be saved." But there comes a vile cry from our soul, "Nay, look to yourself! look to yourself!" Ah, my hearer, look to yourself, and you will be damned. That certainly will come of it. As long as you look to yourself there is no hope for you. It is not a consideration of what you are, but a consideration of what God is, and what Christ is, that can save you. It is looking from yourself to Jesus. O! there be men that quite misunderstand the gospel; they think that righteousness qualifies them to come to Christ; whereas sin is the only qualification for a man to come to Jesus. Good old Crisp says, "Righteousness keeps me from Christ: the whole have no need of a physician, but they that are sick. Sin makes me come to Jesus, when sin is felt; and, in coming to Christ, the more sin I have the more cause I have to hope for mercy." David said, and it was a strange thing, too, "Have mercy upon me, for mine iniquity is great." But, David, why did not you say that it was little? Because, David knew that the bigger his sins were the better reason for asking mercy. The more vile a man is, the more eagerly I invite him to believe in Jesus. A sense of sin is all we have to look for as ministers. We preach to sinners; and let us know that a man will take the title of sinner to himself, and we then say to him, "Look unto Christ, and ye shall be saved." "Look," this is all he demands of thee, and even this he gives thee. If thou lookest to thyself thou art damned; thou art a vile miscreant, filled with loathsomeness, corrupt and corrupting others. But look thou here—seest thou that man hanging on the cross? Dost thou behold his agonized head dropping meekly down upon his breast? Dost thou see that thorny crown, causing drops of blood to trickle down his cheeks? Dost thou see his hands pierced and rent, and his blest feet, supporting the weight of his own frame, rent well nigh in twain with the cruel nails? Sinner! dost thou hear him shriek, "Eloi, Eloi, lama sabbacthani"? Dost thou hear him cry, "It is finished?" Dost thou mark his head hang down in death? Seest thou that side pierced with the spear, and the body taken from the cross? O, come thou hither! Those hands were nailed for thee; those feet gushed gore for thee; that side was opened wide for thee; and if thou wantest to know how thou canst find mercy, there it is. "Look!" "Look unto *me!*" Look no longer to Moses. Look no longer to Sinai. Come thou here and look to Calvary, to Calvary's victim, and to Joseph's grave. And look thou yonder, to the man who near the throne sits with his Father, crowned with light and immortality. "Look, sinner," he says, this morning, to you, "Look unto me, and be ye saved." It is in this way God teaches that there is none beside him; because he makes us look entirely to him, and utterly away from ourselves.

2. But the second thought is, *the means of salvation.* It is, "*Look* unto me, and be ye saved." You have often observed, I am sure, that many people are fond of an intricate worship, an involved religion, one they can hardly understand. They cannot endure worship so simple as ours. Then they must have a man dressed in white, and a man dressed in black; then they must have what they call an altar and a chancel. After a little while, that will not suffice, and they must have flower-pots and candles. The clergyman then becomes a priest, and he must have a variegated dress, with a cross on it. So it goes on: what is simply a plate becomes a paten, and what was once a cup becomes a chalice; and the more complicated the ceremonies are, the better they like them. They like their minister to stand like a superior being. The world likes a religion they cannot comprehend. But have you never noticed how gloriously simple the Bible is? It will not have any of your nonsense; it speaks plain, and nothing but plain things. "*Look!*" There is not an unconverted man who likes this, "Look unto Christ, and be ye saved." No, he comes to Christ like Naaman to Elijah; and, when it is said, "Go, wash in Jordan," he replies, "I verily thought he would come and put his hand on the place, and call on the name of his God. But the idea of telling me to wash in Jordan, what a ridiculous thing! Anybody could do that!" If the prophet had bidden him to do some great thing, would

he not have done it? Ah! certainly he would. And if, this morning, I could preach that any one who walked from here to Bath without his shoes and stockings, or did some impossible thing, should be saved, you would start off to-morrow morning before breakfast. If it would take me seven years to describe the way of salvation, I am sure you would all long to hear it. If only one learned doctor could tell the way to heaven, how would he be run after! And if it were in hard words, with a few scraps of Latin and Greek, it would be all the better. But it is a simple gospel that we have to preach. It is only "Look!" "Ah!" you say, "is that the gospel? I shall not pay any attention to that." But why has God ordered you to do such a simple thing? Just to take down your pride, and to show you that he is God, and that beside him there is none else. O, mark how simple the way of salvation is. It is, "Look! look! look!" Four letters, and two of them alike! "Look unto me, and be ye saved, all the ends of the earth." Some divines want a week to tell what you are to do to be saved; but God the Holy Ghost only wants four letters to do it. "Look unto me, and be ye saved, all the ends of the earth." How simple is that way of salvation! and O, how instantaneous! It takes us some time to move our hand, but a look does not require a moment. So a sinner believes in a moment; and the moment that sinner believes and trusts in his crucified God for pardon, at once he receives salvation in full through his blood. There may be one that came in here this morning unjustified in his conscience, that will go out justified rather than others. There may be some here, filthy sinners one moment, pardoned the next. It is done in an instant. "Look! look! look!" And how universal is it! Because, wherever I am, however far off, it just says, "Look!" It does not say I am to see; it only says, "Look!" If we look on a thing in the dark, we cannot see it; but we have done what we were told. So, if a sinner only looks to Jesus, he will save him; for Jesus in the dark is as good as Jesus in the light; and Jesus, when you cannot see him, is as good as Jesus when you can. It is only, "Look!" "Ah!" says one, "I have been trying to see Jesus this year, but I have not seen him." It does not say, see him, but "Look unto him." And it says that they who looked were lightened. If there is an obstacle before you, and you only look in the right direction, it is sufficient. "Look unto me." It is not seeing Christ so much as looking after him. The will after Christ, the wish after Christ, the desire after Christ, the trusting in Christ, the hanging on Christ, that is what is wanted. "Look! look! look!" Ah! if the man bitten by the serpent had turned his sightless eyeballs towards the brazen serpent, though he had not seen it, he would still have had his life restored. It is looking, not seeing, that saves the sinner.

We say again, how this *humbles* a man! There is a gentleman who says, "Well, if it had been a thousand pounds that would have saved me, I would have thought nothing of it." But your gold and silver is cankered; it is good for nothing. "Then, am I to be saved just the same as my servant Betty?" Yes, just the same: there is no other way of salvation for you. That is to show man that Jehovah is God, and that beside him there is none else. The wise man says, "If it had been to work the most wonderful problem, or to solve the greatest mystery, I would have done it. May I not have some mysterious gospel? May I not believe in some mysterious religion?" No; it is "Look!" "What! am I to be saved just like that Ragged-School boy, who can't read his letters?" Yes, you must, or you will not be saved at all. Another says, "I have been very moral and upright; I have observed all the laws of the land; and, if there is anything else to do, I will do it. I will eat only fish on Fridays, and keep all the fasts of the church, if that will save me." No, sir, that will not save you: your good works are good for nothing. "What! must I be saved in the same way as a harlot or a drunkard?" Yes, sir; there is only one way of salvation for all. "He hath concluded all in unbelief, that he might have mercy upon all." He hath passed a sentence of condemnation on all, that the free grace of God might come upon many to salvation. "Look! look! look!" This is the simple method of salvation. "Look unto me, and be ye saved, all the ends of the earth."

But, lastly, mark how God has cut down the pride of man, and has exalted himself *by the persons whom he has called to look*. "Look unto me, and be ye saved, all the ends of the earth." When the Jew heard Isaiah say that, "Ah!" he exclaimed, "you ought to have said, Look unto me, O Jerusalem, and be saved. That would have been right. But those Gentile dogs, are they to look and be saved?" "Yes," says God; "I will show you Jews, that, though I have given you many privileges, I will exalt others above you; I can do as I will with my own."

Now, who are the ends of the earth? Why, there are poor heathen nations now that are very few degrees removed from brutes, uncivilized and untaught; but if I might go and tread the desert, and find the Bushman in his kraal, or go to the South Seas and find a cannibal, I would say to the cannibal or the Bushman, "Look unto Jesus, and be ye saved, all the ends of the earth." They are some of "the ends of the earth," and the gospel is sent as much to them as to the polite Grecians, the refined Romans, or the educated Britons. But I think "the ends of the earth" imply those who have gone the farthest away from Christ. I say, drunkard, that means you. You have been staggering back, till you have got right to the ends of the earth; you have almost had *delirium tremens;* you cannot be much worse. There is not a man breathing worse than you. *Is there?* Ah! but God, in order to humble your pride, says to you, "Look unto me, and be ye saved." There is another who has lived a life of infamy and sin, until she has ruined herself, and even Satan seems to sweep her out at the back door; but God says, "Look unto me, and be ye saved, all the ends of the earth." Methinks I see one trembling here, and saying, "Ah, I have not been one of these, sir, but I have been something worse; for I have attended the house of God, and I have stifled convictions, and put off all thoughts of Jesus, and now I think he will never have mercy on me." You are one of them. "Ends of the earth!" So long as I find any who feel like that, I can tell them that they are "the ends of the earth." "But," says another, "I am so peculiar; if I did not feel as I do, it would be all very well; but I feel that my case is a peculiar one." That is all right; they are a peculiar people. You will do. But another one says, "There is nobody in the world like me; I do not think you will find a being under the sun that has so many calls, and put them all away, and so many sins on his head. Besides, I have guilt that I should not like to confess to any living creature." One of "the ends of the earth" again; therefore, all I have to do is to cry out, in the Master's name, "Look unto me, and be ye saved, all the ends of the earth: for I am God, and there is none else." But thou sayest, sin will not let thee look. I tell thee, sin will be removed the moment thou dost look. "*But I dare not; he will condemn me; I fear to look.*" He will condemn thee more if thou dost not look. Fear, then, and look; but do not let thy fearing keep thee from looking. "*But he will cast me out.*" Try him. "*But I cannot see him.*" I tell you, it is not seeing, but looking. "*But my eyes are so fixed on the earth, so earthly, so worldly.*" Ah! but, poor soul, he giveth power to look and live. He saith, "Look unto me, and be ye saved, all the ends of the earth."

Take this, dear friends, for a new year's text, both ye who love the Lord, and ye who are only looking for the first time. Christian! in all thy troubles through this year, look unto God and be saved. In all thy trials and afflictions, look unto Christ, and find deliverance. In all thine agony, poor soul, in all thy repentance for thy guilt, look unto Christ, and find pardon. This year remember to put thine eyes heavenward, and thine heart heavenward, too. Remember, this day, that thou bind round thyself a golden chain, and put one link of it in the staple in heaven. Look unto Christ; fear not. There is no stumbling when a man walks with his eyes up to Jesus. He that looked at the stars fell into the ditch; but he that looks at

Christ walks safely. Keep your eyes up all the year long. "Look unto *him*, and be ye saved;" and remember that "*he* is God, and beside *him* there is none else." And thou, poor trembler, what sayest thou? Wilt thou begin the year by looking unto him? You know how sinful you are this morning; you know how filthy you are; and yet it is possible that, before you open your pew door, and get into the aisle, you will be as justified as the apostles before the throne of God. It is possible that, ere your foot treads the threshold of your door, you will have lost the burden that has been on your back, and you will go on your way, singing, "I am forgiven, I am forgiven; I am a miracle of grace; this day is my spiritual birthday." O, that it might be such to many of you, that at last I might say, "Here am I, and the children thou hast given me." Hear this, convinced sinner! "This poor man cried, and the Lord delivered him out of his distresses." O, taste and see that the Lord is good! Now believe on him; now cast thy guilty soul upon his righteousness; now plunge thy black soul into the bath of his blood; now put thy naked soul at the door of the wardrobe of his righteousness; now seat thy famished soul at the feast of plenty. Now "Look!" How simple does it seem! And yet it is the hardest thing in the world to bring men to. They never will do it, till constraining grace makes them. Yet there it is, "Look!" Go thou away with that thought. "Look unto me, and be ye saved, all the ends of the earth: for I am God, and there is none else."

SERMON II

THE BIBLE.

"I have written to him the great things of my law, but they were counted as a strange thing." —HOSEA viii. 12.

THIS is God's complaint against Ephraim. It is no mean proof of his goodness, that he stoops to rebuke his erring creatures; it is a great argument of his gracious disposition, that he bows his head to notice terrestrial affairs. He might, if he pleased, wrap himself with night as with a garment; he might put the stars around his wrist for bracelets, and bind the suns around his brow for a coronet; he might dwell alone, far, far above this world, up in the seventh heaven, and look down with calm and silent indifference upon all the doings of his creatures; he might do as the heathens supposed their Jove did, sit in perpetual silence, sometimes nodding his awful head to make the fates move as he pleased, but never taking thought of the little things of earth, disposing of them as beneath his notice, engrossed within his own being, swallowed up within himself, living alone and retired; and I, as one of his creatures, might stand by night upon a mountain-top, and look upon the silent stars and say, "Ye are the eyes of God, but ye look not down on me; your light is the gift of his omnipotence, but your rays are not smiles of love to me. God, the mighty Creator, has forgotten me; I am a despicable drop in the ocean of creation, a sear-leaf in the forest of beings, an atom in the mountain of existence. He knows me not; I am alone, alone, alone." But it is not so, beloved. Our God is of another order. He notices every one of us; there is not a sparrow or a worm but is found in his decrees. There is not a person upon whom his eye is not fixed. Our most secret acts are known to him. Whatsoever we do, or bear, or suffer, the eye of God still rests upon us, and we are beneath his smile—for we are his people; or beneath his frown—for we have erred from him.

Oh! how ten-thousand-fold merciful is God, that, looking down upon the race of man, he does not smite it out of existence. We see from our text that God looks upon man; for he says of Ephraim, "I have written to him the great things of my law, but they were counted as a strange thing." But see how, when he observes the sin of man, he does not dash him away and spurn him with his foot; he does not shake him by the neck over the gulf of hell, until his brain doth reel and then drop him forever; but rather, he comes down from heaven to plead with his creatures; he argues with them; he puts himself, as it were, upon a level with the sinner—states his grievances and pleads his claim. O Ephraim, I have written unto thee the great things of my law, but they have been unto thee as a strange thing! I come here to-night in God's stead, my friends, to plead with you as God's ambassador, to charge many of you with a sin; to lay it to your hearts by the power of the Spirit, so that you may be convinced of sin, of righteousness, and of a judgment to come. The crime I charge you with is the sin of the text. God has written to you the great things of his law, but they have been unto you as a strange thing. It is concerning this blessed book, the Bible, that I mean to speak to-night. Here lies my text—this Word of God. Here is the theme of my discourse, a theme which demands more eloquence than I possess; a subject upon which a thousand orators might speak at once; a mighty, vast, and comprehensive theme, which might engross all eloquence throughout eternity, and still it would remain unexhausted.

Concerning the Bible, I have three things to say to-night, and they are all in my text. First, its author, "*I* have written;" secondly, its subjects—the great things of God's law; and thirdly, its common treatment—it has been accounted by most men a strange thing.

I. First, then, concerning this book: Who is *the author?* The text says that it is God. "*I* have written to him the great things of my law." Here lies my Bible—who wrote it? I open it, and find it consists of a series of tracts. The first five tracts were written by a man called Moses; I turn on, and I find others. Sometimes I see David is the penman, at other times Solomon. Here I read Micah, then Amos, then Hosea. As I turn further on, to the more luminous pages of the New Testament, I see Matthew, Mark, Luke, and John, Paul, Peter, James, and others; but when I shut up the book, I ask myself, who is the author of it? Do these men jointly claim the authorship? Are they the compositors of this massive volume? Do they between themselves divide the honor? Our holy religion answers, No! This volume is the writing of the living God: each letter was penned with an Almighty finger; each word in it dropped from the everlasting lips; each sentence was dictated by the Holy Spirit. Albeit, that Moses was employed to write his histories with his fiery pen, God guided that pen. It may be that David touched his harp, and let sweet Psalms of melody drop from his fingers; but God moved his hands over the living strings of his golden harp. It may be that Solomon sang canticles of love, or gave forth words of consummate wisdom, but God directed his lips, and made the preacher eloquent. If I follow the thundering Nahum, when his horses plough the waters, or Habakkuk, when he sees the tents of Cushan in affliction; if I read Malachi, when the earth is burning like an oven; if I turn to the smooth page of John, who tells of love, or the rugged, fiery chapters of Peter, who speaks of fire devouring God's enemies; if I turn to Jude, who launches forth anathemas upon the foes of God, everywhere I find God speaking; it is God's voice, not man's; the words are God's words, the words of the Eternal, the Invisible, the Almighty, the Jehovah of this earth. This Bible is God's Bible, and when I see it, I seem to hear a voice springing up from it, saying, "I am the book of God; man, read me. I am God's writing; open my leaf, for I was penned by God; read it, for he is my author, and you will see him visible and manifest everywhere." "I have written to him the great things of my law."

How do you know that God wrote the book? That is just what I shall not try to prove to you. I could if

I pleased, to a demonstration, for there are arguments enough, there are reasons enough, did I care to occupy your time to-night in bringing them before you; but I shall do no such thing. I might tell you, if I pleased, that the grandeur of the style is above that of any mortal writing, and that all the poets who have ever existed could not, with all their works united, give us such sublime poetry and such mighty language as is to be found in the Scriptures. I might insist upon it, that the subjects of which it treats are beyond the human intellect; that man could never have invented the grand doctrines of a Trinity in the Godhead; man could not have told us anything of the creation of the universe; he could never have been the author of the majestic idea of Providence—that all things are ordered according to the will of one great Supreme Being, and work together for good. I might enlarge upon its honesty, since it tells the faults of its writers; its unity, since it never belies itself; its master simplicity, that he who runs may read it; and I might mention a hundred more things, which would all prove, to a demonstration, that the book is of God. But I come not here to prove it. I am a Christian minister, and you are Christians, or profess to be so; and there is never any necessity for Christian ministers to make a point of bringing forward Infidel arguments in order to answer them. It is the greatest folly in the world. Infidels, poor creatures, do not know their own arguments till we tell them, and then they glean their blunted shafts to shoot them at the shield of truth again. It is folly to bring forward these firebrands of hell, even if we are well prepared to quench them. Let men of the world learn error of themselves; do not let us be propagators of their falsehoods. True, there are some preachers who are short of stock, and want them to fill up; but God's own chosen men need not do that; they are taught of God, and God supplies them with matter, with language, with power. There may be some one here to-night who has come without faith, a man of reason, a free-thinker. With him I have no argument at all. I profess not to stand here as a controversialist, but as a preacher of things that I know and feel. But I too have been like him. There was an evil hour when once I shipped the anchor of my faith; I cut the cable of my belief; I no longer moored myself hard by the coasts of Revelation; I allowed my vessel to drift before the wind; I said to reason, "Be thou my captain;" I said to my own brain, "Be thou my rudder;" and I started on my mad voyage. Thank God, it is all over now; but I will tell you its brief history. It was one hurried sailing over the tempestuous ocean of free thought. I went on, and as I went, the skies began to darken; but to make up for that deficiency, the waters were brilliant with corruscations of brilliancy. I saw sparks flying upward that pleased me, and I thought, "If this be free thought, it is a happy thing." My thoughts seemed gems, and I scattered stars with both my hands; but anon, instead of these corruscations of glory, I saw grim fiends, fierce and horrible, start up from the waters, and as I dashed on, they gnashed their teeth, and grinned upon me; they seized the prow of my ship and dragged me on, while I, in part, gloried at the rapidity of my motion, but yet shuddered at the terrific rate with which I passed the old land-marks of my faith. As I hurried forward, with an awful speed, I began to doubt my very existence; I doubted if there were a world, I doubted if there were such a thing as myself. I went to the very verge of the dreary realms of unbelief. I went to the very bottom of the sea of Infidelity. I doubted everything. But here the devil foiled himself: for the very extravagance of the doubt, proved its absurdity. Just when I saw the bottom of that sea, there came a voice which said, "And can this doubt be true?" At this very thought I awoke. I started from that death-dream, which, God knows, might have damned my soul, and ruined this, my body, if I had not awoke. When I arose, faith took the helm; from that moment I doubted not. Faith steered me back; faith cried, "Away, away!" I cast my anchor on Calvary; I lifted my eye to God; and here I am, "alive, and out of hell." Therefore, I speak what I do know. I have sailed that perilous voyage; I have come safe to land. Ask me again to be an Infidel! No; I have tried it; it was sweet at first, but bitter afterwards. Now, lashed to God's gospel more firmly than ever, standing as on a rock of adamant, I defy the arguments of hell to move me; for "I know in whom I have believed, and am persuaded that he is able to keep that which I have committed unto him." But I shall neither plead nor argue this night. You profess to be Christian men, or else you would not be here. Your professions may be lies; what you *say* you are, may be the very contrary to what you *really* are; but still I suppose you all admit that this is the Word of God. A thought or two then upon it. "I have written to him the great things of my law."

First, my friends, stand over this volume, and *admire its authority*. This is no common book. It is not the sayings of the sages of Greece; here are not the utterances of philosophers of past ages. If these words were written by man, we might reject them; but O let me think the solemn thought, that this book is God's handwriting—that these words are God's! Let me look at its date; it is dated from the hills of heaven. Let me look at its letters; they flash glory on my eye. Let me read the chapters; they are big with meaning and mysteries unknown. Let me turn over the prophecies; they are pregnant with unthought-of wonders. Oh, book of books! And wast thou written by my God? Then will I bow before thee. Thou book of vast authority! thou art a proclamation from the Emperor of Heaven; far be it from me to exercise my reason in contradicting thee. Reason, thy place is to stand and find out what this volume means, not to tell what this book ought to say. Come thou, my reason, my intellect, sit thou down and listen, for these words are the words of God. I do not know how to enlarge on this thought. Oh! if you could ever remember that this Bible was actually and really written by God. Oh! if ye had been let into the secret chambers of heaven, if ye had beheld God grasping his pen and writing down these letters—then surely ye would respect them; but they are just as much God's handwriting as if you had seen God write them. This Bible is a book of authority; it is an authorized book, for God has written it. Oh! tremble, tremble, lest any of you despise it; mark its authority, for it is the Word of God.

Then, since God wrote it, mark *its truthfulness.* If I had written it, there would be worms of critics who would at once swarm on it, and would cover it with their evil spawn; had I written it, there would be men who would pull it to pieces at once, and perhaps quite right too. But this is the Word of God; come, search, ye critics, and find a flaw; examine it, from its Genesis to its Revelation, and find an error. This is a vein of pure gold, unalloyed by quartz, or any earthly substance. This is a star without a speck; a sun without a blot; a light without darkness; a moon without its paleness; a glory without a dimness. O Bible! it cannot be said of any other book, that it is perfect and pure; but of thee we can declare all wisdom is gathered up in thee, without a particle of folly. This is the judge that ends the strife, where wit and reason fail. This is the book untainted by any error; but is pure, unalloyed, perfect truth. Why? Because God wrote it. Ah! charge God with error if ye please; tell him that his book is not what it ought to be. I have heard men, with prudish and mock-modesty, who would like to alter the Bible; and (I almost blush to say it) I have heard ministers alter God's Bible, because they were afraid of it. Have you never heard a man say, "He that believeth and is baptized, shall be saved; but he that believeth not"—what does the Bible say?—"Shall be *damned.*" But that does not happen to be polite enough, so they say, "Shall be *condemned.*" Gentlemen, pull the velvet out of your mouths; speak God's word; we want none of your alterations. I have heard men in prayer, instead of saying, "Make your calling and *election* sure," say "Make your calling and *salvation* sure." Pity they were not born when God lived, far—far back, that they might have taught God how to write. Oh, impudence beyond all bounds! Oh, full-blown self-conceit! To attempt to dictate to the All-wise—to teach the Omniscient, and instruct the Eternal. Strange that there should be men so vile as to use the penknife of Jehoiakim, to cut out passages of the word, because they are unpalatable. O ye who dislike certain portions of Holy Writ, rest assured that your taste is corrupt, and that God will not stay for your little opinion. Your dislike is the very reason why God wrote it, because you ought not to be suited; you have no right to be pleased. God wrote what you do not like; he wrote the truth. Oh! let us bend in reverence before it, for God inspired it. It is pure truth. Here from this fountain gushes *aqua vitæ* — the water of life, without a single particle of earth; here from this sun there cometh forth rays of radiance, without the mixture of darkness. Blessed Bible! thou art all truth.

Yet once more, before we leave this point, let us stop and consider *the merciful nature of God*, in having written us a Bible at all. Ah, he might have left us without it, to grope our dark way, as blind men seek the wall; he might have suffered us to wander on with the star of reason as our only guide. I recollect a story of Mr. Hume, who so constantly affirmed that the light of reason is abundantly sufficient. Being at a good minister's house one evening, he had been discussing the question, and declaring his firm belief in the sufficiency of the light of nature. On leaving, the minister offered to hold him a candle to light him down the steps. He said, "No; the light of nature would be enough; the moon would do." It so happened that the moon was covered with a cloud, and he fell down the steps. "Ah!" said the minister, "you had better have had a little light from above, after all, Mr. Hume." So, supposing the light of nature to be sufficient, we had better have a little light from above too, and then we shall be sure to be right. Better have two lights than only one. The light of creation is a bright light. God may be seen in the stars; his name is written in gilt letters on the brow of night; you may discover his glory in the ocean waves, yea, in the trees of the field; but it is better to read it in two books than in one. You will find it here more clearly revealed; for he has written this book himself, and he has given you the key to understand it, if you have the Holy Spirit. Ah, beloved, let us thank God for this Bible; let us love it; let us count it more precious than much fine gold.

But let me say one thing, before I pass on to the second point. If this be the Word of God, what will become of some of you who have not read it for the last month? "Month, sir! I have not read it for this year." Ay, there are some of you who have not read it at all. Most people treat the Bible very politely. They have a small pocket volume, neatly bound; they put a white pocket-handkerchief round it and carry it to their places of worship; when they get home, they lay it up in a drawer till next Sunday morning; then it comes out again for a little bit of a treat, and goes to chapel; that is all the poor Bible gets in the way of an airing. That is your style of entertaining this heavenly messenger. There is dust enough on some of your Bibles to write "damnation" with your fingers. There are some of you who have not turned over your Bibles for a long, long, long while, and what think you? I tell you blunt words, but true words. What will God say at last? When you shall come before him, he shall say, "Did you read my Bible?" "*No.*" "I wrote you a letter of mercy; did you read it?" "*No.*" "Rebel! I have sent thee a letter inviting thee to me; didst thou ever read it?" "*Lord, I never broke the seal; I kept it shut up.*" "Wretch!" says God, "then, thou deservest hell, if I sent thee a loving epistle, and thou wouldst not even break the seal; what shall I do unto thee?" Oh, let it not be so with you. Be Bible-readers; be Bible-searchers.

II. Our second point is: *The subjects on which the Bible treats.* The words of the text are these: "I have written to him the great things of my law." The Bible treats of great things, and of great things only. There is nothing in this Bible which is unimportant. Every verse in it has a solemn meaning; and if we have not found it out yet, we hope yet to do it. You have seen mummies, wrapped round and round with folds of linen. Well, God's Bible is like that; it is a vast roll of white linen, woven in the loom of truth; so you will have to continue unwinding it, roll after roll, before you get the real meaning of it from the very depth; and, when you have found, as you think, a part of the meaning, you will still need to keep on unwinding, unwinding, and all eternity you will be unwinding the words of this wondrous volume. Yet there is nothing in the Bible but great things. Let me divide, so as to be more brief. First, all things in this Bible are great; but, secondly, some things are the greatest of all.

All things in the Bible are great. Some people think it does not matter what doctrines you believe; that it is immaterial what church you attend; that all denominations are alike. Well, I dislike Mrs. Bigotry above almost all people in the world, and I never give her any compliment or praise; but there is another woman I hate equally as much, and that is Mrs. Latitudinarianism—a well-known character, who has made the discovery that all of us are alike. Now, I believe that a man may be saved in any church. Some have been saved in the Church of Rome—a few blessed men whose names I could mention here. I know, blessed be God, that multitudes are saved in the Church of England: she has a host of pious, praying men in her midst. I think that all sections of Protestant Christians have a remnant according to the election of grace; and they had need to have, some of them, a little salt, for otherwise they would go to corruption. But when I say that, do you imagine that I think them all on a level? Are they all alike truthful? One sect says infant baptism is right; another says it is wrong; yet you say they are both right. I cannot see that. One teaches we are saved by free grace; another says that we are not, but are saved by free will; and yet you believe they are both right. I do not understand that. One says that God loves his people, and never leaves off loving them; another says that he did not love his people before they loved him—that he often loves them, and then ceases to love them, and turns them away. They may be both right in the main; but can they both be right when one says "Yes," and the other says "No?" I must have a pair of spectacles, to enable me to look backwards and forwards at the same time, before I can see that. It cannot be, sirs, that they are both right. But some say they differ upon non-essentials. This text says, "I have written to him the *great* things of my law." There is nothing in God's Bible which is not great. Did ever any of you sit down to see which was the purest religion? "Oh," say you, "we never took the trouble. We went just where our father and mother went." Ah! that is a profound reason indeed. You went where your father and mother did. I thought you were sensible people; I did n't think you went where other people pulled you, but went of your own selves. I love my parents above all that breathe, and the very thought that they believed a thing to be true, helps me to think it is correct; but I have not followed them; I belong to a different denomination, and I thank God I do. I can receive them as Christian brethren and sisters; but I never thought that, because they happened to be one thing, I was to be the same. No such thing. God gave me brains, and I will use them; and if you have any intellect, use it too. Never say it does n't matter. Whatever God has put here is of eminent importance: he would not have written a thing that was indifferent. Whatever is here is of some value; therefore, search all questions, try all by the Word of God. I am not afraid to have what I preach tried by this book. Only give me a fair field and no favor, and this book; if I say anything contrary to it, I will withdraw it the next Sabbath-day. By this I stand, by this I fall. Search and see; but don't say, "it does not matter." If God says a thing, it always must be of importance.

But, while all things in God's word are important, *all are not equally important.* There are certain fundamental and vital truths which must be believed, or otherwise no man would be saved. If you want to know what you must believe, if ye would be saved, you will find the great things of God's law between these two covers; they are all contained here. As a sort of digest or summary of the great things of law, I remember an old friend of mine once saying, "Ah! you preach the three R's, and God will always bless you." I said, "What are the three R's?" and he answered, "Ruin, redemption, and regeneration." They contain the sum and substance of divinity. R. for ruin. We were all ruined in the fall; we were all lost when Adam sinned, and we are all ruined by our own transgressions; we are all ruined by our own evil hearts, and our own wicked wills; and we all shall be ruined, unless grace saves us. Then there is a second R. for redemption. We are ransomed by the blood of Christ, a lamb without blemish and without spot; we are rescued by his power; we are ransomed by his merits; we are redeemed by his strength. Then there is R. for regeneration. If we would be pardoned, we must also be regenerated; for no man can partake of redemption unless he is regenerate. Let him be as good as he pleases; let him serve God, as he imagines, as much as he likes; unless he is regenerate, and has a new heart, a new birth, he will still be in the first R. that is ruin. These things contain an epitome of the gospel. I believe there is a better epitome in the five points of Calvanism:—Election according to the fore knowledge of God; the natural depravity and sinfulness of man; particular redemption by the blood of Christ; effectual calling by the power of the Spirit; and ultimate perseverance by the efforts of God's might. I think all those need to be believed, in order to salvation; but I should not like to write a creed like the Athanasian, beginning with "Whosoever shall be saved, before all things it is necessary that he should hold the Catholic faith, which faith is this,"—when I got so far, I should stop, because I should not know what to write. I hold the catholic faith of the Bible, the whole Bible, and nothing but the Bible. It is not for me to draw up creeds; but I ask you to search the Scriptures, for this is the word of life.

God says, "I have written to him the great things of my law." Do you doubt their greatness? Do ye think they are not worth your attention? Reflect a moment, man. Where art thou standing now?

> "Lo, on a narrow neck of land,
> 'Twixt two unbounded seas I stand;
> An inch of time, a moment's space,
> May lodge me in yon heavenly place,
> Or shut me up in hell."

I recollect standing on a seashore once, upon a narrow neck of land, thoughtless that the tide might come up. The tide kept continually washing up on either side, and, wrapped in thoughts, I still stood there, until at last there was the greatest difficulty in getting on shore. You and I stand each day on a narrow neck, and there is one wave coming up there; see, how near it is to your foot; and lo! another follows at every tick of the clock; "our hearts, like muffled drums, are beating funeral marches to the tomb." We are always tending downwards to the grave each moment that we live *This book* tells me that if I am converted, when I die, there is a heaven of joy and love to receive me; it tells me that angels' pinions shall be stretched, and I, borne by strong cherubic wings, shall out-soar the lightning, and mount beyond the stars, up to the throne of God, to dwell forever.

> "Far from a world of grief and sin
> With God eternally shut in."

Oh! it makes the hot tear start from my eye, it makes

my heart too big for this my body, and my brain whirls at the thought of

> "Jerusalem, my happy home,
> Name ever dear to me."

Oh! that sweet scene beyond the clouds; sweet fields arrayed in living green, and rivers of delight. Are not these great things? But then, poor unregenerate soul, the Bible says, if thou art lost, thou art lost forever; it tells thee that if thou diest without Christ, without God, there is no hope for thee; that there is no place without a gleam of hope, where thou shalt read, in burning letters, "Ye knew your duty, but ye did it not;" it tells you, that ye shall be driven from his presence with a "depart, ye cursed." Are not these great things? Yes, sirs, as heaven is desirable, as hell is terrible, as time is short, as eternity is infinite, as the soul is precious, as pain is to be shunned, as heaven is to be sought, as God is eternal, and as his words are sure, these are great things, things ye ought to listen to.

III. Our last point is: *The treatment which the poor Bible receives in this world;* it is accounted a strange thing. What does that mean — the Bible accounted a strange thing? In the first place, it means that it is very strange to some people, because *they never read it.* I remember reading, on one occasion, the sacred story of David and Goliath, and there was a person present, positively grown up to years of maturity, who said to me, "Dear me! what an interesting story; what book is that in?" And I recollect a person once coming to me in private; I spoke to her about her soul, she told me how deeply she felt, how she had a desire to serve God, but she found another law in her members. I turned to a passage in Romans, and read to her, "The good that I would I do not; and the evil which I would not that I do!" She said, "Is that in the Bible? I did not know it." I did not blame her, because she had no interest in the Bible till then; but I did wonder that there could be found persons who knew nothing about such a passage. Ah! you know more about your ledgers than your Bible; you know more about your day-books than what God has written; many of you will read a novel from beginning to end, and what have you got? A mouthful of froth when you have done. But you cannot read the Bible; that solid, lasting, substantial, and satisfying food goes uneaten, locked up in the cupboard of neglect; while anything that man writes, a catch of the day, is greedily devoured. "I have written to him the great things of my law, *but* they were counted as a strange thing." Ye have never read it. I bring the broad charge against you. Perhaps, ye say, I ought not to charge you with any such thing. I always think it better to have a worse opinion of you than too good an one. I charge you with this: you do not read your Bibles. Some of you never have read it through. I know I speak what your heart must say is honest truth. You are not Bible readers. You say you have the Bible in your houses; do I think you are such heathens as not to have a Bible? But when did you read it last? How do you know that your spectacles, which you have lost, have not been there for the last three years? Many people have not turned over its pages for a long time, and God might say unto them, "I have written unto you the great things of my law, but they have been accounted unto you a strange thing."

Others there be who read the Bible; but when they read it, *they say it is so horribly dry.* That young man over there says it is a "bore;" that is the word he uses. He says, "My mother says to me, when you go up to town, read a chapter every day. Well, I thought I would please her, and I said I would. I am sure I wish I had not. I did not read a chapter yesterday, or the day before. We were so busy, I could not help it." You do not love the Bible, do you? "No, there is nothing in it which is interesting." Ah, I thought so. But a little while ago *I* could not see anything in it. Do you know why? Blind men cannot see, can they? But when the Spirit touches the scales of the eyes, they fall off; and when he puts eye-salve on, then the Bible becomes precious. I remember a minister who went to see an old lady, and he thought he would give her some precious promises out of the word of God. Turning to one, he saw written in the margin "P.," and he asked, "What does this mean?" "That means precious, sir." Further down, he saw "T. and P.," and he asked what the letters meant. "That," she said, "means tried and proved, for I have tried and proved it." If you have tried God's word and proved it—if it is precious to your soul, then you are Christains; but those persons who despise the Bible, have "neither part nor lot in the matter." If it is dry to you, you will be dry at last in hell. If you do not esteem it as better than your necessary food, there is no hope for you; for you lack the greatest evidence of your Christianity.

Alas! alas! the worst case is to come. *There are some people who hate the Bible*, as well as despise it. Is there such an one stepped in here? Some of you said, "Let us go and hear what the young preacher has to say to us." This is what he has to say to you: "Behold, ye despisers, and wonder and perish." This is what he hath to say to you: "The wicked shall be turned into hell, and all that forget God." And this, again he has to say to you: "Behold, there shall come in the last days, mockers, like yourselves, walking after your own lusts." But more: he tells you to-night that if you are saved, you must find salvation here. Therefore, despise not the Bible; but search it, read it, and come unto it. Rest thee well assured, O scorner, that thy laughs cannot alter truth, thy jests cannot avert thine inevitable doom. Though in thy hardihood thou shouldst make a league with death, and sign a covenant with hell—yet swift justice shall o'ertake thee, and strong vengeance strike thee low. In vain dost thou jeer and mock, for eternal verities are mightier than thy sophistries, nor can thy smart sayings alter the divine truth of a single word of this volume of Revelation. Oh! why dost thou quarrel with thy best friend, and ill-treat thy only refuge? There yet remains hope, even for the scorner. Hope in a Saviour's veins. Hope in the Father's mercy. Hope in the Holy Spirit's omnipotent agency.

I have done when I have said one word. My friend, the philosopher, says it may be very well for me to urge people to read the Bible; but he thinks there are a great many sciences far more interesting and useful than theology. *Extremely obliged to you for your opinion, sir.* What science do you mean? The science of dissecting beetles and arranging butterflies? "No," you say, "certainly not." The science, then, of arranging stones, and telling us of the strata of the earth? "No, not exactly that." Which science, then? "Oh, all sciences," say you, "are better than the science of the Bible." Ah! sir, that is your opinion; and it is because you are far from God, that you say so. But the science of Jesus Christ is the most excellent of sciences. Let no one turn away from the Bible because it is not a book of learning and wisdom. It is. Would ye know astronomy? It is here: it tells you of the Sun of Righteousness and the Star of Bethlehem. Would you know botany? It is here: it tells you of the plant of renown — the Lily of the Valley, and the Rose of Sharon. Would you know geology and mineralogy? You shall learn it here: for you may read of the Rock of Ages, and the White Stone with the name engraven thereon, which no man knoweth saving he that receiveth it. Would ye study history? Here is the most ancient of all the records of the history of the human race. Whate'er your science is, come and bend o'er this book; your science is here. Come and drink out of this fair fount of knowledge and wisdom, and ye shall find yourselves made wise unto salvation. Wise and foolish, babes and men, gray-headed sires, youths and maidens — I speak to you, I plead with you, I beg of you respect your Bibles, and search them out, for in them ye think ye have eternal life, and these are they which testify of Christ.

I have done. Let us go home and practice what we have heard. I have heard of a woman, who, when she was asked what she remembered of the minister's sermon, said, "I don't recollect anything of it. It was about short weights and bad measures, and I did n't recollect anything but to go home and burn the bushel." So, if you will remember to go home and burn the bushel, if you will recollect to go home and read your Bibles, I shall have said enough. And may God, in his infinite mercy, when you read your Bibles, pour into your soul the illuminating rays of the Sun of Righteousness, by the agency of the ever-adorable Spirit; then you will read to your profit and to your soul's salvation.

We may say of THE BIBLE:

> "God's cabinet of revealed counsel 't is!
> Where weal and woe, are ordered so
> That every man may know which shall be his;
> Unless his own mistake, false application make
>
> It is the index to eternity.
> He cannot miss of endless bliss,
> That takes this chart to steer by,
> Nor can he be mistook, that speaketh by this book.
>
> It is the book of God. What if I should
> Say, God of books, let him that looks
> Angry at that expression, as too bold,
> His thoughts in silence smother, till he find such another."

SERMON III.

THE PERSONALITY OF THE HOLY GHOST.

"And I will pray the Father, and he shall give you another Comforter, that he may abide with you forever; *even* the Spirit of truth; whom the world cannot receive, because it seeth him not, neither knoweth him; but ye know him; for he dwelleth with you, and shall be in you." — JOHN xiv. 16, 17.

You will be surprised to hear me announce that I do not intend this morning to say anything about the Holy Spirit as the Comforter. I propose to reserve that for another discourse.* In this discourse I shall endeavor to explain and enforce certain other doctrines, which I believe are plainly taught in this text, and which I hope God the Holy Ghost may make profitable to our souls. Old John Newton once said, that there were some books which he could not read — they were good and sound enough; but, said he, "they are books of halfpence; you have to take so much in quantity before you have any value; there are other books of silver and others of gold, but I have one book that is a book of bank-notes; and every leaf is a bank-note of immense value." So I found with this text, that I had a bank-note of so large a sum that I

* See next Sermon.

could not tell it out all this morning. I should have to keep you several hours before I could unfold to you the whole value of this precious promise, one of the last which Christ gave to his people.

I invite your attention to this passage because we shall find in it some instruction on four points: first, concerning the true and proper personality of the Holy Ghost; secondly, concerning the united agency of the glorious Three persons in the work of our salvation; thirdly, we shall find something to establish the doctrine of the in-dwelling of the Holy Ghost in the souls of all believers; and fourthly, we shall find out the reason why the carnal mind rejects the Holy Ghost.

I. First of all, we shall have some little instruction concerning the proper *personality of the Holy Spirit.* We are so much accustomed to talk about the influence of the Holy Ghost and his sacred operations and graces, that we are apt to forget that the Holy Spirit is truly and actually a person — that he is a subsistence — an existence; or, as we Trinitarians usually say, one person in the essence of the Godhead. I am afraid that, though we do not know it, we have acquired the habit of regarding the Holy Ghost as an emanation flowing from the Father and the Son, but not as being actually a person himself. I know it is not easy to carry about in our mind the idea of the Holy Spirit as a person. I can think of the Father as a person, because his acts are such as I can understand. I see him hang the world in ether; I behold him swaddling a new-born sea in bands of darkness; I know it is he who formed the drops of hail, who leadeth forth the stars by their hosts, and calleth them by their name; I can conceive of him as a person, because I behold his operations.

I can realize Jesus, the Son of Man, as a real person, because he is bone of my bone, and flesh of my flesh. It takes no great stretch of my imagination to picture the babe in Bethlehem, or behold the "man of sorrows and acquainted with grief," or the king of martyrs, as he was persecuted in Pilate's hall, or nailed to the accursed tree for our sins. Nor do I find it difficult at times to realize the person of my Jesus sitting on his throne in heaven; or girt with clouds and wearing the diadem of all creation, calling the earth to judgment, and summoning us to hear our final sentence. But, when I come to deal with the Holy Ghost, his operations are so mysterious, his doings are so secret, his acts are so removed from everything that is of sense, and of the body, that I cannot so easily get the idea of his being a person; but a person he is. God the Holy Ghost is not an influence, an emanation, a stream of something flowing from the Father; but he is as much an actual person as either God the Son, or God the Father. I shall attempt this morning a little to establish the doctrine, and to show you the truth of it — that God the Holy Spirit is actually a person.

The first proof we shall gather from the pool of holy baptism. Let me take you down, as I have taken others, into the pool now concealed, but which I wish were always open to your view. Let me take you to the baptismal font, where believers put on the name of the Lord Jesus, and you shall hear me pronounce the solemn words, "I baptize thee in the name," — mark, "in the name," not names — "of the Father, and of the Son, and of the Holy Ghost." Every one who is baptized according to the true form laid down in Scripture, must be a Trinitarian: otherwise his baptism is a farce and a lie, and he himself is found a deceiver and a hypocrite before God. As the Father is mentioned, and as the Son is mentioned, so is the Holy Ghost; and the whole is summed up as being a Trinity in unity, by its being said, not the names, but the "name," the glorious name, the Jehovah name, "of the Father, and of the Son, and of the Holy Ghost." Let me remind you that the same thing occurs each time you are dismissed from this house of prayer. In pronouncing the solemn closing benediction, we involve on your behalf the love of Jesus Christ, the grace of the Father, and the fellowship of the Holy Spirit; and thus, according to the apostolic manner, we make a manifest distinction between the persons, showing that we believe the Father to be a person, the Son to be a person, and the Holy Ghost to be a person. Were there no other proofs in Scripture, I think these would be sufficient for every sensible man. He would see that if the Holy Spirit were a mere influence, he would not be mentioned in conjunction with two, whom we all confess to be actual and proper persons.

A second argument arises from the fact, that the Holy Ghost has actually made different appearances on earth. The Great Spirit has manifested himself to man: he has put on a form, so that, whilst he has not been beheld by mortal men, he has been so veiled in an appearance that he was seen, so far as that appearance was concerned, by the eyes of all beholders. See you Jesus Christ our Saviour? There is the river Jordan, with its shelving banks and its willows weeping at its side. Jesus Christ, the Son of God, descends into the stream, and the holy Baptist John plunges him into the waves. The doors of heaven are opened; a miraculous appearance presents itself; a bright light shineth from the sky, brighter than the sun in all its grandeur, and down in a flood of glory descends something which you recognize to be a dove. It rests on Jesus — it sits upon his sacred head, and as the old painters put a halo round the brow of Jesus, so did the Holy Ghost shed a resplendence around the face of him who came to fulfil all righteousness, and therefore commenced with the ordinance of baptism. The Holy Ghost was seen as a dove, to mark his purity and his gentleness, and he came down like a dove *from heaven* to show that it is from heaven alone that he descendeth. Nor is this the only time when the Holy Ghost has been manifest in a visible shape. You see that company of disciples gathered together in an upper room; they are waiting for some promised blessing, and bye-and-bye it shall come. Hark! there is a sound as of a rushing, mighty wind; it fills all the house where they are sitting, and astonished, they look around them, wondering what will come next. Soon a bright light appears, shining upon the heads of each: cloven tongues of fire sat upon them. What were these marvellous appearances of wind and flame but a display of the Holy Ghost in his proper person? I say the fact of an appearance manifests that he must be a person. An influence could not appear — an attribute could not appear: we cannot see attributes — we cannot behold influences. The Holy Ghost must, then, have been a person; since he was beheld by mortal eyes, and came under the cognizance of mortal sense.

Another proof is from the fact, that personal qualities are in Scripture ascribed to the Holy Ghost. First, let me read to you a text in which the Holy Ghost is spoken of as having understanding. In the 1st Epistle to the Corinthians, chap. ii., you will read, "But as it is written, eye hath not seen, nor ear heard, neither hath it entered into the heart of man, the things which God hath prepared for them that love him. But God hath revealed them unto us by his Spirit: for the Spirit searcheth all things, yea, the deep things of God. For what man knoweth the things of a man, save the spirit of man which is in him? Even so the things of God knoweth no man, but the Spirit of God. Here you see an understanding — a power of knowledge is ascribed to the Holy Ghost. Now, if there be any persons here whose minds are of so preposterous a complexion that they would ascribe one attribute to another, and would speak of a mere influence having understanding, then I give up all the argument. But I believe every rational man will admit, that when anything is spoken of as having an understanding, it must be an existence — it must, in fact, be a person. In the 12th chapter, v. 10, of the same Epistle, you will find a *will* ascribed to the Holy Spirit. "But all these worketh that one and the self-same spirit, dividing to every man severally as he will." So it is plain that the Spirit has a will. He does not come from God simply at God's will, but he has a will of his own, which is always in keeping with the will of the infinite Jehovah, but is, nevertheless, distinct and separate; therefore, I say he is a person. In another text, *power* is ascribed to the Holy Ghost, and power is a thing which can only be ascribed to an existence. In Rom. xv. 13, it is written, "Now the God of hope fill you with all joy and peace in believing, that ye may abound in hope through the power of the Holy Ghost." I need not insist upon it, because it is self-evident, that wherever you find understanding, will, and power, you must also find an existence; it cannot be a mere attribute, it cannot be a metaphor, it cannot be a personified influence; but it must be a person.

But I have a proof, which, perhaps, will be more telling upon you than any other. Acts and deeds are ascribed to the Holy Ghost; therefore, he must be a person. You read in the first chapter of the Book of Genesis, that the Spirit brooded over the surface of the earth, when it was as yet all disorder and confusion. This world was once a mass of chaotic matter; there was no order; it was like the valley of darkness and of the shadow of death. God the Holy Ghost spread his wings over it; he sowed the seeds of life in it; the germs from which all beings sprang were implanted by him; he impregnated the earth so that it became capable of life. Now, it must have been a person who brought order out of confusion: it must have been an existence who hovered over this world and made it what it now is. But do we not read in Scripture something more of the Holy Ghost? Yes, we are told that "holy men of old spake as they were moved by the Holy Ghost.' When Moses penned the Pentateuch, the Holy Ghost moved his hand; when David wrote the Psalms, and discoursed sweet music on his harp, it was the Holy Spirit that gave his fingers their seraphic motion; when Solomon dropped from his lips the words of the proverbs of wisdom, or when he hymned the Canticles of love, it was the Holy Ghost who gave him words of knowledge and hymns of rapture. Ah! and what fire was that which touched the lips of the eloquent Isaiah? What hand was that which came upon Daniel?

What might was that which made Jeremiah so plaintive in his grief? or what was that which winged Ezekiel and made him, like an eagle, soar into mysteries aloft, and see the Mighty Unknown beyond our reach? Who was it that made Amos, the herdsman, a prophet? who taught the rugged Haggai to pronounce his thundering sentences? who showed Habakkuk the horses of Jehovah marching through the waters? or who kindled the burning eloquence of Nahum? who caused Malachi to close up the book with the muttering of the word curse? Who was it in each of these save the Holy Ghost? and must it not have been a person who spake in and through these ancient witnesses? We must believe it. We cannot avoid believing it when we read that "holy men of old spake as they were moved by the Holy Ghost." And when has the Holy Ghost ceased to have an influence upon men? We find that still he deals with his ministers and with all his saints. Turn to the Acts, and you will find that the Holy Ghost said, "Separate me Paul and Barnabas for the work." I never heard of an attribute saying such a thing. The Holy Spirit said to Peter, "Go to the Centurion, and what I have cleansed, that call not thou common." The Holy Ghost caught away Philip after he had baptized the Eunuch, and carried him away to another place; and the Holy Ghost said to Paul, "Thou shalt not go into that city, but shall turn into another." And we know that the Holy Ghost was lied unto by Ananias and Sapphira, when it was said, "Thou hast not lied unto man, but unto God." Again, that power which we feel every day, who are called to preach — that wondrous spell which makes our lips so potent — that power which gives us thoughts which are like birds from a far-off region, not the natives of our soul — that influence which I sometimes strangely feel, which, if it does not give me poetry and eloquence, gives me a might I never felt before, and lifts me above my fellow-man — that majesty with which he clothes his ministers, till in the midst of the battle they cry aha! like the war horse of Job, and move themselves like leviathans in the water — that power which gives us might over men, and causes them to sit and listen as if their ears were chained, as if they were entranced by the power of some magician's wand — that power must come from a person; it must come from the Holy Ghost.

But is it not said in Scripture, and do we not feel it, dear brethren, that it is the Holy Ghost who regenerates the soul? It is the Holy Ghost who quickens us. "You hath he quickened who were dead in trespasses and sins." It is the Holy Spirit who imparts the first germ of life, convincing us of sin, of righteousness, and of judgment to come. And is it not the Holy Spirit, who, after that flame is kindled, still fans it with the breath of his mouth and keeps it alive? Its author is its preserver. Oh! can it be said that it is the Holy Ghost who strives in men's souls; that it is the Holy Ghost who brings them to the foot of Sinai, and then guides them into the sweet place that is called Calvary — can it be said that he does all these things, and yet is not a person? It may be said, but it must be said by fools; for he never can be a wise man who can consider that these things can be done by any other than a glorious person — a divine existence.

Allow me to give you one more proof, and I shall have done. Certain feelings are ascribed to the Holy

Ghost, which can only be understood upon the supposition that he is actually a person. In the 4th chapter of Ephesians, v. 30, it is said that the Holy Ghost can be grieved: "Grieve not the Holy Spirit of God, whereby ye are sealed unto the day of redemption." In Isaiah, chap. lxiii. v. 10, it is said that the Holy Ghost can be vexed: "But they rebelled, and vexed his Holy Spirit; therefore he was turned to be their enemy, and he fought against them." In Acts, chap. vii. v. 51, you read that the Holy Ghost can be resisted: "Ye stiff-necked and uncircumcized in heart and ears, ye do always resist the Holy Ghost; as your fathers did, so do ye." And in the 5th chapter, v. 9, of the same book, you will find that the Holy Ghost may be tempted. We are there informed that Peter said to Ananias and Sapphira, "How is it that ye have agreed together to tempt the Spirit of the Lord?" Now, these things could not be emotions which might be ascribed to a quality or an emanation; they must be understood to relate to a person; an influence could not be grieved; it must be a person who can be grieved, vexed, or resisted.

And now, dear brethren, I think I have fully established the point of the personality of the Holy Ghost; allow me now, most earnestly, to impress upon you the absolute necessity of being sound upon the doctrine of the Trinity. I knew a man, a good minister of Jesus Christ he is now, and I believe he was before he turned his eyes unto heresy — he began to doubt the glorious divinity of our blessed Lord, and for years did he preach the heterodox doctrine, until one day he happened to hear a very eccentric old minister preaching from the text, "But there the *glorious Lord* shall be unto us a place of broad rivers and streams, wherein shall go no galley with oars, neither shall gallant ship pass thereby. Thy tacklings are loosed; they could not well strengthen their mast, they could not spread the sail." "Now," said the old minister, "you give up the Trinity, and your tacklings are loosed, you cannot strengthen your masts. Once give up the doctrine of three persons, and your tacklings are all gone; your mast, which ought to be a support to your vessel, is a rickety one, and shakes." A gospel without a Trinity! it is a pyramid built upon its apex. A gospel without the Trinity! it is a rope of sand that cannot hold together. A gospel without the Trinity! then, indeed, Satan can overturn it. But, give me a gospel with the Trinity, and the might of hell cannot prevail against it; no man can any more overthrow it than a bubble could split a rock, or a feather break in halves a mountain. Get the thought of the three persons, and you have the marrow of all divinity. Only know the Father, and know the Son, and know the Holy Ghost to be one, and all things will appear clear. This is the golden key to the secrets of nature; this is the silken clue of the labyrinths of mystery, and he who understands this, will soon understand as much as mortals e'er can know.

II. Now for our second point — the *united agency* of the three persons in the work of our salvation. Look at the text, and you will find all the three persons mentioned. "I"— that is the Son — "will pray the Father, and he shall give you another Comforter." There are the three persons mentioned, all of them doing something for our salvation. "I will pray," says the Son. "I will send," says the Father. "I will comfort," says the Holy Ghost. Now, let us, for a few moments, discourse upon this wondrous theme—the unity of the three persons with regard to the great purpose of the salvation of the elect. When God first made man, he said, "Let *us* make man," not let *me*, but, "Let us make man in our own image." The covenant Elohim said to each other, "Let us unitedly become the creator of man." "So, when in ages far gone by, in eternity, they said, "Let us save man;" it was not the Father who said, "Let *me* save man," but the three persons conjointly said, with one consent, "Let *us* save man." It is to me a source of sweet comfort to think that it is not one person of the Trinity that is engaged for my salvation; it is not simply one person of the Godhead who vows that he will redeem me; but it is a glorious trio of Godlike ones, and the three declare, unitedly, "*We* will save man."

Now, observe here, that each person is spoken of as performing a separate office. "I will pray," says the Son; that is intercession. "I will send," says the Father; that is donation. "I will comfort," says the Holy Spirit; that is supernatural influence. O! if it were possible for us to see the three persons of the Godhead, we should behold one of them standing before the throne, with outstretched hands, crying day and night, "O Lord, how long?" We should see one girt with Urim and Thummim, precious stones, on which are written the twelve names of the tribes of Israel; we should behold him, crying unto his Father, "Forget not thy promises, forget not thy covenant;" we should hear him make mention of our sorrows, and tell forth our griefs on our behalf, for he is our intercessor. And could we behold the Father, we should not see him a listless and idle spectator of the intercession of the Son, but we should see him with attentive ear listening to every word of Jesus, and granting every petition. Where is the Holy Spirit all the while? Is he lying idle? O no; he is floating over the earth, and when he sees a weary soul, he says, "Come to Jesus, he will give you rest;" when he beholds an eye filled with tears, he wipes away the tears, and bids the mourner look for comfort on the cross; when he sees the tempest-tossed believer, he takes the helm of his soul and speaks the word of consolation; he helpeth the broken in heart, and bindeth up their wounds; and, ever on his mission of mercy, he flies around the world, being everywhere present. Behold, how the three persons work together. Do not then say, "I am grateful to the Son"—so you ought to be, but God the Son no more saves you than God the Father. Do not imagine that God the Father is a great tyrant, and that God the Son had to die to make him merciful. It was not to make the Father's love flow towards his people. Oh no. One loves as much as the other; the three are conjoined in the great purpose of rescuing the elect from damnation.

But you must notice another thing in my text, which will show the blessed unity of the three—the one person promises to the other. The Son says, "I will pray the Father." "Very well," the disciples may have said, "We can trust you for that." "And he will send you." You see, here is the Son signing a bond on behalf of the Father. "He will send you another Comforter." There is a bond on behalf of the Holy Spirit too. "And he will abide with you forever." One person speaks for the other, and how could they, if there were any disagreement between them? If one wished to save, and the other not, they could not promise on another's behalf. But whatever the Son says, the Father listens to; whatever the Father promises, the Holy Ghost works; and, whatever the Holy Ghost injects into the soul, that God the Father fulfils. So, the three together mutually promise on one another's behalf. There is a bond with three names appended — Father, Son, and Holy Ghost. By three immutable things, as well as by two, the Christian is secured beyond the reach of death and hell. A Trinity of securities, because there is a Trinity of God.

III. Our third point is, the *indwelling* of the Holy Ghost in believers. Now, beloved, these first two things have been matters of pure doctrine; this is the subject of experience. The indwelling of the Holy Ghost is a subject so profound, and so having to do with the inner man, that no soul will be able truly and really to comprehend what I say, unless it has been taught of God. I have heard of an old minister, who told a fellow of one of the Cambridge colleges, that he understood a language that *he* never learnt in all his life. "I have not," he said, "even a smattering of Greek, and I know no Latin, but thank God, I can talk the language of Canaan, and that is more than you can." So, beloved, I shall now have to talk a little of the language of Canaan. If you cannot comprehend me, I am much afraid it is because you are not of Israelitish extraction; you are not a child of God, nor an inheritor of the kingdom of heaven.

We are told in the text, that Jesus would send the Comforter, who would abide in the saints forever; who would dwell with them, and be in them. Old Ignatius, the martyr, used to call himself Theophorus, or the God-bearer, "because," said he, "I bear about with me the Holy Ghost." And truly every Christian is a God-bearer. "Know ye not that ye are the temples of the Holy Ghost? for he dwelleth in you." That man is no Christian who is not the subject of the indwelling of the Holy Spirit; he may talk well, he may understand theology, and be a sound Calvinist; he will be the child of nature finely dressed, but not the living child. He may be a man of so profound an intellect, so gigantic a soul, so comprehensive a mind, and so lofty an imagination, that he may dive into all the secrets of nature, may know the path which the eagle's eye hath not seen, and go into depths where the ken of mortals reacheth not, but he shall not be a Christian with all his knowledge, he shall not be a son of God with all his researches, unless he understands what it is to have the Holy Ghost dwelling in him, and abiding in him; yea, and that forever.

Some people call this fanaticism, and they say, "You are a Quaker; why not follow George Fox?" Well, we would not mind that much: we would follow any one who followed the Holy Ghost. Even he, with all his eccentricities, I doubt not, was, in many cases, actually inspired by the Holy Spirit; and whenever I find a man in whom there rests the Spirit of God, the spirit within me leaps to hear the spirit within him, and we feel that we are one. The Spirit of God in one Christian soul recognizes the Spirit in another. I recollect talking with a good man, as I believe he was, who was insisting that it was impossible for us to know whether we had the Holy Spirit within us or not. I should like him to be here this morning, because I would read this verse to him, "But ye know him, for he dwelleth with you, and shall be in you." Ah! you think you cannot tell whether you have the Holy Spirit or not. Can I tell whether I am alive or not? If I were touched by electricity, could I tell whether I was or not? I suppose I should; the shock would be strong enough to make me know where I stood. So, if I have God within me—if I have Deity tabernacling in my breast—if I have God the Holy Ghost resting in my heart, and making a temple of my body, do you think I shall know it? Call ye it fanaticism if you will, but I trust that there are some of us who know what it is to be always, or generally, under the influence of the Holy Spirit—always in one sense, generally in another. When we have difficulties, we ask the direction of the Holy Ghost. When we do not understand a portion of Holy Scripture, we ask God the Holy Ghost to shine upon us. When we are depressed, the Holy Ghost comforts us. You cannot tell what the wondrous power of the indwelling of the Holy Ghost is; how it pulls back the hand of the saint when he would touch the forbidden thing; how it prompts him to make a covenant with his eyes; how it binds his feet, lest they should fall in a slippery way; how it restrains his heart, and keeps him from temptation. O ye, who know nothing of the indwelling of the Holy Ghost, despise it not. O despise not the Holy Ghost, for it is the unpardonable sin. "He that speaketh a word against the Son of Man, it shall be forgiven him, but he that speaketh against the Holy Ghost, it shall never be forgiven him, either in this life, or that which is to come." So saith the Word of God. Therefore, tremble, lest in anything ye despise the influences of the Holy Spirit.

But before closing this point, there is one little word that pleases me very much, that is "forever." You knew I should not miss that; you were certain I could not let it go without observation. "Abide with you forever." I wish I could get an Arminian here to finish my sermon. I fancy I see him taking that word "forever." He would say, "for — forever;" he would have to stammer and stutter; for he could never get it out all at once. He might stand and pull it about, and at last he would have to say, "the translation is wrong." And then I suppose the poor man would have to prove that the original was wrong too. Ah! but blessed be God we can read it — "He shall abide with you forever." Once give me the Holy Ghost, and I shall never lose him till "forever" has run out; till eternity has spun its everlasting rounds.

IV. Now we have to close up with a brief remark on the reason why the world rejects the Holy Ghost. It is said, "Whom the world cannot receive, because it seeth him not, neither knoweth him." You know what is sometimes meant by "the world" — those whom God in his wondrous sovereignty passed over when he chose his people: the preterite ones; those passed over in God's wondrous preterition — not the reprobates who were condemned to damnation by some awful decree; but those passed over by God, when he chose out his elect. These cannot receive the Spirit. Again, it means all in a carnal state are not able to procure themselves this divine influence; and, thus it is true, "Whom the world cannot receive."

The unregenerate world of sinners despises the

Holy Ghost, "because it seeth him not." Yes, I believe this is the great secret why many laugh at the idea of the existence of the Holy Ghost — because they see him not. You tell the worldling, "I have the Holy Ghost within me." He says, "I cannot see it." He wants it to be something tangible — a thing he can recognize with his senses. Have you ever heard the argument used by a good old Christian against an Infidel doctor? The doctor said there was no soul, and asked, "Did you ever see a soul?" "No," said the Christian. "Did you ever hear a soul?" "No." "Did you ever smell a soul?" "No." "Did you ever taste a soul?" "No." "Did you ever feel a soul?" "Yes," said the man — "I feel I have one within me." "Well," said the doctor, "there are four senses against one; you have only one on your side." "Very well," said the Christian, "Did you ever see a pain?" "No." "Did you ever hear a pain?" "No." "Did you ever smell a pain?" "No." "Did you ever taste a pain?" "No." "Did you ever feel a pain?" "Yes." "And that is quite enough, I suppose, to prove there is a pain?" "Yes." So the worldling says there is no Holy Ghost, because he cannot see it. Well, but we feel it. You say that is fanaticism, and that we never felt it. Suppose you tell me that honey is bitter, I reply, "No, I am sure you cannot have tasted it; taste it and try." So with the Holy Ghost; if you did but feel his influence, you would no longer say there is no Holy Spirit, because you cannot see it. Are there not many things, even in nature, which we cannot see? Did you ever see the wind? No; but ye know there is wind, when ye behold the hurricane tossing the waves about, and rending down the habitations of men; or when, in the soft evening zephyr, it kisses the flowers, and maketh dew-drops hang in pearly coronets around the rose. Did ye ever see electricity? No; but ye know there is such a thing, for it travels along the wires for thousands of miles, and carries our messages; though you cannot see the thing itself, you know there is such a thing. So you must believe there is a Holy Ghost working in us, both to will and to do, even though it is beyond our senses.

But the last reason why worldly men laugh at the doctrine of the Holy Spirit, is, because they do not know it. If they know it by heartfelt experience, and if they recognized its agency in the soul; if they had ever been touched by it; if they had been made to tremble under a sense of sin; if they had had their hearts melted, they would never have doubted the existence of the Holy Ghost.

And now, beloved, it says, "He dwelleth with you, and shall be in you." We will close up with that sweet recollection — the Holy Ghost dwells in all believers, and shall be with them.

One word of comment and advice to the saints of God, and to sinners, and I have done. Saints of the Lord! ye have this morning heard that God the Holy Ghost is a person; ye have had it proved to your souls. What follows from this? Why, it followeth how earnest ye should be in prayer *to* the Holy Spirit, as well as *for* the Holy Spirit. Let me say that this is an inference that you should lift up your prayers to the Holy Ghost: that you should cry earnestly unto him; for he is able to do exceeding abundantly above all you can speak or think. See this mass of people. What is to convert it? See this crowd. Who is to make my influence permeate through the mass? You know this place now has a mighty influence, and, God blessing us, it will have an influence not only upon this city, but upon England at large; for we now employ the press as well as the pulpit; and certainly, I should say, before the close of the year, more than two hundred thousand of my productions will be scattered through the land — words uttered by my lips, or written by my pen. But how can this influence be rendered for good? How shall God's glory be promoted by it? Only by incessant prayer for the Holy Spirit; by constantly calling down the influence of the Holy Ghost upon us; we want him to rest upon every page that is printed, and upon every word that is uttered. Let us then be doubly earnest in pleading with the Holy Ghost, that he would come and own our labors; that the whole church at large may be revived thereby, and not ourselves only, but the whole world share in the benefit.

Then, to the ungodly, I have this one closing word to say. Ever be careful how you speak of the Holy Ghost. I do not know what the unpardonable sin is, and I do not think any man understands it; but it is something like this: "He that speaketh a word against the Holy Ghost, it shall never be forgiven him." I do not know what that means; but tread carefully! There is danger; there is a pit which our ignorance has covered by sand; tread carefully! you may be in it before the next hour. If there is any strife in your heart to-day, perhaps you will go to the ale-house and forget it. Perhaps there is some voice speaking in your soul, and you will put it away. I do not tell you you will be resisting the Holy Ghost, and committing the unpardonable sin; but it is somewhere there. Be very careful. O there is no crime on earth, so black as the crime against the Holy Spirit! Ye may blaspheme the Father, and ye shall be damned for it, unless ye repent; ye may blaspheme the Son, and hell shall be your portion, unless ye are forgiven; but blaspheme the Holy Ghost, and thus saith the Lord: "There is no forgiveness, either in this world nor in the world which is to come." I cannot tell you what it is; I do not profess to understand it; but there it is. It is the danger signal; stop! man, stop! If thou hast despised the Holy Spirit—if thou hast laughed at his revelations, and scorned what Christians call his influence, I beseech thee, stop! This morning seriously deliberate. Perhaps some of you have actually committed the unpardonable sin; stop! Let fear stop you; sit down. Do not drive on so rashly as you have done, Jehu! O slacken your reins! Thou who art such a profligate in sin—thou who hast uttered such hard words against the Trinity, stop! Ah, it makes us all stop. It makes us all draw up, and say, "Have I not perhaps so done?" Let us think of this; and let us not at any time trifle either with the words or the acts of God the Holy Ghost.

SERMON IV.

THE COMFORTER.

"But the Comforter, *which* is the Holy Ghost, whom the Father will send in my name, he shall teach you all things and bring all things to your remembrance, whatsoever I have said unto you." — JOHN xiv. 26.

GOOD old Simeon called Jesus the consolation of Israel; and so he was. Before his actual appearance, his name was the day-star; cheering the darkness, and prophetic of the rising sun. To him they looked with the same hope which cheers the nightly watcher, when from the lonely castle-top he sees the fairest of the stars, and hails her as the usher of the morn. When he was on earth, he must have been the consolation of all those who were privileged to be his companions. We can imagine how readily the disciples would run to Christ to tell him of their griefs, and how sweetly, with that matchless intonation of his voice, he would speak to them, and bid their fears be gone. Like children, they would consider him as their Father; and to him every want, every groan, every sorrow, every agony, would at once be carried; and he, like a wise physician, had a balm for every wound; he had mingled a cordial for their every care; and readily did he dispense some mighty remedy to allay all the fever of their troubles. Oh! it must have been sweet to have lived with Christ. Surely, sorrows were then but joys in masks, because they gave an opportunity to go to Jesus to have them removed. Oh! would to God, some of us may say, that we could have lain our weary heads upon the bosom of Jesus, and that our birth had been in that happy era, when we might have heard his kind voice, and seen his kind look, when he said, "Let the weary ones come unto me."

But now he was about to die. Great prophecies were to be fulfilled; and great purposes were to be answered; and therefore, Jesus must go. It behoved him to suffer, that he might be made a propitiation for our sins. It behoved him to slumber in the dust awhile, that he might perfume the chamber of the grave to make it—

"No more a charnel house to fence
The relics of lost innocence."

It behoved him to have a resurrection, that we, who shall one day be the dead in Christ, might rise first, and in glorious bodies stand upon earth. And it behoved him that he should ascend up on high, that he might lead captivity captive; that he might chain the fiends of hell; that he might lash them to his chariot-wheels, and drag them up high heaven's hill, to make them feel a second overthrow from his right arm, when he should dash them from the pinnacles of heaven down to the deeper depths beneath. "It is right I should go away from you," said Jesus, "for if I go not away, the Comforter will not come." Jesus must go. Weep, ye disciples: Jesus must be gone. Mourn, ye poor ones, who are to be left without a Comforter. But hear how kindly Jesus speaks: "I will not leave you comfortless, I will pray the Father, and he shall send you another Comforter, who shall be with you, and shall dwell in you forever." He would not leave those few poor sheep alone in the wilderness; he would not desert his children, and leave them fatherless. Albeit that he had a mighty mission which did fill his heart and hand; albeit he had so much to perform, that we might have thought that even his gigantic intellect would be overburdened; albeit he had so much to suffer, that we might suppose his whole soul to be concentrated upon the thought of the sufferings to be endured. Yet it was not so; before he left, he gave soothing words of comfort; like the good Samaritan, he poured in oil and wine, and we see what he promised: "I will send you another Comforter — one who shall be just what I have been, yea, even more; who shall console you in your sorrows, remove your doubts, comfort you in your afflictions, and stand as my vicar on earth, to do that which I would have done had I tarried with you."

Before I discourse of the Holy Ghost as the Comforter, I must make one or two remarks on the different translations of the word rendered "Comforter." The Rhemish translation, which you are aware is adopted by Roman Catholics, has left the word untranslated, and gives it "Paraclete." "But the Paraclete, which is the Holy Ghost, whom the Father will send in my name, he shall teach you all things." This is the original Greek word, and it has some other meanings beside "Comforter." Sometimes it means the monitor or instructor: "I will send you another monitor, another teacher." Frequently it means "Advocate;" but the most common meaning of the word is that which we have here: I will send you another *Comforter.*" However, we cannot pass over those other two interpretations without saying something upon them.

"I will send you another teacher." Jesus Christ had been the official teacher of his saints whilst on earth. They called no man Rabbi except Christ. They sat at no men's feet to learn their doctrines; but they had them direct from the lips of him who "spake as never man spake." "And now," says he, "when I am gone, where shall you find the great infallible teacher? Shall I set you up a pope at Rome, to whom you shall go, and who shall be your infallible oracle? Shall I give you the councils of the church to be held to decide all knotty points?" Christ said no such thing. "I am the infallible paraclete, or teacher, and when I am gone, I will send you another teacher, and he shall be the person who is to explain Scripture; he shall be the authoritative oracle of God, who shall make all dark things light, who shall unravel mysteries, who shall untwist all knots of revelation, and shall make you understand what you could not discover, had it not been for his influence." And, beloved, no man ever learns anything aright, unless he is taught of the Spirit. You may learn election, and you may know it so that you shall be damned by it, if you are not taught of the Holy Ghost; for I have known some who have learned election to their soul's destruction: they have learned it so that they said they were of the elect, whereas, they had no marks, no evidences, and no works of the Holy Ghost in their souls. There is a way of learning truth in Satan's college, and holding it in licentiousness; but if so, it shall be to your souls as poison to your veins, and prove your everlasting ruin. No man can know Jesus Christ unless he is taught of God. There is no doctrine of the Bible which can be safely, thoroughly, and truly learned, except by the agency of the one authoritative teacher. Ah! tell me not of systems of divinity; tell me not of schemes of theology; tell me not of infallible commentators, or most learned and most arrogant doctors; but tell me of the Great Teacher, who shall instruct us, the sons of God, and shall make us wise to understand all things. He is *the* Teacher; it matters not what this man or that man says; I rest on no man's boasting authority, nor will you. Ye are not to be carried away with the craftiness of men, nor sleight of words; this is the authoritative oracle — the Holy Ghost resting in the hearts of his children.

The other translation is *advocate*. Have you ever thought how the Holy Ghost can be said to be an advocate? You know Jesus Christ is called the wonderful, the counsellor, the mighty God; but how can the Holy Ghost be said to be an advocate? I suppose it is thus: he is an advocate on earth to plead against the enemies of the cross. How was it that Paul could so ably plead before Felix and Agrippa? How was it that the Apostles stood unawed before the magistrates, and confessed their Lord? How has it come to pass, that in all times God's ministers have been made fearless as lions, and their brows have been firmer than brass; their hearts sterner than steel, and their words like the language of God? Why, it was simply for this reason: that it was not the man who pleaded, but it was God the Holy Ghost pleading through him. Have you never seen an earnest minister, with hands uplifted and eyes dropping tears, pleading with the sons of men? Have you never admired that portrait from the hand of old John Bunyan?—a grave person with eyes lifted up to heaven, the best of books in his hand, the law of truth written on his lips, the world behind his back, standing as if he pleaded with men, and a crown of gold hanging over his head. Who gave that minister so blessed a manner, and such goodly matter? Whence came his skill? Did he acquire it in the college? Did he learn it in the seminary? Ah, no. He learned it of the God of Jacob; he learned it of the Holy Ghost; for the Holy Ghost is the great counsellor who teaches us how to advocate his cause aright.

But, besides this, the Holy Ghost is the advocate in men's hearts. Ah! I have known men reject a doctrine until the Holy Ghost began to illuminate them. We who are the advocates of the truth, are often very poor pleaders; we spoil our cause by the words we use; but it is a mercy that the brief is in the hand of a special pleader, who will advocate successfully, and overcome the sinner's opposition. Did you ever know him fail once? Brethren, I speak to your souls: has not God in old times convinced you of sin? Did not the Holy Ghost come and prove that you were guilty, although no minister could ever get you out of your self-righteousness? Did he not advocate Christ's righteousness? Did he not stand and tell you that your works were filthy rags? And when you had well-nigh still refused to listen to his voice, did he not fetch hell's drum and make it sound about your ears; bidding you look through the vista of future years, and see the throne set, and the books open, and the sword brandished, and hell burning, and fiends howling, and the damned shrieking forever? And did he not convince you of the judgment to come? He is a mighty advocate when he pleads in the soul, of sin, of righteousness, and of the judgment to come. Blessed advocate! plead in my heart; plead with my conscience. When I sin, make conscience bold to tell me of it; when I err, make conscience speak at once; and when I turn aside to crooked ways, then advocate the cause of righteousness, and bid me sit down in confusion, knowing my guiltiness in the sight of God.

But there is yet another sense in which the Holy Ghost advocates, and that is, he advocates our cause with Jesus Christ, with groanings that cannot be uttered. O my soul! thou art ready to burst within me. O my heart! thou art swelled with grief. The hot tide of my emotion would well-nigh overflood the channels of my veins. I long to speak, but the very desire chains my tongue. I wish to pray, but the fervency of my feeling curbs my language. There is a groaning within that cannot be uttered. Do you know who can utter that groaning? who can understand it, and who can put it into heavenly language, and utter it in a celestial tongue, so that Christ can hear it? O yes; it is God the Holy Spirit; he advocates our cause with Christ, and then Christ advocates it with his Father. He is the advocate who maketh intercession for us, with groanings that cannot be uttered.

Having thus explained the Spirit's office as a teacher and advocate, we now come to the translation of our version, the Comforter; and here I shall have three divisions: first, the *comforter;* secondly, the *comfort;* and thirdly, the *comforted.*

I. First, then, the Comforter. Briefly let me run over in my mind, and in your minds too, the characteristics of this glorious Comforter. Let me tell you some of the attributes of his comfort, so that you may understand how well adapted he is to your case.

And first, we will remark that God the Holy Ghost is a very *loving* Comforter. I am in distress, and I want consolation. Some passer by hears of my sorrow, and he steps within, sits down, and essays to cheer me; he speaks soothing words, but he loves me not; he is a stranger; he knows me not at all; he has only come in to try his skill. And what is the consequence? His words run o'er me like oil upon a slab of marble; they are like the pattering rain upon the rock; they do not break my grief; it stands unmoved as adamant, because he has no love for me. But let some one who loves me dear as his own life, come and plead with me, then truly his words are music; they taste like honey: he knows the password of the doors of my heart, and my ear is attentive to every word: I catch the intonation of each syllable as it falls, for it is like the harmony of the harps of heaven. Oh! there is a voice in love, it speaks a language which is its own: it has an idiom and a brogue which none can mimic; wisdom cannot imitate it; oratory cannot attain unto it; it is love alone which can reach the mourning heart; love is the only handkerchief which can wipe the mourner's tears away. And is not the Holy Ghost a loving comforter? Dost thou know, O saint, how much the Holy Spirit loves thee? Canst thou measure the love of the Spirit? Dost thou know how great is the affection of his soul towards thee? Go measure heaven with thy span; go weigh the mountains in the scales; go take the ocean's water, and tell each drop; go count the sand upon the sea's wide shore; and when thou hast accomplished this, thou canst tell how much he loveth thee. He has loved thee long, he has loved thee well, he loved thee ever, and he still shall love thee; surely he is the person to comfort thee, because he loves. Admit him, then, to your heart, O Christian, that he may comfort you in your distress.

But next, he is a *faithful* Comforter. Love sometimes proveth unfaithful. "Oh! sharper than a serpent's tooth" is an unfaithful friend! Oh! far more bitter than the gall of bitterness, to have a friend turn from me in my distress! Oh! woe of woes, to have one who loves me in my prosperity, forsake me in the dark day of my trouble. Sad indeed; but such is not God's Spirit. He ever loves, and loves even to the end — a faithful Comforter. Child of God, you are in trouble. A little while ago, you found him a sweet and loving Comforter; you obtained relief from him when others were but broken cisterns; he sheltered you in his bosom, and carried you in his arms. Oh, wherefore dost thou distrust him now? Away with thy fears; for he is a faithful Comforter. "Ah! but," thou sayest, "I fear I shall be sick, and shall be deprived of his ordinances." Nevertheless, he shall visit thee on thy sick bed, and sit by thy side, to give thee consolation. "Ah! but I have distresses greater than you can conceive of; wave upon wave rolleth over me; deep calleth unto deep, at the noise of the Eternal's waterspouts." Nevertheless, he will be faithful to his promise. "Ah! but I have sinned." So thou hast, but sin cannot sever thee from his love; he loves thee still. Think not, O poor downcast child of God, because the scars of thine old sins have marred thy beauty, that he loves thee less because of that blemish. O no! He loved thee when he foreknew thy sin; he loved thee with the knowledge of what the aggregate of thy wickedness would be; and he does not love thee less now. Come to him in all boldness of faith; tell him thou hast grieved him, and he will forget thy wandering, and will receive thee again; the kisses of his love shall be bestowed upon thee, and the arms of his grace shall embrace thee. He is faithful: trust him, he will never deceive you; trust him, he will never leave you.

Again, he is an *unwearied* Comforter. I have sometimes tried to comfort persons, and have been tired. You, now and then, meet with the case of a nervous person. You ask, "What is your trouble?" You are told; and you essay, if possible, to remove it; but while you are preparing your artillery to battle the trouble, you find that it has shifted its quarters, and is occupying quite a different position. You change your argument and begin again; but lo, it is again gone, and you are bewildered. You feel like Hercules, cutting off the ever-growing heads of the Hydra, and you give up your task in despair. You meet with persons whom it is impossible to comfort, reminding one of the man who locked himself up in fetters, and threw the key away, so that nobody could unlock him. I have found some in the fetters of despair. "O, I am the man," say they, "that has seen affliction; pity me, pity me, O, my friends;" and the more you try to comfort such people, the worse they get; and, therefore, out of all heart, we leave them to wander alone, among the tombs of their former joys. But the Holy Ghost is never out of heart with those whom he wishes to comfort. He attempts to comfort us, and we run away from the sweet cordial; he gives some sweet draught to cure us, and we will not drink it; he gives some wondrous potion to charm away all our troubles, and we put it away from us. Still he pursues us; and though we say that we will not be comforted, he says we shall be, and when he has said, he does it; he is not to be wearied by all our sins, nor by all our murmurings.

And oh, how *wise* a Comforter is the Holy Ghost. Job had comforters, and I think he spoke the truth, when he said, "Miserable comforters are ye all." But I dare say they esteemed themselves wise; and when the young man Elihu rose to speak, they thought he had a world of impudence. Were they not "grave and reverend seniors?" Did not they comprehend his grief and sorrow? If they could not comfort him, who could? But they did not find out the cause. They thought he was not really a child of God, that he was self-righteous, and they gave him the wrong physic. It is a bad case when the doctor mistakes a disease, and gives a wrong prescription, and so, perhaps, kills the patient. Sometimes, when we go and visit people, we mistake their disease; we want to comfort them on this point, whereas they do not require any such comfort at all, and they would be better left alone, than spoiled by such unwise comforters as we are. But oh, how wise the Holy Spirit is! he takes the soul, lays it on the table, and dissects it in a moment; he finds out the root of the matter, he sees where the complaint is, and then he applies the knife where something is required to be taken away, or puts a plaster where the sore is; and he never mistakes. O, how wise is the blessed Holy Ghost; from every comforter I turn and leave them all, for thou art he who alone givest the wisest consolation.

Then mark, how *safe* a Comforter the Holy Ghost is. All comfort is not safe, mark that. There is a young man over there very melancholy. You know how he became so. He stepped into the house of God and heard a powerful preacher, and the word was blessed, and convinced him of sin. When he went home, his father and the rest found there was something different about him, " Oh," they said, "John is mad, he is crazy;" and what said his mother? " Send him into the country for a week; let him go to the ball, or the theatre." John, did you find any comfort there? " Ah, no; they made me worse, for while I was there, I thought hell might open and swallow me up." Did you find any relief in the gayeties of the world? "No," say you, "I thought it was idle waste of time." Alas! this is miserable comfort, but it is the comfort of the worldling; and, when a Christian gets into distress, how many will recommend him this remedy and the other. " Go and hear Mr. So-and-so preach;" "have a few friends at your house;" "read such-and-such a consoling volume;" and very likely it is the most unsafe advice in the world. The devil will sometimes come to men's souls as a false comforter; and he will say to the soul, "what need is there to make all this ado about repentance? you are no worse than other people;" and he will try to make the soul believe, that what is presumption, is the real assurance of the Holy Ghost; thus he deceives many by false comfort. Ah! there have been many, like infants, destroyed by elixirs, given to lull them to sleep; many have been ruined by the cry of " peace, peace," when there is no peace; hearing gentle things, when they ought to be stirred to the quick. Cleopatra's asp was brought in a basket of flowers; and men's ruin often lurks in fair and sweet speeches. But the Holy Ghost's comfort is safe, and you may rest on it. Let him speak the word, and there is a reality about it; let him give the cup of consolation, and you may drink it to the bottom; for in its depths there are no dregs, nothing to intoxicate or ruin, it is all safe.

Moreover, the Holy Ghost is an *active* Comforter: he does not comfort by words, but by deeds. Some comfort by, "Be ye warmed, and be ye filled, giving nothing." But the Holy Ghost gives, he intercedes with Jesus; he gives us promises, he gives us grace, and so he comforts us. Mark again, he is always a *successful* Comforter; he never attempts what he cannot accomplish.

Then, to close up, he is an *ever-present* Comforter, so that you never have to send for him. Your God is always near you; and when you need comfort in your distress, behold the word is nigh thee; it is in thy mouth, and in thy heart. He is an ever-present help in time of trouble. I wish I had time to expand these thoughts, but I cannot.

II. The second thing is, the comfort. Now, there are some persons who make a great mistake about the influence of the Holy Spirit. A foolish man who had a fancy to preach in a certain pulpit, though in truth he was quite incapable of the duty, called upon the minister, and assured him solemnly, that it had been revealed to him by the Holy Ghost that he was to preach in his pulpit. "Very well," said the minister, "I suppose I must not doubt your assertion, but as it has not been revealed to me that I am to let you preach, you must go your way, until it is." I have heard many fanatical persons say the Holy Spirit revealed this and that to them. Now, that is very generally revealed nonsense. The Holy Ghost does not reveal anything fresh now. He brings old things to our remembrance. "He shall teach you all things, and bring all things to your remembrance, whatsoever I have told you." The canon of revelation is closed, there is no more to be added; God does not give a fresh revelation, but he rivets the old one. When it has been forgotten, and laid in the dusty chamber of our memory, he fetches it out and cleans the picture, but does not paint a new one. There are no new doctrines, but the old ones are often revived. It is not, I say, by any new revelation that the Spirit comforts. He does so by telling us old things over again; he brings a fresh lamp to manifest the treasures hidden in Scripture; he unlocks the strong chests in which the truth has long lain, and he points to secret chambers filled with untold riches; but he coins no more, for enough is done. Believer! there is enough in the Bible for thee to live upon forever. If thou shouldst outnumber the years of Methuselah, there would be no need for a fresh revelation; if thou shouldst live till Christ should come upon the earth, there would be no necessity for the addition of a single word; if thou shouldst go down as deep as Jonah, or even descend as David said he did, into the belly of hell, still there would be enough in the Bible to comfort thee without a supplementary sentence. But Christ says, "He shall take of mine, and show it unto you." Now, let me just tell you briefly, what it is the Holy Ghost tells us.

Ah! does he not whisper to the heart, "Saint, be of

good cheer—there is one who died for thee; look to Calvary, behold his wounds, see the torrent gushing from his side—there is thy purchaser, and thou art secure. He loves thee with an everlasting love, and this chastisement is meant for thy good; each stroke is working thy healing; by the blueness of the wound thy soul is made better." "Whom he loveth he chasteneth, and scourgeth every son whom he receiveth." Doubt not his grace, because of thy tribulation; but believe that he loveth thee as much in seasons of trouble, as in times of happiness. And then, moreover, he says, "What is all thy suffering compared with that of thy Lord's? or what, when weighed in the scales of Jesus' agonies, is all thy distress?" And especially at times does the Holy Ghost take back the veil of heaven, and lets the soul behold the glory of the upper world! Then it is that the saint can say, "O thou art a Comforter to me!"

> "Let cares like a wild deluge come,
> And storms of sorrow fall;
> May I but safely reach my home,
> My God, my heaven, my all."

Some of you could follow, were I to tell of manifestations of heaven. You, too, have left sun, moon, and stars at your feet, while, in your flight, outstripping the tardy lightning, you have seemed to enter the gates of pearl, and tread the golden streets, borne aloft on wings of the Spirit. But here we must not trust ourselves; lest, lost in reverie, we forget our theme.

III. And now, thirdly, who are the comforted persons? I like, you know, at the end of my sermon to cry out, "Divide! divide!" There are two parties here—some who are comforted, and others who are the comfortless ones — some who have received the consolations of the Holy Ghost, and some who have not. Now let us try and sift you, and see which is the chaff, and which is the wheat; and may God grant that some of the chaff may, this night, be transformed into his wheat!

You may say, "How am I to know whether I am a recipient of the comfort of the Holy Ghost?" You may know it by one rule. If you have received one blessing from God, you will receive all other blessings too. Let me explain myself. If I could come here as an auctioneer, and sell the gospel off in lots, I should dispose of it all. If I could say, here is justification through the blood of Christ — free; giving away, gratis; many a one would say, "I will have justification; give it me: I wish to be justified; I wish to be pardoned." Suppose I took sanctification, the giving up of all sin, a thorough change of heart, leaving off drunkenness and swearing; many would say, "I don't want that; I should like to go to heaven, but I do not want that holiness; I should like to be saved at last, but I should like to have my drink still; I should like to enter glory, but then I must have an oath or two on the road." Nay, but, sinner, if thou hast one blessing, thou shalt have all. God will never divide the gospel. He will not give justification to that man, and sanctification to another — pardon to one and holiness to another. No, it all goes together. Whom he calls, them he justifies; whom he justifies, them he sanctifies; and whom he sanctifies, them he also glorifies. O! if I could lay down nothing but the *comforts* of the gospel, ye would fly to them as flies do to honey. When ye come to be ill, ye send for the clergyman.

Ah! you all want your minister then to come and give you consoling words. But, if he be an honest man, he will not give some of you a particle of consolation. He will not commence pouring oil when the knife would be better. I want to make a man feel his sins before I dare tell him anything about Christ. I want to probe into his soul and make him feel that he is lost before I tell him anything about the purchased blessing. It is the ruin of many to tell them, "Now just believe on Christ, and that is all you have to do." If, instead of dying, they get better, they rise up whitewashed hypocrites—that is all. I have heard of a city missionary who kept a record of two thousand persons who were supposed to be on their death-bed, but recovered, and whom he should have put down as converted persons had they died; and how many do you think lived a Christian life afterwards out of the two thousand? Not two. Positively he could only find one who was found to live afterwards in the fear of God. Is it not horrible that when men and women come to die, they should cry, "comfort, comfort?" and that hence their friends conclude that they are children of God, while, after all, they have no right to consolation, but are intruders upon the enclosed grounds of the blessed God. O God, may these people ever be kept from having comfort when they have no right to it! Have you the other blessings? Have you had the conviction of sin? Have you ever felt your guilt before God? Have your souls been humbled at Jesus' feet? And have you been made to look to Calvary alone for your refuge? If not, you have no right to consolation. Do not take an atom of it. The Spirit is a convincer before he is a Comforter; and you must have the other operations of the Holy Spirit, before you can derive anything from this.

And now I have done. You have heard what this babbler hath said once more. What has it been? Something about the Comforter. But let me ask you, before you go, what do you know about the Comforter? Each one of you, before descending the steps of this chapel, let this solemn question thrill through your souls — What do you know of the Comforter? O! poor souls, if ye know not the Comforter, I will tell you what you shall know. You shall know the Judge! If ye know not the Comforter on earth, ye shall know the Condemner in the next world, who shall cry, "Depart, ye cursed, into everlasting fire in hell." Well might Whitfield call out, "O earth, earth, earth, hear the word of the Lord!" If ye were to live here forever, ye might slight the gospel; if ye had a lease of your lives, ye might despise the Comforter. But, sirs, ye must die. Since last we met together, probably some have gone to their long last home; and ere we meet again in this sanctuary, some here will be amongst the glorified above, or amongst the damned below. Which will it be? Let your soul answer. If to-night you fell down dead in your pews, or where you are standing in the gallery, where would you be? in *heaven* or in *hell?* Ah! deceive not yourselves; let conscience have its perfect work; and if, in the sight of God, you are obliged to say, "I tremble and fear lest my portion should be with unbelievers," listen one moment, and then I have done with thee. "He that believeth and is baptized shall be saved, and he that believeth not shall be damned." Weary sinner, hellish sinner, thou who art the devil's castaway, reprobate, profligate, harlot, robber, thief, adulterer, fornicator, drunkard, swearer, Sabbath-breaker — list! I speak to thee as well as to the rest. I exempt no man. God hath said there is no exemption here. "*Whosoever* believeth on the name of Jesus Christ shall be saved." Sin is no barrier: thy guilt is no obstacle. Whosoever — though he were as black as Satan, though he were filthy as a fiend — whosoever this night believes, shall have every sin forgiven, shall have every crime effaced; shall have every iniquity blotted out; shall be saved in the Lord Jesus Christ, and shall stand in heaven safe and secure. That is the glorious gospel. God apply it to your hearts, and give you faith in Jesus!

"We have listened to the preacher —
Truth by him has now been shown;
But we want a GREATER TEACHER,
From the everlasting throne:
APPLICATION
Is the work of God *alone*."

SERMON V.

CHRIST CRUCIFIED.

"But we preach Christ crucified, unto the Jews a stumbling-block, and unto the Greeks foolishness; but unto them which are called, both Jews and Greeks, Christ the power of God, and the wisdom of God." — 1 Cor. i. 23, 24.

What contempt hath God poured upon the wisdom of this world! How hath he brought it to nought, and made it appear as nothing. He has allowed it to work out its own conclusions, and prove its own folly. Men boasted that they were wise; they said that they could find out God to perfection; and in order that their folly might be refuted once and forever, God gave them the opportunity of so doing. He said, "Worldly wisdom, I will try thee. Thou sayest that thou art mighty, that thine intellect is vast and comprehensive, that thine eye is keen, and thou canst find all secrets; now, behold, I try thee; I give thee one great problem to solve. Here is the universe; stars make its canopy, fields and flowers adorn it, and the floods roll o'er its surface; my name is written therein; the invisible things of God may be clearly seen in the things which are made." "Philosophy, I give thee this problem — find me out. Here are my works — find me out. Discover in the wondrous world which I have made, the way to worship me acceptably. I give thee space enough to do it—there are data enough. Behold the clouds, the earth, and the stars. I give thee time enough; I will give thee four thousand years, and I will not interfere; but thou shalt do as thou wilt with thine own world. I will give thee men enough; for I will make great minds and vast, whom thou shalt call lords of earth; thou shalt have orators, thou shalt have philosophers. Find me out, O reason; find me out, O wisdom; find me out, if thou canst; find me out unto perfection; and if thou canst not, then shut thy mouth forever, and then will I teach thee that the wisdom of God is wiser than the wisdom of man; yea, that the foolishness of God is wiser than men." And how did the wisdom of man work out the problem? How did wisdom perform her feat? Look upon the heathen nations; there you see the result of wisdom's researches. In the time of Jesus Christ, you might have beheld the earth covered with the slime of pollution, a Sodom on a large scale—corrupt, filthy, depraved; indulging in vices which we dare not mention; revelling in lust too abominable even for our imagination to dwell upon for a moment. We find the men prostrating themselves before blocks of wood and stone, adoring ten thousand gods more vicious than themselves. We find, in fact, that reason wrote out her lines with a finger covered with blood and filth, and that she forever cut herself out from all her glory by the vile deeds she did. She would not worship God. She would not bow down to him who is "clearly seen," but she worshipped any creature—the reptile that crawled, the crocodile, the viper—everything might be a god; but not, forsooth, the God of heaven. Vice might be made into a ceremony, the greatest crime might be exalted into a religion; but true worship she knew nothing of. Poor reason! poor wisdom! how art thou fallen from heaven; like Lucifer, thou son of the morning! thou art lost; thou hast written out thy conclusion, but a conclusion of consummate folly. "After that in the wisdom of God, the world by wisdom knew not God, it pleased God by the foolishness of preaching to save them that believe."

Wisdom had had its time, and time enough; it had done its all, and that was little enough; it had made the world worse than it was before it stepped upon it, and "now," says God, "foolishness shall overcome wisdom; now ignorance, as ye call it, shall sweep away science; now (saith God,) humble, child-like faith shall crumble to the dust all the colossal systems your hands have piled." He calls his warriors. Christ puts his trumpet to his mouth, and up come the warriors, clad in fishermen's garb, with the brogue of the lake of Galilee —poor humble mariners. Here are the warriors, O wisdom, that are to confound thee; these are the heroes who shall overcome thy proud philosophers; these men are to plant their standard upon thy ruined walls, and bid them fall forever; these men and their successors are to exalt a gospel in the world which ye may laugh at as absurd, which ye may sneer at as folly, but which shall be exalted above the hills, and shall be glorious even to the highest heavens. Since that day, God has always raised up successors of the apostles. I claim to be a successor of the apostles; not by any lineal descent, but because I have the same roll and charter as any apostle, and am as much called to preach the gospel as Paul himself; if not as much owned by the conversion of sinners, yet, in a measure, blessed of God; and, therefore, here I stand, foolish as Paul might be, foolish as Peter, or any of those fishermen; but still with the might of God I grasp the sword of truth, coming here to "preach Christ and him crucified, unto the Jews a stumbling-block, and unto the Greeks foolishness; but unto them which are called, both Jews and Greeks, Christ the power of God, and the wisdom of God."

Before I enter upon our text, let me very briefly tell you what I believe preaching Christ and him crucified is. My friends, I do not believe it is preaching Christ and him crucified, to give people a batch of philosophy every Sunday morning and evening, and neglect the truths of this Holy Book. I do not believe it is preaching Christ and him crucified, to leave out the main cardinal doctrines of the Word of God, and preach a religion which is all a mist and a haze, without any definite truths whatever. I take it *that* man does not preach Christ and him crucified, who can get through a sermon without mentioning Christ's name once; nor does that man preach Christ and him crucified, who leaves out the Holy Spirit's work, who never says a word about the Holy Ghost, so that indeed the hearers might say, "We do not so much as know whether there be a Holy Ghost." And I have my own private opinion, that there is no such thing as preaching Christ and him crucified, unless you preach what now-a-days is called Calvinism. I have my own ideas, and those I always state boldly. It is a nickname to call it Calvanism. Calvinism is the gospel, and nothing else. I do not believe we can preach the gospel, if we do not preach justification by faith without works; nor unless we preach the sovereignty of God in his dispensation of grace; nor unless we exalt the electing, unchangeable, eternal, immutable, conquering love of Jehovah; nor, I think, can we preach the gospel, unless we base it upon the peculiar redemption which Christ made for his elect and chosen people; nor can I comprehend a gospel which lets saints fall away after they are called, and suffers the children of God to be burned in the fires of damnation, after having believed. Such a gospel I abhor. The gospel of the Bible is not such a gospel as that. We preach Christ and him crucified in a different fashion, and to all gainsayers we reply, "We have not so learned Christ."

There are three things in the text: first, a gospel rejected, "Christ crucified, to the Jews a stumbling-block, and to the Greeks foolishness;" secondly, a gospel triumphant, "unto those who are called, both Jews and Greeks;" and thirdly, a gospel admired; it is to them who are called "the power of God and the wisdom of God."

I. First, we have here *a gospel rejected.* One would have imagined that, when God sent his gospel to men, all men would meekly listen, and humbly receive its truths. We should have thought that God's ministers had but to proclaim that life is brought to light by the gospel, and that Christ is come to save sinners, and every ear would be attentive, every eye would be fixed, and every heart would be wide open to receive the truth. We should have said, judging favorably of our fellow-creatures, that there would not exist in the world a monster so vile, so depraved, so polluted, as to put so much as a stone in the way of the progress of truth; we could not have conceived such a thing; yet that conception is the truth. When the gospel was preached, instead of being accepted and admired, one universal hiss went up to heaven; men could not bear it; its first preacher they dragged to the brow of the hill, and would have sent him down headlong; yea, they did more — they nailed him to the cross, and there they let him languish out his dying life in agony such as no man hath borne since. All his chosen ministers have been hated and abhorred by worldlings; instead of being listened to, they have been scoffed at; treated as if they were the offscouring of all things, and the very scum of mankind. Look at the holy men in the old times, how they were driven from city to city, persecuted, afflicted, tormented, stoned to death, wherever the enemy had power to do so. Those friends of men, those real philanthropists, who came with hearts big with love, and hands full of mercy, and lips pregnant with celestial fire, and souls that burned with holy influence; those men were treated as if they were spies in the camp, as if they were deserters from the common cause of mankind; as if they were enemies, and not, as they truly were, the best of friends. Do not suppose, my friends, that men like the gospel any better now than they did then. There is an idea that you are growing better. I do not believe it. You are growing worse. In many respects men may be better, — outwardly better; but the heart within is still the same. The human heart of to-day dissected, would be just like the human heart a thousand years ago; the gall of bitterness within that breast of yours, is just as bitter as the gall of bitterness in that of Simon of old. We have in our hearts the same latent opposition to the truth of God; and hence we find men, even as of old, who scorn the gospel.

I shall, in speaking of the gospel rejected, endeavor to point out the two classes of persons who equally despise the truth. The Jews make it a stumbling-block, and the Greeks account it foolishness. Now these two very respectable gentlemen—the Jew and the Greek—I am not going to make these ancient individuals the object of my condemnation, but I look upon them as members of a great parliament, representatives of a great constituency, and I shall attempt to show that, if all the race of Jews were cut off, there would be still a great number in the world who would answer to the name of Jews, to whom Christ is a stumbling-block; and that if Greece were swallowed up by some earthquake, and ceased to be a nation, there would still be the Greek unto whom the gospel would be foolishness. I shall simply introduce the Jew and the Greek, and let them speak a moment to you, in order that you may see the gentlemen who represent you; the representative men; the persons who stand for many of you, who as yet are not called by divine grace.

The first is a Jew to him the gospel is a stumbling-block. A respectable man the Jew was in his day; all formal religion was concentrated in his person; he went up to the temple very devoutly; he tithed all he had, even to the mint and the cummin. You would see him fasting twice in the week, with a face all marked with sadness and sorrow. If you looked at him, he had the law between his eyes; there was the phylactery, and the borders of his garments of amazing width, that he might never be supposed to be a Gentile dog; that no one might ever conceive that he was not an Hebrew of pure descent. He had a holy ancestry; he came of a pious family; a right good man was he. He could not like those Sadducees at all, who had no religion. He was thoroughly a religious man; he stood up for his synagogue; he would not have that temple on Mount Gerizim; he could not bear the Samaritans, he had no dealings with them; he was a religionist of the first order, a man of the very finest kind; a specimen of a man who is a moralist, and who loves the ceremonies of the law. Accordingly, when he heard about Christ, he asked who Christ was. "The Son of a carpenter." Ah! "The son of a carpenter, and his mother's name was Mary, and his father's name Joseph." "That of itself is presumption enough," said he; "positive proof, in fact, that he cannot be the Messiah." And what does he say? Why, he says, "Woe unto you, Scribes and Pharisees, hypocrites." "That won't do." Moreover, he says, "It is not by the works of the flesh that any man can enter into the kingdom of heaven." The Jew tied a double knot in his phylactery at once; he thought he would have the borders of his garment made twice as broad. *He* bow to the Nazarene! No, no; and if so much as a disciple crossed the street, he thought the place polluted, and would not tread in his steps. Do you think he would give up his old father's religion, the religion which came from Mount Sinai, that old religion that lay in the ark and the overshadowing cherubim? He give that up! not he. A vile imposter — that is all Christ was in his eyes. He thought so. "A stumbling-block to me; I cannot hear about it; I will not listen to it." Accordingly, he turned a deaf ear to all the preacher's eloquence, and listened not at all. Farewell, old Jew! Thou sleepest with thy fathers, and thy generation is a wandering race, still walking the earth. Farewell! I have done with thee. Alas! poor wretch, that Christ, who was thy stumbling-block, shall be thy judge, and on thy head shall be that loud curse. "His blood be on us and on our children." But I am going to find out Mr. Jew here in Exeter Hall — persons who answer to his description — to whom Jesus Christ is a stumbling-block. Let me introduce you to yourselves, some of you. You were of a pious family too, were you not? Yes. And you have a religion which you love; you love it so far as the chrysalis of it goes, the outside, the covering, the husk. You would not have one rubric altered, nor one of those dear old arches taken down, nor the stained glass removed, for all the world; and any man who should say a word against such things, you would set down as a heretic at once. Or, perhaps, you do not go to such a place of worship, but you love some plain old meeting-house, where your forefathers worshipped, called a dissenting chapel. Ah! it is a beautiful plain place; you love it, you love its ordinances, you love its exterior; and if any one spoke against the place, how vexed you would feel. You think that what they do there, they ought to do everywhere; in fact, your church is a model one; the place where you go is exactly the sort of place for everybody; and if I were to ask you why you hope to go to heaven, you would perhaps say, "Because I am a Baptist," or, "Because I am an Episcopalian," or whatever other sect you belong to. There is yourself; I know Jesus Christ will be to you a stumbling-block. If I come and tell you, that all your going to the house of

God is good for nothing; if I tell you that all those many times you have been singing and praying, all pass for nothing in the sight of God, because you are a hypocrite and a formalist. If I tell you that your heart is not right with God, and that unless it is so, all the external is good for nothing, I know what you will say, — "I shan't hear that young man again." It is a stumbling-block. If you had stepped in anywhere where you had heard formalism exalted: if you had been told "this must you do, and this other must you do, and then you will be saved," you would highly approve of it. But how many are there externally religious, with whose characters you could find no fault, but who have never had the regenerating influence of the Holy Ghost; who never were made to lie prostrate on their face before Calvary's cross; who never turned a wistful eye to yonder Saviour crucified; who never put their trust in him that was slain for the sons of men. They love a superficial religion, but when a man talks deeper than that, they set it down for cant. You may love all that is external about religion, just as you may love a man for his clothes — caring nothing for the man himself. If so, I know you are one of those who reject the gospel. You will hear me preach; and while I speak about the externals, you will hear me with attention; whilst I plead for morality, and argue against drunkenness, or show the heinousness of Sabbath-breaking, all well and good; but if once I say, "Except ye be converted, and become as little children, ye can in no wise enter into the kingdom of God;" if once I tell you that you must be elected of God: that you must be purchased with the Saviour's blood — that you must be converted by the Holy Ghost — you say, "He is a fanatic! Away with him, away with him! We do not want to hear that any more." Christ crucified, is to the Jew — the ceremonialist — a stumbling-block.

But there is another specimen of this Jew to be found. He is thoroughly orthodox in his sentiments. As for forms and ceremonies, he thinks nothing about them. He goes to a place of worship where he learns sound doctrine. He will hear nothing but what is true. He likes that we should have good works and morality He is a good man, and no one can find fault with him. Here he is, regular in his Sunday pew. In the market he walks before men in all honesty — so you would imagine. Ask him about any doctrine, and he can give you a disquisition upon it. In fact, he could write a treatise upon anything in the Bible, and a great many things besides. He knows almost everything; and here, up in this dark attic of the head, his religion has taken up its abode; he has a best parlor down in his heart, but his religion never goes there — that is shut against it. He has money in there — Mammon, worldiness; or he has something else — self-love, pride. Perhaps he loves to hear experimental preaching; he admires it all; in fact, he loves anything that is sound. But then, he has not any sound in himself; or rather, it is all sound, and there is no substance. He likes to hear true doctrine; but it never penetrates his inner man. You never see him weep. Preach to him about Christ crucified, a glorious subject, and you never see a tear roll down his cheek; tell him of the mighty influence of the Holy Ghost — he admires you for it, but he never had the hand of the Holy Spirit on his soul; tell him about communion with God, plunging in Godhead's deepest sea, and being lost in its immensity — the man loves to hear, but he never experiences, he has never communed with Christ; and accordingly, when you once begin to strike home; when you lay him on the table, take out your dissecting knife, begin to cut him up, and show him his own heart, let him see what it is by nature, and what it must become by grace — the man starts, he cannot stand that; he wants none of that — Christ received in the heart, and accepted. Albeit that he loves it enough in the head, 't is to him a stumbling-block, and he casts it away. Do you see yourselves here, my friends? See yourselves as others see you? See yourselves as God sees you? For so it is, here be many to whom Christ is as much a stumbling-block now as ever he was. O ye formalists! I speak to you; O ye who have the nutshell, but abhor the kernel; O ye who like the trappings and the dress, but care not for that fair virgin who is clothed therewith; O ye who like the paint and the tinsel, but abhor the solid gold, I speak to you; I ask you, does your religion give you solid comfort? Can you stare death in the face with it, and say, "I know that my Redeemer liveth?" Can you close your eyes at night, and your vesper song shall be:

> "I to the end must endure,
> As sure as the earnest is given?"

Can you bless God for affliction? Can you plunge in, accoutred as ye are, and swim through all the floods of trial? Can you march triumphant through the lion's den, laugh at affliction, and bid defiance to hell? Can you? No! Your gospel is an effeminate thing — a thing of words and sounds, and not of power. Cast it from you, I beseech you; it is not worth your keeping; and when you come before the throne of God, you will find it will fail you, and fail you so that you shall never find another; for lost, ruined, destroyed, ye shall find that Christ, who is now σκανδαλον, a stumbling-block, will be your judge.

I have found out the Jew, and I have now to discover the Greek. He is a person of quite a different exterior to the Jew. As to the phylactery, to him it is all rubbish; and as to the broad hemmed garment, he despises it. He does not care for the forms of religion; he has an intense aversion, in fact, to broad-brimmed hats, or to everything which looks like outward show. He likes eloquence; he admires a smart saying; he loves a quaint expression; he likes to read the last new book; he is a Greek, and to him the gospel is foolishness. The Greek is a gentleman found everywhere, now-a-days; manufactured sometimes in colleges, constantly made in schools, produced everywhere. He is on the exchange, in the market; he keeps a shop, rides in a carriage; he is noble, a gentleman; he is everywhere, even in court. He is thoroughly wise. Ask him anything, and he knows it. Ask for a quotation from any of the old poets, or any one else, and he can give it you. If you are a Mohammedan, and plead the claims of your religion, he will hear you very patiently. But if you are a Christian, and talk to him of Jesus Christ, "Stop your cant," he says, "I don't want to hear anything about that." This Grecian gentleman believes all philosophy except the true one; he studies all wisdom except the wisdom of God; he likes all learning except spiritual learning; he loves everything except that which God approves; he likes everything which man makes, and nothing which comes from God;

it is foolishness to him, confounded foolishness. You have only to discourse about one doctrine in the Bible, and he shuts his ears; he wishes no longer for your company — it is foolishness. I have met this gentleman a great many times. Once, when I saw him, he told me he did not believe in any religion at all; and when I said I did, and had a hope that when I died I should go to heaven, he said he dared say it was very comfortable, but he did not believe in religion, and that he was sure it was best to live as nature dictated. Another time he spoke well of all religions, and believed they were very good in their place, and all true; and he had no doubt that, if a man were sincere in any kind of religion, he would be all right at last. I told him I did not think so, and that I believed there was but one religion revealed of God — the religion of God's elect, the religion which is the gift of Jesus. He then said I was a bigot, and wished me good morning. It was to him foolishness. He had nothing to do with me at all. He either liked no religion, or every religion. Another time I held him by the coat button, and I discussed with him a little about faith. He said, "It is all very well, I believe that is true Protestant doctrine." But presently I said something about election, and he said, "I don't like that; many people have preached that and turned it to bad account." I then hinted something about free grace; but that he could not endure, it was to him foolishness. He was a polished Greek, and thought that if he were not chosen, he ought to be. He never liked that passage, "God hath chosen the foolish things of this world to confound the wise, and the things which are not, to bring to nought things that are." He thought it was very discreditable to the Bible; and when the book was revised, he had no doubt it would be cut out. To such a man — for he is here this morning, very likely come to hear this reed shaken of the wind — I have to say this: Ah! thou wise man, full of worldly wisdom; thy wisdom will stand thee here, but what wilt thou do in the swellings of Jordan? Philosophy may do well for thee to lean upon whilst thou walkest through this world; but the river is deep, and thou wilt want something more than that. If thou hast not the arm of the Most High to hold thee up in the flood and cheer thee with promises, thou wilt sink, man; with all thy philosophy, thou wilt sink; with all thy learning, thou shalt sink, and be washed into that awful ocean of eternal torment, where thou shalt be forever. Ah! Greeks, it may be foolishness to you, but ye shall see the man your judge, and then shall ye rue the day that e'er ye said that God's gospel was foolishness.

II. Having spoken thus far upon *the gospel rejected*, I shall now briefly speak upon the gospel triumphant. "Unto us who are called, both Jews and Greeks, it is the power of God, and the wisdom of God." Yonder man rejects the gospel, despises grace, and laughs at it as a delusion. Here is another man who laughed at it too; but God will fetch him down upon his knees. Christ shall not die for nothing. The Holy Ghost shall not strive in vain. God hath said, "My word shall not return unto me void, but it shall accomplish that which I please, and it shall prosper in the thing whereto I sent it." "He shall see of the travail of his soul, and shall be abundantly satisfied." If one sinner is not saved, another shall be. The Jew and the Greek shall never depopulate heaven. The choirs of glory shall not lose a single songster by all the opposition of Jews and Greeks; for God hath said it; some shall be called; some shall be saved; some shall be rescued.

> "Perish the virtue, as it ought, abhorred,
> And the fool with it, who insults his Lord.
> The atonement a Redeemer's love has wrought
> Is not for you — the righteous need it not.
> See'st thou yon harlot wooing all she meets,
> The worn-out nuisance of the public streets,
> Herself from morn to night, from night to morn,
> Her own abhorrence, and as much your scorn:
> The gracious shower, unlimited and free,
> Shall fall on her, when Heaven denies it thee.
> Of all that wisdom dictates, this the drift,
> That man is dead in sin, and life a gift."

If the righteous and good are not saved, if they reject the gospel, there are others who are to be called, others who shall be rescued; for Christ will not lose the merits of his agonies, or the purchase of his blood. "*Unto us who are called.*" I received a note this week asking me to explain that word, *called;* because in one passage it says, "many are called but few are chosen," while in another it appears that all who are called must be chosen. Now, let me observe that there are two calls. As my old friend, John Bunyan, says, the hen has two calls, the common cluck, which she gives daily and hourly, and the special one, which she means for her little chickens. So there is a general call, a call made to every man; every man hears it. Many are called by it; all you are called this morning in that sense, but very few are chosen. The other is a special call, the children's call. You know how the bell sounds over the workshop, to call the men to work — that is a general call. A father goes to the door and calls out, "John, it is dinner-time"—that is the special call. Many are called with the general call, but they are not chosen; the special call is for the children only, and that is what is meant in the text, "Unto us who are called, both Jews and Greeks, the power of God and the wisdom of God." That call is always a special one. While I stand here and call men, nobody comes; while I preach to sinners universally, no good is done; it is like the sheet lightning you sometimes see on the summer's evening, beautiful, grand; but whoever heard of anything being struck by it? But the special call is the forked flash from heaven; it strikes somewhere; it is the arrow sent in between the joints of the harness. The call which saves is like that of Jesus, when he said "Mary," and she said unto him "Rabboni." Do you know anything about that special call, my beloved? Did Jesus ever call you by name? Canst thou recollect the hour when he whispered thy name in thine ear, when he said, "Come to me?" If so, you will grant the truth of what I am going to say next about it—that it is an effectual call. There is no resisting it. When God calls, with his special call, there is no standing out. Ah! I know I laughed at religion; I despised, I abhorred it; but that call! Oh, I would not come. But God said, "Thou shalt come. All that the Father giveth to me shall come." "Lord, I will not." "But thou shalt," said God. And I have gone up to God's house sometimes almost with a resolution that I would not listen, but listen I must. Oh, how the word came into my soul! Was there a power of resistance? No; I was thrown down; each bone seemed to be broken; I was saved by effectual grace. I appeal to your experience, my friends. When God took you in hand, could you withstand him? You stood against your minister times enough. Sickness did not break you down; disease did not bring you to God's feet; eloquence did not convince you; but when God puts his hand to the work, ah! then what a change. Like Saul, with his horses going to Damascus, that voice from heaven said, "I am Jesus whom thou persecutest." "Saul, Saul, why persecutest thou me?" There was no going further then. That was an effectual call. Like that, again, which Jesus gave to Zaccheus, when he was up in the tree; stepping under the tree, he said, "Zaccheus, come down, to-day I must abide in thy house." Zaccheus was taken in the net; he heard his own name; the call sank into his soul; he could not stop up in the tree, for an almighty impulse drew him down. And I could tell you some singular instances of persons going to the house of God and having their characters described, limned out to perfection, so that they have said, "He is painting me, he is painting me." Just as I might say to that young man here, who stole his master's gloves yesterday, that Jesus calls him to repentance. It may be that there is such a person here; and when the call comes to a peculiar character, it generally comes with a special power. God gives his ministers a brush, and shows them how to use it in painting life-like portraits, and thus the sinner hears the special call. I cannot give the special call; God alone can give it, and I leave it with him. Some must be called. Jew and Greek may laugh, but still there are some who are called, both Jews and Greeks.

Then, to close up this second point, it is a great mercy that many a Jew has been made to drop his self righteousness; many a legalist has been made to drop his legalism, and come to Christ; and many a Greek has bowed his genius at the throne of God's gospel. We have a few such. As Cowper says:

"We boast some rich ones whom the gospel sways,
And one who wears a coronet, and prays;
Like gleanings of an olive tree they show,
Here and there one upon the topmost bough."

III. Now we come to our third point, *a gospel admired;* unto to us who are called of God, it is the power of God, and the wisdom of God. Now, beloved, this must be a matter of pure experience between your souls and God. If you are called of God this morning, you will know it. I know there are times when a Christian has to say,

"'T is a point I long to know,
Oft it causes anxious thought;
Do I love the Lord or no?
Am I his, or am I not?"

But, if a man never in his life knew himself to be a Christian, he never was a Christian. If he never had a moment of confidence, when he could say, "Now I know in whom I have believed," I think I do not utter a harsh thing when I say, that that man could not have been born again; for I do not understand how a man can be born again and not know it; I do not understand how a man can be killed and then made alive again, and not know it; how a man can pass from death unto life, and not know it; how a man can be brought out of darkness into marvellous liberty without knowing it. I am sure I know it when I shout out my old verse:

"Now freed from sin, I walk at large,
My Saviour's blood 's my full discharge;
At his dear feet content I lay,
A sinner saved, and homage pay."

There are moments when the eyes glisten with joy: and we can say, "we are persuaded, confident, certain." I do not wish to distress any one who is under doubt. Often gloomy doubts will prevail; there are seasons when you fear you have not been called, when you doubt your interest in Christ. Ah! what a mercy it is that it is not your hold of Christ that saves you, but his hold of you! What a sweet fact that it is not how you grasp his hand, but his grasp of yours, that saves you. Yet I think you ought to know, some time or other, whether you are called of God. If so, you will follow me in the next part of my discourse, which is a matter of pure experience; unto us who are saved, it is "Christ the power of God, and the wisdom of God."

The gospel is, to the true believer, a thing of power. It is Christ, the power of God. Power, sir! Aye, there is a power in God's gospel. Power, sir! Aye, a mighty power. Once I, like Mazeppa, bound on the wild horse of my lust, bound hand and foot, incapable of resistance, was galloping on with hell's wolves behind me, howling for my body and my soul, as their just and lawful prey. There came a mighty hand which stopped that wild horse, cut my bands, set me down, and brought me into liberty. Is there power, sir? Aye, there is power; and he who has felt it, must acknowledge it. There was a time when I lived in the strong old castle of my sins, and rested on my works. There came a trumpeter to the door, and bade me open it. I with anger chid him from the porch, and said he ne'er should enter. There came a goodly personage, with loving countenance; his hands were marked with scars, where nails were driven, and his feet had nail-prints too; he lifted up his cross, using it as a hammer; at the first blow the gate of my prejudice shook; at the second it trembled more, at the third down it fell, and in he came; and he said, "Arise, and stand upon thy feet, for I have loved thee with an everlasting love." A thing of power! Ah! it is a thing of power. I have felt it *here*, in this heart; I have the witness of the Spirit within, and know it is a thing of might, because it has conquered me; it has bowed me down.

> "His free grace alone, from the first to the last,
> Hath won my affection, and held my soul fast."

The gospel, to the Christian, is a thing of power. What is it that makes the young man devote himself, as a missionary, to the cause of God, to leave father and mother, and go into distant lands? It is a thing of power that does it; it is the gospel. What is it that constrains yonder minister, in the midst of the cholera, to climb up that creaking staircase, and stand by the bed of some dying creature who has that dire disease? It must be a thing of power which leads him to venture his life; it is love of the cross of Christ which bids him do it. What is that which enables one man to stand up before a multitude of his fellows, all unprepared it may be, but determined that he will speak nothing but Christ, and him crucified? What is it that enables him to cry, like the war horse of Job, in battle, Aha! and move glorious in might? It is a thing of power that does it: it is Christ crucified. And what emboldens that timid female to walk down that dark lane some wet evening, that she may go and sit beside the victim of a contagious fever? What strengthens her to go through that den of thieves, and pass by the profligate and profane? What influences her to enter into that charnel house of death, and there sit down and whisper words of comfort? Does gold make her do it? They are too poor to give her gold. Does fame make her do it? She shall never be known nor written among the mighty women of this earth. What makes her do it? Is it love of merit? No; she knows she has no desert before high heaven. What impels her to it? It is the power, the thing of power; it is the cross of Christ: she loves it, and she therefore says,

> "Were the whole realm of nature mine,
> That were a present far too small;
> Love so amazing, so divine,
> Demands my soul, my life, my all."

But I behold another scene. A martyr is going to the stake; the halbert men are around him; the crowds are mocking, but he is marching steadily on. See, they bind him, with a chain around his middle, to the stake; they heap faggots all about him; the flame is lighted up; listen to his words: "Bless the Lord, O my soul, and all that is within me, bless his holy name." The flames are kindling round his legs; the fire is burning him even to the bone; see him lift up his hands and say, "I know that my Redeemer liveth, and though the fire devour this body, yet in my flesh shall I see the Lord." Behold him clutch the stake and kiss it, as if he loved it, and hear him say, "For every chain of iron that man girdeth me with, God shall give me a chain of gold; for all these faggots, and this ignominy and shame, he shall increase the weight of my eternal glory." See all the under parts of his body are consumed; still he lives in the torture; at last he bows himself, and the upper part of his body falls over; and as he falls you hear him say, "Into thy hands I commend my Spirit." What wondrous magic was on him, sirs? What made that man strong? What helped him to bear that cruelty? What made him stand unmoved in the flames? It was the thing of power; it was the cross of Jesus crucified. For "unto us who are saved it is the power of God."

But behold another scene far different. There is no crowd there; it is a silent room. There is a poor pallet, a lonely bed: a physician standing by. There is a young girl: her face is blanched by consumption; long hath the worm eaten her cheek, and though sometimes the flush came, it was the death flush of the deceitful consumption. There she lieth, weak, pale, wan, worn, dying, yet behold a smile upon her face, as if she had seen an angel. She speaketh, and there is music in her voice. Joan of Arc of old was not half so mighty as that girl. She is wrestling with dragons on her death-bed; but see her composure, and hear her dying sonnet:

"Jesus, lover of my soul,
Let me to thy bosom fly,
While the nearer waters roll,
While the tempest still is high.
Hide me, O my Saviour, hide,
Till this storm of life be past,
Safe into the haven guide,
O receive my soul at last."

And with a smile she shuts her eye on earth, and opens it in heaven. What enables her to die like that? It is the thing of power; it is the cross; it is Jesus crucified.

I have little time to discourse upon the other point, and it be far from me to weary you by a lengthened and prosy sermon, but we must glance at the other statement: Christ is, to the called ones, the wisdom of God as well as the power of God. To a believer, the gospel is the perfection of wisdom, and if it appear not so to the ungodly, it is because of the perversion of judgment consequent on their depravity.

An idea has long possessed the public mind, that a religious man can scarcely be a wise man. It has been the custom to talk of Infidels, Atheists, and Deists, as men of deep thought and comprehensive intellect; and to tremble for the Christian controversialist, as if he must surely fall by the hand of his enemy. But this is purely a mistake; for the gospel is the sum of wisdom; an epitome of knowledge; a treasure-house of truth; and a revelation of mysterious secrets. In it we see how justice and mercy may be married; here we behold inexorable law entirely satisfied, and sovereign love bearing away the sinner in triumph. Our meditation upon it enlarges the mind; and as it opens to our soul in successive flashes of glory, we stand astonished at the profound wisdom manifest in it. Ah, dear friends! if ye seek wisdom, ye shall see it displayed in all its greatness; not in the balancing of the clouds, nor the firmness of earth's foundations; not in the measured march of the armies of the sky, nor in the perpetual motions of the waves of the sea; not in vegetation with all its fairy forms of beauty, nor in the animal with its marvellous tissue of nerve, and vein, and sinew; nor even in man, that last and loftiest work of the Creator. But turn aside and see this great sight!—an incarnate God upon the cross; a substitute atoning for mortal guilt; a sacrifice satisfying the vengeance of Heaven, and delivering the rebellious sinner. Here is essential wisdom; enthroned, crowned, glorified. Admire, ye men of earth, if ye be not blind; and ye who glory in your learning bend your heads in reverence, and own that all your skill could not have devised a gospel at once so just to God, so safe to man.

Remember, my friends, that while the gospel is in itself wisdom, it also confers wisdom on its students; she teaches young men wisdom and discretion, and gives understanding to the simple. A man who is a believing admirer and a hearty lover of the truth as it is in Jesus, is in a right place to follow with advantage any other branch of science. I confess I have a shelf in my head for everything now. Whatever I read I know where to put it; whatever I learn I know where to stow it away. Once when I read books, I put all my knowledge together in glorious confusion; but ever since I have known Christ, I have put Christ in the centre as my sun, and each science revolves round it like a planet, while minor sciences are satellites to these planets. Christ is to me the wisdom of God. I can learn everything now. The science of Christ crucified is the most excellent of sciences, she is to me the wisdom of God. O, young man, build thy studio on Calvary! there raise thine observatory, and scan by faith the lofty things of nature. Take thee a hermit's cell in the garden of Gethsemane, and lave thy brow with the waters of Siloa. Let the Bible be thy standard classic — thy last appeal in matters of contention. Let its light be thine illumination, and thou shalt become more wise than Plato, more truly learned than the seven sages of antiquity.

And now, my dear friends, solemnly and earnestly, as in the sight of God, I appeal to you. You are gathered here this morning, I know, from different motives; some of you have come from curiosity; others of you are my regular hearers; some have come from one place and some from another. What have you heard me say this morning? I have told you of two classes of persons who reject Christ; the religionist, who has a religion of form and nothing else; and the man of the world, who calls our gospel foolishness. Now, put your hand upon your heart, and ask yourself this morning, "Am I one of these?" If you are, then walk the earth in all your pride; then go as you came in: but know that for all this the Lord shall bring thee unto judgment; know thou that thy joys and delights shall vanish like a dream, "and, like the baseless fabric of a vision," be swept away forever. Know thou this, moreover, O man, that one day in the halls of Satan, down in hell, I perhaps may see thee amongst those myriad spirits who revolve forever in a perpetual circle with their hands upon their hearts. If thine hand be transparent, and thy flesh transparent, I shall look through thy hand and flesh, and see thy heart within. And how shall I see it? Set in a case of fire — in a case of fire! And there thou shalt revolve forever with the worm gnawing within thy heart, which ne'er shall die — a case of fire around thy never-dying, ever-tortured heart. Good God! let not these men still reject and despise Christ; but let this be the time when they shall be called.

To the rest of you who are called, I need say nothing. The longer you live, the more powerful will you find the gospel to be; the more deeply Christ-taught you are, the more you live under the constant influence of the Holy Spirit, the more you will know the gospel to be a thing of power, and the more also will you understand it to be a thing of wisdom. May every blessing rest upon you; and may God come up with us in the evening!

SERMON VI.

THE POWER OF THE HOLY GHOST.

"The power of the Holy Ghost."—Rom. xv. 13.

Power is the special and peculiar prerogative of God, and God alone. "Twice have I heard this; that power belongeth unto God." God is God; and power belongeth to him. If he delegates a portion of it to his creatures, yet still it is *his* power. The sun, although he is "like a bridegroom coming out of his chamber, and rejoiceth as a strong man to run his race," yet has no power to perform his motions except as God directs him. The stars, although they travel in their orbits, and none could stay them, yet have neither might nor force, except that which God daily infuses into them. The tall archangel, near his throne, who outshines a comet in its blaze, though he is one of those who excel in strength, and hearken to the voice of the commands of God, yet has no might except that which his Maker gives to him. As for Leviathan, who so maketh the sea to boil like a pot, that one would think the deep were hoary; as for Behemoth, who drinketh up Jordan at a draught, and boasteth that he can snuff up rivers; as for those majestic creatures that are found on earth, they owe their strength to him who fashioned their bones of steel, and made their sinews of brass. And when we think of man, if he has might or power, it is so small and insignificant, that we can scarcely call it such; yea, when it is at its greatest—when he sways his sceptre, when he commands hosts, when he rules nations—still the power belongeth unto God; and it is true, "Twice have I heard this, that power belongeth unto God." This exclusive prerogative of God, is to be found in each of the three persons of the glorious Trinity. The Father hath power; for by his word were the heavens made, and all the hosts of them; by his strength all things stand, and through him they fulfil their destiny. The Son hath power; for, like his Father, he is the Creator of all things; "Without him was not anything made that was made," and "by him all things consist." And the Holy Spirit hath power. It is concerning the power of the Holy Ghost that I shall speak this morning; and may you have a practical exemplification of that attribute in your own hearts, when you shall feel that the influence of the Holy Ghost is being poured out upon me, so that I am speaking the words of the living God to your souls, and bestowed upon you when you are feeling the effects of it in your own spirits.

We shall look at the power of the Holy Ghost in three ways this morning. First, *the outward and visible displays of it;* second, *the inward and spiritual manifestations of it;* and third, *the future and expected works thereof.* The power of the Spirit will thus, I trust, be made clearly present to your souls.

I. First, then, we are to view the power of the Spirit

in the *outward and visible displays of it.* The power of the Spirit has not been dormant; it has exerted itself. Much has been done by the Spirit of God already; more than could have been accomplished by any being except the Infinite, Eternal, Almighty Jehovah, of whom the Holy Spirit is one person. There are four works which are the outward and manifest signs of the power of the Spirit; creation works; resurrection works; works of attestation, or of witness; and works of grace. Of each of these works I shall speak very briefly.

1. First, the Spirit has manifested the omnipotence of his power in *creation works;* for though not very frequently in Scripture, yet sometimes creation is ascribed to the Holy Ghost, as well as to the Father and the Son. The creation of the heavens above us, is said to be the work of God's Spirit. This you will see at once by referring to the sacred Scriptures, Job xxvi. 13th verse, "By his Spirit he hath garnished the heavens; his hand hath formed the crooked serpent." All the stars of heaven are said to have been placed aloft by the Spirit, and one particular constellation called the "crooked serpent," is specially pointed out as his handiwork. He looseth the bands of Orion; he bindeth the sweet influences of the Pleiades, and binds Arcturus with his suns. He made all those stars that shine in heaven. The heavens were garnished by his hands, and he formed the crooked serpent by his might. So, also, in those continued acts of creation which are still performed in the world; as the bringing forth of man and animals, their birth and generation. These are ascribed also to the Holy Ghost. If you look at the 104th Psalm, at the 29th verse you will read, "Thou

hidest thy face, they are troubled; thou takest away their breath, they die, and return to their dust. Thou sendest forth thy Spirit, they are created; and thou renewest the face of the earth." So that the creation of every man is the work of the Spirit; and the creation of all life, and all flesh-existence in this world, is as much to be ascribed to the power of the Spirit, as the first garnishing of the heavens, or the fashioning of the crooked serpent. But if you look in the first chapter of Genesis, you will there see more particularly set forth that peculiar operation of power upon the universe which was put forth by the Holy Spirit; you will then discover what was his special work. In the 2d verse of the first chapter of Genesis, we read, "And the earth was without form, and void; and darkness was upon the face of the deep. And the Spirit of God moved upon the face of the waters." We know not how remote the period of the creation of this globe may be—certainly many millions of years before the time of Adam. Our planet has passed through various stages of existence, and different kinds of creatures have lived on its surface, all of which have been fashioned by God. But before that era came, wherein man should be its principal tenant and monarch, the Creator gave up the world to confusion. He allowed the inward fires to burst up from beneath, and melt all the solid matter, so that all kinds of substances were commingled in one vast mass of disorder. The only name you could give to the world then, was, that it was a chaotic mass of matter; what it should be, you could not guess or define. It was entirely "without form and void; and darkness was upon the face of the deep." The Spirit came, and stretching his broad wings, bade the darkness disperse, and as he moved over it, all the different portions of matter came into their places, and it was no longer "without form, and void;" but became round, like its sister planets, and moved, singing the high praises of God—not discordantly, as it had done before, but as one great note in the vast scale of creation. Milton very beautifully describes this work of the Spirit, in thus bringing order out of confusion, when the King of Glory, in his powerful Word and Spirit, came to create new worlds:

"On heavenly ground they stood; and from the shore
They view'd the vast immeasurable abyss
Outrageous as a sea, dark, wasteful, wild,
Up from the bottom turn'd by furious winds
And surging waves, as mountains, to assault
Heaven's height, and with the centre mix the pole.

"Silence, ye troubled waves, and thou deep, peace,
Said then the Omnific Word; your discord end.
Then on the watery calm
His brooding wings the Spirit of God outspread
And vital virtue infused, and vital warmth
Throughout the fluid mass."

This you see, then, is the power of the Spirit. Could we have seen that earth all in confusion, we should have said, "Who can make a world out of this?" The answer would have been, "The power of the Spirit can do it. By the simple spreading of his dove-like wings, he can make all the things come together. Upon that there shall be order where there was nought but confusion." Nor is this all the power of the Spirit. We have seen some of his works in creation. But there was one particular instance of creation in which the Holy Spirit was more especially concerned; viz., the formation of the body of our Lord Jesus Christ. Though our Lord Jesus Christ was born of a woman, and made in the likeness of sinful flesh, yet, the power that begat him was entirely in God the Holy Spirit— as the Scriptures express it, "The Holy One of Israel shall overshadow thee." He was begotten, as the Apostles' Creed says, begotten of the Holy Ghost. "That holy thing which is born of thee shall be called the Son of the Highest." The corporeal frame of the Lord Jesus Christ was a master-piece of the Holy Spirit. I suppose his body to have excelled all others in beauty; to have been like that of the first man, the very pattern of what the body is to be in heaven, when it shall shine forth in all its glory. That fabric, in all its beauty and perfection, was modelled by the Spirit. "In his book were all the members written, when as yet there were none of them." He fashioned and formed him; and here again we have another instance of the creative energy of the Spirit.

2. A second manifestation of the Holy Spirit's power is to be found in the *resurrection of the Lord Jesus Christ.* If ye have ever studied this subject, ye have perhaps been rather perplexed to find that sometimes the resurrection of Christ is ascribed to himself. By his own power and godhead he could not be held by the bond of death, but as he willingly gave up his life he had power to take it again. In another portion of Scripture, you find it ascribed to God the Father: "He raised him up from the dead:" "Him hath God the Father exalted." And many other passages of similar import. But, again, it is said in Scripture that Jesus Christ was raised by the Holy Spirit. Now, all these things were true. He was raised by the Father

because the Father said, "Loose the prisoner—let him go. Justice is satisfied. My law requires no more satisfaction—vengeance has had its due—let him go." Here he gave an official message which delivered Jesus from the grave. He was raised by his own majesty and power, because he had a right to come out; and he felt he had, and therefore "burst the bonds of death: he could be no longer holden of them." But he was raised by the Spirit as to that energy which his mortal frame received, by the which it rose again from the grave after having lain there for three days and nights. If you want proofs of this you must open your Bibles again, 1 Peter, iii. 18. "For Christ also hath once suffered for sins, the just for the unjust, that he might bring us to God, being put to death in the flesh but quickened by the Spirit." And a further proof you may find in Romans, viii. 11. (I love sometimes to be textual, for I believe the great fault of Christians is that they do not search the Scriptures enough, and I will make them search them when they are here if they do not do so anywhere else.) "But if the Spirit of him that raised up Jesus from the dead dwell in you, he that raised up Christ from the dead shall also quicken your mortal bodies by his Spirit that dwelleth in you."

The resurrection of Christ, then, was effected by the agency of the Spirit! and here we have a noble illustration of his omnipotence. Could you have stepped, as angels did, into the grave of Jesus, and seen his sleeping body, you would have found it cold as any other corpse. Lift up the hand; it falls by the side. Look at the eye; it is glazed. And there is a death-thrust which must have annihilated life. See his hands: the blood distills not from them. They are cold and motionless. Can that body live? Can it start up? Yes; and be an illustration of the might of the Spirit. For when the power of the Spirit came on him, as it was when it fell upon the dry bones of the valley, "he arose in the majesty of his divinity, and, bright and shining, astonished the watchmen so that they fled away; yea, he arose no more to die, but to live forever, King of kings and Prince of the kings of the earth."

3. The third of the works of the Holy Spirit, which have so wonderfully demonstrated his power, are *attestation works.* I mean by this, works of witnessing. When Jesus Christ went into the stream of baptism in the river Jordan, the Holy Spirit descended upon him like a dove, and proclaimed him God's beloved son. That was what I style an attestation work. And when afterwards Jesus Christ raised the dead, when he healed the leper, when he spoke to diseases and they fled apace, when demons rushed in thousands from those who were possessed of them, it was done by the power of the Spirit. The Spirit dwelt in Jesus without measure, and by that power all those miracles were worked. These were attestation works. And when Jesus Christ was gone, you will remember that master attestation of the Spirit, when he came like a rushing mighty wind upon the assembled apostles, and cloven tongues sat upon them; and you will remember how he attested their ministry, by giving them to speak with tongues as he gave them utterance; and how, also, miraculous deeds were wrought by them, how they taught, how Peter raised Dorcas, how he breathed life into Enticus, how great deeds were wrought by the apostles as well as their

Master — so that "mighty signs and wonders were done by the Holy Ghost, and many believed thereby." Who will doubt the power of the Holy Spirit after that? Ah! those Socinians who deny the existence of the Holy Ghost and his absolute personality, what will they do when we get them on creation, resurrection, and attestation? They must rush in the very teeth of Scripture. But mark! it is a stone upon which if any man fall he shall be bruised; but if it fall upon him, as it will do if he resists it, it shall grind him to powder. The Holy Spirit has power omnipotent, even the power of God.

4. Once more, if we want another outward and visible sign of the power of the Spirit, we may look at the *works of grace*. Behold a city where a soothsayer hath the power — who has given out himself to be some great one — a Philip enters it and preaches the Word of God; straightway a Simon Magus loses his power and himself seeks for the power of the Spirit to be given to him, fancying it might be purchased with money. See, in modern times, a country where the inhabitants live in miserable wigwams, feeding on reptiles and the meanest creatures; observe them bowing down before their idols and worshipping their false gods, and so plunged in superstition, so degraded and debased, that it became a question whether they had souls or not; behold a Moffat go with the Word of God in his hand, hear him preach as the Spirit gives him utterance, and accompanies that Word with power. They cast aside their idols — they hate and abhor their former lusts; they build houses, wherein they dwell; they become clothed, and in their right mind. They break the bow, and cut the spear in sunder; the unciv-

ilized became civilized; the savage becomes polite; he who knew nothing begins to read the Scriptures: thus out of the mouths of Hottentots God attests the power of his mighty Spirit. Take a household in this city — and we could guide you to many such — the father is a drunkard; he has been the most desperate of characters; see him in his madness, and you might just as well meet an unchained tiger as meet such a man. He seems as if he could rend a man to pieces who should offend him. Mark his wife. She, too, has a spirit in her, and when he treats her ill she can resist him; many broils have been seen in that house, and often has the neighborhood been disturbed by the noise created there. As for the poor little children — see them in their rags and nakedness, poor untaught things. Untaught, did I say? They are taught and well taught in the devil's school, and are growing up to be the heirs of damnation. But some one whom God has blessed by his Spirit is guided to the house. He may be but an humble city missionary, perhaps, but he speaks to such a one: Oh! says he, come and listen to the voice of God. Whether it is by his own agency, or a minister's preaching, the Word, which is quick and powerful, cuts to the sinner's heart. The tears run down his cheeks — such as had never been seen before. He shakes and quivers. The strong man bows down — the mighty man trembles — and those knees that never shook begin to knock together. That heart which never quailed before now begins to shake before the power of the Spirit. He sits down on an humble bench by the penitent; he lets his knees bend, whilst his lips utter a child's prayer; but, whilst a child's prayer, a prayer of a child of God. He becomes a changed character. Mark the reformation in his house! That wife of his becomes the decent matron. Those children are the credit of the house, and in due time they grow up like olive branches round his table, adorning his house like polished stones. Pass by the house — no noise or broils, but songs of Zion. See him — no drunken revelry; he has drained his last cup, and, now foreswearing it, he comes to God and is his servant. Now, you will not hear at midnight the bacchanalian shout; but should there be a noise, it will be the sound of the solemn hymn of praise to God. And, now, is there not such a thing as the power of the Spirit? Yes! and these must have witnessed it, and seen it. I know a village, once perhaps the most profane in England — a village inundated by drunkenness and debauchery of the worst kind, where it was impossible almost for an honest traveller to stop in the public house without being annoyed by blasphemy; a place noted for incendiaries and robbers. One man, the ringleader of all, listened to the voice of God. That man's heart was broken. The whole gang came to hear the gospel preached, and they sat and seemed to reverence the preacher as if he were a God, and not a man. These men became changed and reformed; and every one who knows the place affirms that such a change had never been wrought but by the power of the Holy Ghost. Let the gospel be preached and the Spirit poured out, and you will see that it has such power to change the conscience, to ameliorate the conduct, to raise the debased, to chastise and to curb the wickedness of the race, that you must glory in it. I say, there is nought like the power of the Spirit. Only let that come, and, indeed, everything can be accomplished.

II. Now for the second point, *the inward and spiritual power of the Holy Spirit.* What I have already spoken of may be seen; what I am about to speak of must be felt, and no man will apprehend what I say with truth unless he has felt it. The other, even the Infidel must confess; the other, the greatest blasphemer cannot deny, if he speaks the truth; but this is what the one will laugh at as enthusiasm, and what the other will say is but the invention of our fevered fancies. However, we have a more sure word of testimony than all that they may say. We have a witness within. We know it is the truth, and we are not afraid to speak of the inward spiritual power of the Holy Ghost. Let us notice two or three things wherein the inward and spiritual power of the Holy Ghost is very greatly to be seen and extolled.

First, in that the Holy Ghost has *a power over men's hearts.* Now, men's hearts are very hard to affect. If you want to get at them for any worldly object, you can do it. A cheating world can win man's heart; a little gold can win man's heart; a trump of fame and a little clamor of applause can win man's heart. But there is not a minister breathing that can win man's heart himself. He can win his ears and make them listen; he can win his eyes, and fix those eyes upon him; he can win the attention, but the heart is very slippery. Yes! the heart is a fish that troubles all gospel fishermen to hold. You may sometimes pull it almost all out of the water; but, slimy as an eel, it slippeth between your fingers, and you have not captured it after all. Many a man has fancied that he has caught the heart, but has been disappointed. It would take a strong hunter to overtake the hart on the mountains. It is too fleet for human foot to approach. The Spirit alone has power over man's heart. Do you ever try your power on a heart? If any man thinks that a minister can convert the soul, I wish he would try. Let him go and be a Sabbath-school teacher. He shall take his class, he shall have the best books that can be obtained, he shall have the best rules, he shall draw his lines of circumvallation about his spiritual Sebastopol, he shall take the best boy in his class, and if he is not tired in a week I shall be very much mistaken. Let him spend four or five Sabbaths in trying; but he will say, "the young fellow is incorrigible." Let him try another. And he will have to try another, and another, and another, before he will manage to convert one. He will soon find "it is not by might nor power, but by my Spirit, saith the Lord." Can a minister convert? Can he touch the heart? David said, "Your hearts are as fat as grease." Aye, that is quite true; and we cannot get through so much grease at all. Our sword cannot get at the heart, it is encased in so much fatness; it is harder than a nether millstone. Many a good old Jerusalem blade has been blunted against the hard heart. Many a piece of the true steel that God has put into the hands of his servants has had the edge turned by being set up against the sinner's heart. We cannot reach the soul, but the Holy Spirit can. "My beloved can put in his hand by the hole in the door, and my bowels will move for sin." He can give a sense of blood-bought pardon that shall dissolve a heart of stone. He can

"Speak with that voice which wakes the dead,
And bids the sinner rise;
And makes the guilty conscience dread
The death that never dies."

He can make Sinai's thunders audible; yea, and he can make the sweet whisperings of Calvary enter into the soul. He has power over the heart of man. And here is a glorions proof of the omnipotence of the Spirit that he has rule over the heart.

But if there is one thing more stubborn than the heart, it is *the will.* "My lord Will-be-will," as Bunyan calls him in his "Holy War," is a fellow who will not easily be bent. The will, especially in some men, is a very stubborn thing; and in all men, if the will is once stirred up to opposition, there is nothing can be done with them. *Free-will* somebody believes in. *Free-will* many dream of. Free-will! wherever is that to be found? Once there was Free-will in Paradise, and a terrible mess Free-will made there; for it spoiled all Paradise and turned Adam out of the garden. Free-will was once in heaven; but it turned the glorious archangel out, and a third part of the stars of heaven fell into the abyss. I want nothing to do with Free-will, but I will try to see whether I have got a Free-will within. And I find I have. Very free will to evil, but very poor will to that which is good. Free-will enough when I sin, but when I would do good, evil is present with me, and how to do that which I would I find not. Yet some boast of Free-will. I wonder whether those who believe in it have any more power over persons' wills than I have? I know I have not any. I find the old proverb very true, "One man can bring a horse to the water, but a hundred cannot make him drink." I find that I can bring you all to the water, and a great many more than can get into this chapel; but I cannot make you drink; and I don't think a hundred ministers could make you drink. I have read old Rowland Hill, and Whitfield, and several others, to see what they did; but I cannot discover a plan of turning your wills. I cannot coax you, and you will not yield by any manner of means. I do not think any man has power over his fellow-creature's will, but the Spirit of God has. "I will make them willing in the day of my power." He maketh the unwilling sinner so willing that he is impetuous after the gospel; he who was obstinate now hurries to the cross. He who laughed at Jesus now hangs on his mercy; and he who would not believe is now made by the Holy Spirit to do it, not only willingly, but eagerly; he is happy, is glad to do it, rejoices in the sound of Jesus' name, and delights to run in the way of God's commandments. The Holy Spirit has power over the will.

And yet there is one thing more which I think is rather worse than the will. You will guess what I mean. The will is somewhat worse than the heart to bend, but there is one thing that excels the will in its naughtiness, and that is the *imagination.* I hope that my will is managed by Divine Grace. But I am afraid my imagination is not at times. Those who have a fair share of imagination know what a difficult thing it is to control. You cannot restrain it. It will break the reins. You will never be able to manage it. The imagination will sometimes fly up to God with such a power that eaglés' wings cannot match it. It sometimes has such might that it can almost see the King in his beauty, and the land which is very far off. With regard to myself, my imagination will sometimes take me over the gates of iron, across that infinite unknown, to the very gates of pearl, and discovers the blessed glorified. But, if it is potent one way, it is another: for my imagination has taken me down to the vilest kennels and sewers of earth. It has given me thoughts so dreadful, that, while I could not avoid them, yet I was thoroughly horrified at them. These thoughts will come; and when I feel in the holiest frame, the most devoted to God, and the most earnest in prayer, it often happens that that is the very time when the plague breaks out the worst. But I rejoice and think of one thing, that I can cry out when this imagination comes upon me. I know it is said in the Book of Leviticus, when an act of evil was committed, if the maiden cried out against it, then her life was to be spared. So it is with the Christian. If he cries out, there is hope. Can you chain your imagination? No; but the power of the Holy Ghost can. Ah, it shall do it! and it does do it at last, it does it even on earth.

III. But the last thing was, the *future and desired effects;* for, after all, though the Holy Spirit has done so much, he cannot say, "It is finished." Jesus Christ could exclaim concerning his own labor, "It is finished." But the Holy Spirit cannot say that. He has more to do yet: and until the consummation of all things, when the Son himself becomes subject to the Father, it shall not be said by the Holy Spirit, "It is finished." What, then, has the Holy Spirit to do?

First, he has to *perfect us in holiness.* There are two kinds of perfection which a Christian needs: one is the perfection of justification in the person of Jesus; and the other is, the perfection of sanctification worked in him by the Holy Spirit. At present corruption still rests even in the breasts of the regenerate. At present the heart is partially impure. At present there are still lusts and evil imaginations. But, oh! my soul rejoices to know that the day is coming when God shall finish the work which he has begun; and he shall present my soul, not only perfect in Christ, but perfect in the Spirit, without spot or blemish, or any such thing. And is it true that this poor depraved heart is to become as holy as that of God? And is it true that this poor spirit, which often cries, "O wretched man that I am, who shall deliver me from the body of this sin and death!" shall get rid of sin and death?—I shall have no evil things to vex my ears, and no unholy thoughts to disturb my peace. Oh happy hour! may it be hastened! Just before I die sanctification will be finished; but not till that moment shall I ever claim perfection in myself. But at that moment when I depart, my spirit shall have its last baptism in the Holy Spirit's fire. It shall be put in the crucible for its last trying in the furnace; and then, free from all dross, and fine, like a wedge of pure gold, it shall be presented at the feet of God without the least degree of dross or mixture. O glorious hour! O blessed moment! Methinks I long to die if there were no heaven, if I might but have that last purification, and come up from Jordan's stream most white from the washing. Oh! to be washed white, clean, pure, perfect! Not an angel more pure than I shall be—yea, not God himself more holy! And I shall be able to say, in a double sense, "Great God, I am clean—through Jesus' blood I am clean, through the Spirit's work I am clean too!" Must you not extol the power of the Holy Ghost in thus making us fit to stand before our Father in heaven?

Another great work of the Holy Spirit, which is not accomplished is, *the bringing on of the latter-day glory.* In a few more years—I know not when, I know not how—the Holy Spirit will be poured out in a far different style from the present. There are diversities of operations; and during the last few years it has been the case that the diversified operations have consisted in very little pouring out of the Spirit. Ministers have gone on in dull routine, continually preaching—preaching—preaching, and little good has been done. I do hope that perhaps a fresh era has dawned upon us, and that there is a better pouring out of the Spirit even now. For the hour is coming, and it may be even now is, when the Holy Ghost shall be poured out again in such a wonderful manner, that many shall run to and fro, and knowledge shall be increased—the knowledge of the Lord shall cover the earth as the waters cover the surface of the great deep; when his kingdom shall come, and his will shall be done on earth even as it is in heaven. We are not going to be dragging on forever like Pharoah, with the wheels off his chariot. My heart exults, and my eyes flash with the thought that very likely I shall live to see the out-pouring of the Spirit; when "the sons and the daughters of God again shall prophesy, and the young men shall see visions, and the old men shall dream dreams." Perhaps there shall be no miraculous gifts—for they will not be required; but yet there shall be such a miraculous amount of holiness, such an extraordinary fervor of prayer, such a real communion with God, and so much vital religion, and such a spread of the doctrines of the cross, that every one will see that verily the Spirit is poured out like water, and the rains are descending from above. For that let us pray; let us continually labor for it, and seek it of God.

One more work of the Spirit, which will especially manifest his power—*the general resurrection.* We have reason to believe from Scripture, that the resurrection of the dead, whilst it will be effected by the voice of God and of his Word, (the Son,) shall also be brought about by the Spirit. That same power which raised Jesus Christ from the dead, shall also quicken your mortal bodies. The power of the resurrection is, perhaps, one of the finest proofs of the works of the Spirit. Ah! my friends, if this earth could but have its mantle torn away for a little while, if the green sod could be cut from it, and we could look about six feet deep into its bowels, what a world it would seem! What should we see? Bones, carcasses, rottenness, worms, corruption. And you would say, Can these dry bones live? Can they start up? Yes! "in a moment! in the twinkling of an eye, at the last trump, the dead shall be raised." He speaks; they are alive! See them scattered! bone comes to his bone! See them naked; flesh comes upon them! See them still lifeless; "Come from the four winds, O breath, and breathe upon these slain!" When the wind of the Holy Spirit comes, they live; and they stand upon their feet an exceeding great army.

I have thus attempted to speak of the power of the Spirit, and I trust I have shown it to you. We must now have a moment or two for practical inference. The Spirit is very powerful, Christian! What do you infer from that fact? Why, that you never need distrust the power of God to carry you to heaven. O how that sweet verse was laid to my soul yesterday!

"His tried Almighty arm
Is raised for your defence;
Where is the power can reach you there?
Or what can pluck you thence?"

The power of the Holy Spirit is your bulwark, and all his omnipotence defends you. Can your enemies overcome omnipotence? then they can conquer you. Can they wrestle with Deity, and hurl him to the ground? then they might conquer you. For the power of the Spirit is our power; the power of the Spirit is our might.

Once again, Christians, if this is the power of the Spirit, *why should you doubt anything?* There is your son. There is that wife of yours, for whom you have supplicated so frequently; do not doubt the Spirit's power. "Though he tarry, wait for him." There is thy husband, O holy woman! and thou hast wrestled for his soul. And though he is ever so hardened and desperate a wretch, and treats thee ill, there is power in the Spirit. And, O ye who have come from barren churches, with scarcely a leaf upon the tree, do not doubt the power of the Spirit to raise you up. For it shall be a "pasture for flocks, a den of wild asses," open but deserted, until the Spirit is poured out from on high. And then the parched ground shall be made a pool, and the thirsty land springs of water; and in the habitations of dragons, where each lay shall be grass with reeds and rushes. And, O ye members of Park-street! ye who remember what your God has done for you especially, never distrust the power of the Spirit. Ye have seen the wilderness blossom like Carmel, ye have seen the desert blossom like the rose; trust him for the future. Then go out and labor with this conviction, that the power of the Holy Ghost is able to do anything. Go to your Sunday-school; go to your tract distribution; go to your missionary enterprise; go to your preaching in your rooms, with the conviction that the power of the Spirit is our great help.

And now, lastly, to you sinners. What is there to be said to you about this power of the Spirit? Why, to me, there is some hope for some of you. I cannot save you; I cannot get at you. I make you cry sometimes—you wipe your eyes, and it is all over. But I know my Master can. That is my consolation. Chief of sinners, there is hope for thee! This power can save you as well as anybody else. It is able to break your heart, though it is an iron one; to make your eyes run with tears, though they have been like rocks before. His power is able this morning, if he will, to change your heart, to turn the current of all your ideas; to make you at once a child of God, to justify you in Christ. There is power enough in the Holy Spirit. Ye are not straightened in him, but in your own bowels. He is able to bring sinners to Jesus; he is able to make you willing in the day of his power. Are you willing this morning? Has he gone so far as to make you desire his name; to make you wish for Jesus? Then, O sinner! whilst he draws you, say, "Draw me, I am wretched without thee." Follow him, follow him; and, while he leads, tread you in his footsteps, and rejoice that he has begun a good work in you, for there is an evidence that he will continue it even unto the end. And, O desponding one! put thy trust in the power of the Spirit. Rest on the blood of Jesus, and thy soul is safe, not only now, but throughout eternity. God bless you, my hearers. Amen.

SERMON VII.

THE CHURCH OF CHRIST.

"And I will make them and the places round about my hill a blessing; and I will cause the shower to come down in his season; there shall be showers of blessing."—EZEKIEL xxxiv. 26.

THE chapter (Ezek. xxxiv.) that I read at the commencement of the service is a prophetical one; and, I take it, it has relation, not to the condition of the Jews during the captivity and their subsequent happiness when they should return to their land, but to a state into which they should fall after they had been restored to their country under Nehemiah and Ezra, and in which state they still continue to the present day. The prophet tells us that the shepherds then, instead of feeding the flock, fed themselves; they trod the grass, instead of allowing the sheep to eat it, and they fouled the waters with their feet. That is an exact description of the state of Judea after the captivity; for then there arose the Scribes and Pharisees, who took the key of knowledge, and would not enter themselves nor allow others to enter; who laid heavy burdens on men's shoulders, and would not touch them with one of their fingers; who made religion to consist entirely in sacrifices and ceremonies, and imposed such a burden on the people, that they cried out, "What a weariness it is!" That same evil has continued with the poor Jews to the present day; and should you read the nonsense of the Talmud and the Gemara, and see the burdens they laid upon them, you would say, "Verily, they have idle shepherds;" they give the sheep no food; they trouble them with fanciful superstitions and silly views, and instead of telling them that the Messiah is already come, they delude them with the idea that there is a Messiah yet to come, who shall restore Judea, and raise it to its glory. The Lord pronounces a curse upon these Pharisees and Rabbis, these who "thrust with side and with shoulder," those evil shepherds who will not suffer the sheep to lie down, neither will feed them with good pasture. But, after having described this state, he prophecies better times for the poor Jew. The day is coming when the careless shepherds shall be as nought; when the power of the Rabbis shall cease, when the traditions of the Mishna and the Talmud shall be cast aside. The hour is approaching, when the tribes shall go up to their own country; when Judea, so long a howling wilderness, shall once more blossom like the rose; when, if the temple itself be not restored, yet on Zion's hill shall be raised some Christian building, where the chants of solemn praise shall be heard, as erst of old the Psalms of David were sung in the tabernacle. Not long shall it be, ere they shall come — shall come from distant lands, where'er they rest or roam; and she who has been the offscouring of all things, whose name has been a proverb and a byword, shall become the glory of all lands. Dejected Zion shall raise her head, shaking herself from dust, and darkness, and the dead. Then shall the Lord feed his people, and make them and the places round about his hill a blessing. I think we do not attach sufficient importance to the restoration of the Jews. We do not think enough of it. But certainly, if there is anything promised in the Bible it is this. I imagine that you cannot read the Bible without seeing clearly that there is to be an actual restoration of the children of Israel. "Thither they shall go up; they shall come with weeping unto Zion, and with supplications unto Jerusalem." May that happy day soon come! For when the Jews are restored, then the fulness of the Gentiles shall be gathered in; and as soon as they return, then Jesus will come upon Mount Zion to reign with his ancients gloriously, and the halcyon days of the Millennium shall then dawn; we shall then know every man to be a brother and a friend; Christ shall rule, with universal sway.

This, then, is the meaning of the text; that God would make Jerusalem and the places round about his hill a blessing. I shall not, however, use it so this morning, but I shall use it in a more confined sense — or, perhaps, in a more enlarged sense — as it applies to the church of Jesus Christ, and to this particular church with which you and I stand connected. "I will make them and the places round about my hill a blessing; and I will cause the shower to come down in his season; there shall be showers of blessing."

There are two things here spoken of. First, *Christ's church is to be a blessing;* secondly, *Christ's church is to be blessed.* These two things you will find in the different sentences of the text.

I. First, *Christ's church is to be a blessing.* "I will

make them and the places round about my hill a blessing." The object of God, in choosing a people before all worlds, was not only to save that people, but through them to confer essential benefits upon the whole human race. When he chose Abraham, he did not elect him simply to be God's friend, and the recipient of peculiar privileges; but he chose him to make him, as it were, the conservator of truth. He was to be the ark in which the truth should be hidden. He was to be the keeper of the covenant in behalf of the whole world; and when God chooses any men by his sovereign-electing grace, and makes them Christ's, he does it not only for their own sake, that they may be saved, but for the world's sake. For, know ye not that "ye are the light of the world?" — "A city set upon a hill, which cannot be hid?" "Ye are the salt of the earth;" and when God makes you salt, it is not only that ye may have salt in yourselves, but that like salt ye may preserve the whole mass. If he makes you leaven, it is that, like the little leaven, you may leaven the whole lump. Salvation is not a selfish thing; God does not give it for us to keep to ourselves, but that we may thereby be made the means of blessing to others; and the great day shall declare that there is not a man living on the surface of the earth but has received a blessing in some way or other through God's gift of the gospel. The very keeping of the wicked in life, and granting of the reprieve, was purchased with the death of Jesus; and through his sufferings and death, the temporal blessings which both we and they enjoy are bestowed on us. The gospel was sent that it might first bless those that embrace it, and then expand, so as to make them a blessing to the whole human race.

In thus speaking of the church as a blessing, we shall notice three things. First, here is *divinity* — "*I* will make them a blessing;" secondly, here is *personality of religion* — "I will make *them* a blessing;" and thirdly, here is *the development of religion* — "and the places round about my hill."

1. First, with regard to this blessing which God will cause his church to be, here is *divinity*. It is God the everlasting Jehovah speaking: he says, "*I* will make them a blessing." None of us can bless others unless God has first blessed us. We need divine workmanship. "I will make them a blessing by helping them, and by constraining them." God makes his people a blessing by helping them. What can we do without God's help? I stand and preach to thousands, or it may be hundreds; what have I done, unless a greater than man has been in the pulpit with me? I work in the Sabbath-schools; what can I do, unless the Master is there, teaching the children with me? We want God's aid in every position; and once give us that assistance, and there is no telling with how little labor we may become a blessing. Ah! a few words sometimes will be more of a blessing than a whole sermon. You take some little prattler on your knee; and some few words that you say to him he remembers, and makes use of in after years. I knew a gray-headed old man, who was in the habit of doing this. He once took a boy to a certain tree, and said, "Now, John, you kneel down at that tree, and I will kneel down with you." He knelt down and prayed, and asked God to convert him and save his soul. "Now," said he, "perhaps you will come to this tree again; and if you are not converted, you will remember that I

asked under this tree that God would save your soul." That young man went away, and forgot the old man's prayer; but it chanced as God would have it that he walked down that field again, and saw a tree. It seemed as if the old man's name was cut in the bark. He recollected what he prayed for, and that the prayer was not fulfilled; but he dare not pass the tree without kneeling down to pray himself; and there was his spiritual birthplace. The simplest observation of the Christian shall be made a blessing, if God help him. "His leaf also shall not wither"—the simplest word he speaks shall be treasured up; "and whatsoever he doeth shall prosper."

But there is *constraint* here. "I will *make* them a blessing." I will give them to be a blessing; I will constrain them to be a blessing. I can say myself, that I never did anything which was a blessing to my fellow creatures, without feeling compelled to do it. I thought of going to a Sabbath school to teach. On a certain day, some one called—asked me—begged me—prayed me to take his class. I could not refuse to go; and there I was held, hand and foot, by the superintendent, and was compelled to go on. I was asked to address the children; I thought I could not, but no one else was there to do it, so I stood up and stumbled out a few words. And I recollect the first occasion on which I attempted to preach to the people—I am sure I had no wish to do it—but there was no one else in the place, and the congregation must go away without a single word of warning or address. How could I suffer it? I felt forced to address them. And so it has been with whatever I have laid my hand to. I have always felt a kind of impulse which I could not resist;

but, moreover, felt placed by Providence in such a position, that I had no wish to avoid the duty, and if I had desired it, could not have helped myself. And so it is with God's people. If they will go through their lives, wherever they have been made a blessing, they will find that God seems to have thrust them into the vineyard. Such-and-such a man was once rich. What good was he in the world? He did but loll in his carriage; he did but little good, and was of little service to his fellow-creatures. Says God, "I will make him a blessing:" so he strips away his riches, and brings him into low circumstances. He is then brought into association with the poor, and his superior education and intellect make him a blessing to them. God *makes* him a blessing. Another man was naturally very timid; he would not pray at the prayer meeting, he would hardly like to join the church: soon he gets into a position in which he cannot help himself. "I will *make* him a blessing." And as sure as ever you are a servant of God, he will *make* you a blessing. He will have none of his gold in the lump; he will hammer it out, and make it a blessing. I verily believe there are some in my congregation, to whom God has given power to preach his name: they do not know it, perhaps, but God will make it known by-and-by. I would have every man look and see, whether God is making him do a certain thing; and when once he feels the impulse, let him by no means ever check it. I am somewhat of a believer in the doctrine of the Quakers, as to the impulses of the Spirit, and I fear lest I should check one of them. If a thought crosses my mind, "Go to such a person's house," I always like to do it, because I do not know but what it may be from the

Spirit. I understand this verse to mean something like that. "I will make them a blessing." I will force them to do good. If I cannot make a sweet scent come from them in any other way, I will pound them in the mortar of affliction. If they have seed, and the seed cannot be scattered in any other way, I will send a rough wind to blow the downy seed everywhere." "I will *make* them a blessing." If you have never been *made* a blessing to any one, depend upon it you are not a child of God; for Jehovah says, "I *will* make them a blessing."

2. But notice, next, the *personality* of the blessing. "I will make *them* a blessing." "I will make each member of the church a blessing." Many people come up to the house of prayer, where the church assembles: and you say, "Well, what are you doing at such-and-such a place where you attend?" "Well, *we* are doing so-and-so." "How do you spell we?" "It is a plain monosyllable," say you. Yes, but do you put *I* in "we?" "No." There are a great many people who could easily spell "we" without an *I* in it; for though they say, "*We* have been doing so-and-so," they do not say, "How much have *I* done? Did I do anything in it? Yes; this chapel has been enlarged; what did I subscribe? Twopence!" Of course it is done. Those who paid the money have done it. "We preach the gospel." Do we, indeed? "Yes, we sit in our pew and listen a little, and do not pray for a blessing. We have got such a large Sunday school." Did you ever teach in it? "We have got a very good working society." Did you ever go to work in it? That is not the way to spell "we." It is, "I will make *them* a blessing." When Jerusalem was built every man began nearest

his own house. That is where you must begin to build or do something. Do not let us tell a lie about it. If we do not have some share in the building, if we neither handle the trowel nor the spear, let us not talk about *our* church; for the text says, "I will make *them* a blessing," every one of them.

"But, sir, what can I do? I am nothing but a father at home; I am so full of business, I can only see my children a little." But in your business, do you ever have any servants? "No; I am a servant myself." You have fellow-servants? "No; I work alone." Do you work alone, then, and live alone, like a monk in a cell? I don't believe that. But you have fellow-servants at work; cannot you say a word to their conscience? "I don't like to intrude religion into business." Quite right, too; so say I; when I am at business, let it be business; when you are at religion, let it be religion. But do you never have an opportunity? Why, you cannot go into an omnibus, or a railway carriage, but what you can say something for Jesus Christ. I have found it so, and I don't believe I am different from other people. *Cannot do anything?* Cannot you put a tract in your hat, and drop it where you go? Cannot you speak a word to a child? Where does this man come from, that cannot do anything? There is a spider on the wall; but he taketh hold on kings' palaces, and spinneth his web to rid the world of noxious flies. There is a nettle in the corner of the churchyard; but the physician tells me it has its virtues. There is a tiny star in the sky; but that is noted in the chart, and the mariner looks at it. There is an insect under water; but it builds a rock. God made all these things for something; but here is a man that God made, and gave him nothing at all to do! I do not believe it. God never makes useless things; he has no superfluous workmanship. I care not what you are; you have somewhat to do. And oh! may God show you what it is, and then make you do it, by the wondrous compulsion of his providence and his grace.

3. But we have to notice, in the third place, *the development of gospel blessing*. "I will make them a blessing;" but it does not end there. "And the places round about my hill." Religion is an expansive thing. When it begins in the heart, at first it is like a tiny grain of mustard seed; but it gradually increases, and becomes a great tree, so that the birds of the air lodge in the branches thereof. A man cannot be religious to himself. "No man liveth to himself, and no man dieth to himself." You have heard a score of times, that if you do but drop a pebble in a brook it causes a small ring at first, then another outside of that, and then another, and then another, till the influence of the pebble is perceptible over the entire bosom of the water. So it is when God makes his people a blessing. "I will make a minister a blessing to one or two; I will then make him a blessing to a hundred; I will then make him a blessing to thousands; and then I will make those thousands a blessing. I will make each one individually a blessing, and when I have done that, I will make all the places round about a blessing. "I will make them a blessing." I hope we shall never be satisfied, as members of Park-street, until we are a blessing, not only to ourselves, but to all the places round about our hill. What are the places round about our hill? I think they are, first, our agencies; sec-

ondly, our neighborhood; thirdly, the churches adjacent to us.

First, there are our agencies. There is our Sabbath-school: how near that is to our hill? I speak a great deal about this, because I want it to be brought into notice. I intend to preach a practical sermon this morning, to move some of you to come and teach in the Sabbath-school; for there we require some suitable men, to "come up to the help of the Lord, to the help of the Lord against the mighty." Therefore I mention the Sabbath-school as a place very near to the hill; it ought to be just at the very foot of it; yea, it ought to be so near the hill that very many may pass from it to the church. Then there is our Visiting and Christian Instruction Society, which we have for the visiting of this neighborhood. I trust that has been made a blessing. God has sent among us a man who labors zealously and earnestly in visiting the sick. I have, as the superintendent of my beloved brother, the missionary, a regular account of his labors; his report has most highly gratified me, and I am able to bear testimony to the fact, that he is very efficiently laboring around us. I want that society to have all your sympathy and strength. I consider him as a Joshua, with whom you are to go forth by hundreds to those who live in the neighborhood. Do you know what dark places there are? Walk down a street a little to the right. See the shops open on a Sunday. Some, thank God, that used to open them, now come and worship with us. We shall have more yet; for "the earth is the Lord's and the fulness thereof," and why should not we have it? My brethren, as you visit the sick, or distribute tracts from door to door, make this your prayer — that this society, being one of the places round about our hill, may be made a blessing! Let me not forget any agency connected with this church. There are several more which are places round about our hill; and the Lord has just put it into my heart to fashion other societies, which shall be made a blessing to this hill, and in a little while you shall hear thereof. We have several brethren in this congregation to whom God has given a mouth of utterance; these are about to form themselves into a society for proclaiming the Word of God. Where God has so blessed his church, and made us to be so noted and named amongst the people, why should we not keep on? We have been brought up to a great pitch of fervency and love; now is the time for doing something. While the iron is hot, why not strike and fashion it? I believe we have the materials, not only for making a church here that shall be the glory of the Baptist Churches in London, but for making churches everywhere throughout the metropolis; and we have more schemes on hand, which, matured by sober judgment, and backed by prudence, shall yet make this metropolis more honored than it has been by the sound of the pure gospel and the proclamation of the pure Word of God. May God make all our agencies — the places round about our hill — a blessing.

But next, there is the neighborhood. I am paralyzed sometimes, when I think that we are of so little service to the neighborhood, though this is a green oasis in the midst of a great spiritual desert. Just at the back of us we could find you hundreds of Roman Catholics, and men of the very worst character; and it is sad to think that we cannot make this place a blessing to them. It is made a great blessing to you, my hearers, but you do not come from this district; you come from anywhere and nowhere, some of you, I suppose. People say, "There is something doing in that chapel; look at the crowd; but we cannot get in!" This one thing I ask — never come here to gratify your curiosity. You that are members of other congregations, just consider it your duty to stay at home. There are many stray sheep about. I would rather have them than you. Keep your own place. I do not want to rob other ministers. Do not come here from charity. We are much obliged to you for your kindly intentions; but we would rather have your room than your company, if ye are members of other churches. We want sinners to come — sinners of every sort; but do not let us have that sort of men whose ears are everlastingly itching for some new preacher; who are saying, "I want something else, I want something else." Oh! do, I beseech you, for God's sake, be of some good; and if you are running about from one place to another, you can never expect to be. Do ye know what is said of rolling stones? Ah! ye have heard of that. They "gather no moss." Now, don't be rolling stones, but keep at home. God, however, so help us, as to make us a blessing to the neighborhood! I long to see something done for the people around. We must open our arms to them: we must go out into the open air to them; we must and will preach God's gospel to them. Let, then, the people around listen to the word of the gospel; and may it be said, "That place is the cathedral of Southwark!" So it is now. Out of it goes a blessing; God is pouring out a blessing upon it.

What else do we mean by the places round about our hill? We mean, the churches adjacent. I cannot but rejoice in the prosperity of many churches around us; but as our beloved brother, Mr. Sherman, said, last Thursday morning, "It is not invidious to say, that there are very few churches that are in a prosperous state, and that, taking the churches at large, they are in a deplorable condition. It is only here and there," said he, "that God is pouring out his Spirit; but most of the churches are lying, like barges at Blackfriar's Bridge when the tide is down — right in the mud; and all the king's horses and all the king's men cannot pull them off, till the tide comes and sets them afloat." Who can tell, then, what good may be done by this church? If there is a light in this candlestick, let others come and light their candles by it. If there is a flame here, let the flame spread, until all the neighboring churches shall be lit up with the glory. Then, indeed, shall we be made the rejoicing of the earth; for there is never a revival in one spot, but it shall affect others. Who shall tell, then, where it shall end?

> "Fly abroad, thou mighty gospel;
> Win and conquer, never cease."

And it never will cease, when God once makes the places round about his hill a blessing.

II. The second point is, that God's people are not only to be a blessing, but *they are to be blessed.* For read the second part of the verse. "And I will cause the shower to come down in his season; there shall be showers of blessing." It is somewhat singular, as a prognostication of the showers of blessings we hope to receive here, that God sent us showers on the first day of opening. If I were a believer in omens, I should pray, that as it rained the first day, so may it rain every day since. When it stops may the chapel be shut up; for we only want it open so long as showers of grace continue to descend.

First, here is *sovereign mercy.* Listen to these words: "I will give them the shower in its season." Is it not sovereign, divine mercy; for who can say, "I will give them showers," except God? Can the false prophet who walks amongst the benighted Hottentots? He says he is a rain-maker, and can give them showers; but can he do it? Is there an imperial monarch, or the most learned man on earth, who can say, "I will give them the showers in their season?" No; there is only one fist wherein all the clouds are held; there is only one hand in which all the channels of the mighty ocean above the firmament are contained; there is only one voice that can speak to the clouds, and bid them beget the rain. "Out of whose womb came the ice? and the hoary frost of heaven, who hath gendered it?" "Who sendeth down the rain upon the earth? who scattereth the showers upon the green herb? Do not I, the Lord?" Who else could do it? Is not rain in God's power? and who could send it, except him? We know that Catholics pretend that they can get grace without getting it from God directly; for they believe that God puts all his grace into the pope, and then that runs down into smaller pipes, called cardinals and bishops, through which it runs into the priests; and, by turning the tap with a shilling, you can get as much grace as you like. But it is not so with God's grace. He says, "I will give them showers." Grace is the gift of God, and is not to be created by man.

Notice, next, it is *needed* grace. "I will give them

showers." What would the ground do without showers? You may break the clods, you may sow your seeds; but what can you do without the rain? Ah! you may prepare your barn, and sharpen your sickles; but your sickles will be rusted before you have any wheat, unless there are showers. They are needed. So is the divine blessing.

> "In vain Apollos sow the seed,
> And Paul may plant in vain;

In vain you come here, in vain you labor, in vain you give your money:

> "Till God the plenteous shower bestows,
> And sends salvation down."

Then, next, it is *plenteous grace*. "I will send them showers." It does not say, "I will send them drops," but "I will send them showers." "It seldom rains but it pours." So it is with grace. If God gives a blessing, he usually gives it in such a measure that there is not room enough to receive it. Where are we going to hold God's blessing that we have obtained already? I told the people on Thursday that God had promised us, that if we brought the tithes into the storehouse, he would send us such a blessing that we would not have room to hold it. We have tried it, and the promise has been fulfilled, as it always will be as long as we rely upon it. Plenteous grace! Ah! we shall want plenteous grace, my friends; plenteous grace to keep us humble, plenteous grace to make us prayerful, plenteous grace to make us holy, plenteous grace to make us zealous, plenteous grace to make us truthful, plenteous grace to preserve us through this life, and at last to land us in heaven. We cannot do without showers of grace. How many are there here that have been dry in a shower of grace? Why, there is a shower of grace here; but how is it that it does not fall on some of the people? It is because they put up the umbrella of their prejudice; and though they sit here, even as God's people sit, even when it rains, they have such a prejudice against God's Word, they do not want to hear it, they do not want to love it, and it runs off again. Nevertheless, the showers are there; and we will thank God for them where they do fall.

Again, it is *seasonable grace.* "I will give them the shower in its season." There is nothing like seasonable grace. There are fruits, you know, that are best in their season, and they are not good at any other time; and there are graces that are good in their season, but we do not always require them. A person vexes and irritates me; I want grace just at that moment to be patient: I have not got it, and I get angry; ten minutes after I am ever so patient; but I have not had grace in its season. The promise is, "I will give them the shower in its season." Ah! poor waiting soul, what is thy season this morning? Is it the season of drought? Then that is the season for showers. Is it a season of great heaviness and black clouds? Then that is the season for showers. What is your season this morning, business man? Lost money all the week, have you? Now is the season to ask for showers. It is night-time; now the dew falls. The dew does not fall in the day—it falls in the night; the night of affliction, trial, and trouble. There stands the promise; only go and plead it. "I will give them the shower in its season."

We have one thought more, and then we have done. Here is a *varied* blessing. "I will give thee *showers* of blessing." The word is in the plural. All kinds of blessings God will send. The rain is all of one kind when it comes; but grace is not all of one kind, or it does not produce the same effect. When God sends rain upon the church, he "sends showers of blessing." There are some ministers who think, that if there is a shower on their church, God will send a shower of work. Yes, but if he does, he will send a shower of comfort. Others think that God will send a shower of gospel truth. Yes, but if he sends that, he will send a shower of gospel holiness. For all God's blessings go together. They are like the sweet sister graces that danced hand in hand. God sends showers of blessings. If he gives comforting grace, he will also give converting grace; if he makes the trumpet blow for the bankrupt sinner, he will also make it sound a shout of joy for the sinner that is pardoned and forgiven. He will send "showers of blessing."

Now, then, there is a promise in that Bible. We have tried to explain and enlarge upon it. What shall we do with it?

> "In that book there hidden lies
> A pearl of price unknown."

Well, we have examined this rich promise; we as a church are looking at it; we are saying, "Is that ours?" I think most of the members will say, "It is; for God has poured out upon us showers of blessing in their season." Well, then, if the promise is ours the precept is ours, as much as the promise. Ought we not to ask God to continue to make us a blessing? Some say I did so-and-so when I was a young man; but supposing you are fifty, you are not an old man now. Is there not something you can do? It is all very well to talk about what you have done; but what are you doing now? I know what it is with some of you; you shined brightly once, but your candle has not been snuffed lately, and so it does not shine so well. May God take away some of the worldly cares, and snuff the candles a little! You know there were snuffers and snuffer-trays provided in the temple for all the candles, but no extinguishers; and if there should be a poor candle here this morning, with a terrific snuff, that has not given a light for a long while, you will have no extinguisher from me, but I hope you will always have a snuffing. I thought the first time when I came to the lamps this morning it would be to snuff them. That has been the intention of my sermon — to snuff you a little — to set you to work for Jesus Christ. O Zion, shake thyself from the dust! O Christian, raise thyself from thy slumbers! Warrior, put on thy armor! Soldier, grasp thy sword! The captain sounds the alarm of war. O sluggard! why sleepest thou? O heir of heaven, has not Jesus done so much for thee, that thou shouldst live to him? O beloved brethren, purchased with redeeming mercies, girt about with loving-kindness and with tenderness,

"Now for a shout of sacred joy,"

and after that, to the battle! The little seed has grown to this: who knoweth what it shall be? Only let us together strive, without variance. Let us labor for Jesus. Never did men have so fair an opportunity, for the last hundred years. "There is a time that, taken at the flood, leads on to fortune." Shall you take it at the flood? Over the bar, at the harbor's mouth! O ship of heaven, let thy sails be out; led not thy canvas be furled; and the wind will blow us across the seas of difficulty that lie before us. O! that the latter day might have its dawning even in this despised habitation! O my God! from this place cause the first wave to spring, which shall move another, and then another, till the last great wave shall sweep over the sands of time, and dash against the rocks of eternity, echoing as it falls, "Hallelujah! Hallelujah! Hallelujah! the Lord God Omnipotent reigneth!"

SERMON VIII.

THE ETERNAL NAME.

"His name shall endure forever."—PSALM lxxii. 17.

No one here requires to be told that this is the name of Jesus Christ, which "shall endure forever." Men have said of many of their works, "they shall endure forever;" but how much have they been disappointed! In the age succeeding the flood, they made the brick, they gathered the slime, and when they had piled old Babel's tower, they said, "This shall last forever." But God confounded their language; they finished it not. By his lightnings he destroyed it, and left it a monument of their folly. Old Pharoah and the Egyptian monarchs heaped up their pyramids, and they said "They shall stand forever," and so indeed they do stand but the time is approaching when age shall devour even these. So with all the proudest works of man, whether they have been his temples or his monarchies, he has written "everlasting" on them; but God has ordained their end, and they have passed away. The most stable things have been evanescent as shadows and the bubbles of an hour, speedily destroyed at God's bidding. Where is Nineveh, and where is Babylon? Where th cities of Persia? Where are the high places of Edom? Where are Moab, and the princes of Ammon? Where are the temples or the heroes of Greece? Where the millions that passed from the gates of Thebes? Where are the hosts of Xerxes, or where the vast armies of the Roman emperors? Have they not passed away? And though in their pride they said, "This monarchy is an everlasting one; this queen of the seven hills shall be called the eternal city," its pride is dimmed; and she who sat alone, and said, "I shall be no widow, but a queen forever," she hath fallen, hath fallen, and in a little while she shall sink like a millstone in the flood, her name being a curse and a byword, and her site the habitation of dragons and of owls. Man calls his works eternal — God calls them fleeting; man conceives that they are built of rock — God says, "Nay, sand, or worse than that — they are air." Man says he erects them for eternity — God blows but for a moment, and where are they? Like baseless fabrics of a vision, they are passed and gone forever.

It is pleasant, then, to find that there is one thing which is to last forever. Concerning that one thing we hope to speak to-night, if God will enable me to preach, and you to hear. "His name shall endure forever." First, *the religion* sanctified by his name shall endure forever; secondly, *the honor* of his name shall endure forever; and thirdly, *the saving, comforting power* of his name shall endure forever.

I. First, *the religion of the name of Jesus is to endure forever.* When imposters forged their delusions, they had hopes that peradventure they might in some distant age carry the world before them; and if they saw a few followers gather around their standard, who offered incense at their shrine, then they smiled, and said, "My religion shall outshine the stars and last through eternity." But how mistaken have they been! How many false systems have started up and passed away! Why, some of us have seen, even in our short lifetime, sects that rose like Jonah's gourd, in a single night, and passed away as swiftly. We, too, have beheld prophets rise, who have had their hour — yea, they have had their day, as dogs all have; but, like the dogs, their day has passed away, and the imposter, where is he? And the arch-deceiver, where is he? Gone and ceased. Specially might I say this of the various systems of Infidelity. Within a hundred and fifty years, how has the boasted power of reason changed! It has piled up one thing, and then another day it has laughed at its own handiwork, demolished its own castle, and constructed another, and the next day a third. It has a thousand dresses. Once it came forth like a fool with its bells, heralded by Voltaire; then it came out a braggard bully, like Tom Paine; then it changed its course, and assumed another shape, till, forsooth, we have it in the base, bestial seculiarism of the present day, which looks for nought but the earth, keeps its nose upon the ground, and like the beast, thinks this world is enough; or looks for another through seeking this. Why, before one hair on this head shall be gray, the last secularist shall have passed away; before many of us are fifty years of age, a new Infidelity shall come, and to those who say, "Where will saints be?" we can turn round and say, "Where are you?" And they will answer, "We have altered our names." They will have altered their name, assumed a fresh shape put on a new form of evil, but still their nature will be the same; opposing Christ, and endeavoring to blaspheme his truths. On all their systems of religion, or non-religion — for that is a system too — it may be written, "Evanescent; fading as the flower, fleeting as the meteor, frail and unreal as a vapor." But of Christ's religion, it shall be said, "His name shall endure forever." Let me now say a few things — not to prove it, for that I do not wish to do — but to give you some hints whereby, possibly, I may one day prove it to other people, that Jesus Christ's religion must inevitably endure forever.

And first, we ask those who think it shall pass away, *when was there a time when it did not exist?* We ask them whether they can point their finger to a period when the religion of Jesus was an unheard-of thing? "Yes," they will reply, "before the days of Christ and his apostles." But we answer, "Nay, Bethlehem was not the birthplace of the gospel; though Jesus was born there, there was a gospel long before the birth of Jesus, and a preached one too; although not preached in all its simplicity and plainness, as we hear it now. There was a gospel in the wilderness of Sinai, although it might be confused with the smoke of the incense, and only to be seen through slaughtered victims; yet, there was a gospel there." Yea, more, we take them back to the fair trees of Eden, where the fruits perpetually ripened, and summer always rested, and amid these groves we tell them there was a gospel, and we let them hear the voice of God, as he spoke to recreant man, and said, "The seed of the woman shall bruise the serpent's head." And having taken them thus far back, we ask, "Where were false religions born? Where was their cradle?" They point us to Mecca, or they turn their fingers to Rome, or they speak of Confucius, or the dogmas of Budha. But we say, you only go back to a distant obscurity; we take you to the primeval age; we direct you to the days of purity; we take you back to the time when Adam first trod the earth; and then we ask you whether it is not likely that, as the first-born, it will not also be the last to die? and as it was born so early, and still exists, whilst a thousand ephemera have become extinct, whether it does not look most possible, that when all others shall have perished, like the bubble upon the wave, this only shall swim, like a good ship upon the ocean, and still shall bear its myriad souls, not to the land of shades, but across the river of death to the plains of heaven?

We ask next, supposing Christ's gospel to become extinct, *what religion is to supplant it?* We inquire of the wise man, who says Christianity is soon to die, "Pray, sir, what religion are we to have in its stead? Are we to have the delusions of the heathen, who bow before their gods, and worship images of wood and stone? Will ye have the orgies of Bacchus, or the obscenities of Venus? Would ye see your daughters once more bowing down before Thammuz, or performing obscene rites as of old?" Nay, ye would not endure such things; ye would say, "It must not be tolerated by civilized men." Then what would ye have? Would ye have Romanism and its superstitions? Ye will say, "No, God help us, never." They may do what they please with Britain; but she is too wise to take old Popery back again, while Smithfield lasts, and there is one of the signs of martyrs there; aye, while there breathes a man who marks himself a freeman, and swears by the constitution of Old

England, we cannot take Popery back again. She may be rampant with her superstitions and her priestcraft; but with one consent my hearers reply, "We will not have Popery." Then what will ye choose? Shall it be Mahometanism? Will ye choose that, with all its fables, its wickedness and libidinousness? I will not tell you of it. Nor will I mention the accursed imposture of the West that has lately arisen. We will not allow Polygamy, while there are men to be found who love the social circle, and cannot see it invaded. We would not wish, when God hath given to man one wife, that he should drag in twenty, as the companions of that one. We cannot prefer Mormonism; we will not, and we shall not. Then what shall we have in the place of Christianity? "Infidelity," you cry, do you, sirs? And would you have that? Then what would be the consequence? What do many of them promote? Communist views, and the real disruption of all society as at present established. Would you desire Reigns of Terror here, as they had in France? Do you wish to see all society shattered, and men wandering like monster icebergs on the sea, dashing against each other, and being at last utterly destroyed? God save us from Infidelity! What can you have, then? Nought. There is nothing to supplant Christianity. What religion shall overcome it? There is not one to be compared with it. If we tread the globe round, and search from Britain to Japan, there shall be no religion found, so just to God, so safe to man.

We ask the enemy once more, suppose a religion were to be found which would be preferable to the one we love, *by what means would you crush ours?* How would you get rid of the religion of Jesus? and how would you extinguish his name? Surely, sirs, ye would never think of the old practice of persecution, would you? Would ye once more try the efficacy of stakes and fires, to burn out the name of Jesus? Would ye give us the boots and instruments of torture? Try it, sirs, and ye shall not quench Christianity. Each martyr, dipping his finger in his blood, would write its honors on the heavens as he died; and the very flame that mounted up to heaven would emblazon the skies with the name of Jesus. Persecution has been tried. Turn to the Alps; let the valleys of Piedmont speak; let Switzerland testify; let France, with its St. Bartholomew; let England, with all its massacres, speak. And if ye have not crushed it yet, shall ye hope to do it? Shall ye? Nay, a thousand are to be found, and ten thousand if it were necessary, who are willing to march to the stake to-morrow: and when they are burned, if ye could take up their hearts, ye would see engraven upon each of them the name of Jesus. "His name shall endure forever;" for how can ye destroy our love to it? "Ah, but," ye say, "we would try gentler means than that." Well, what would ye attempt? Would ye invent a better religion? We bid you do it, and let us hear it; we have not yet so much as believed you capable of such a discovery. What then? Would ye wake up one that should deceive us and lead us astray? We bid you do it; for it is not possible to deceive the elect. Ye may deceive the multitude, but God's elect shall not be led astray. They have tried us. Have they not given us Popery? Have they not assailed us with Puseyism? Are they not tempting us with Arminianism by the wholesale? And do we therefore renounce God's truth? No: we have taken this for our motto, and by it we will stand. "The Bible, the whole Bible, and nothing but the Bible," is still the religion of Protestants; and the selfsame truth which moved the lips of Chrysostom the old doctrine that ravished the heart of Augustine, the old faith which Athanasius declared, the good old doctrine that Calvin preached, is our gospel now, and God helping us, we will stand by it till we die. How will ye quench it? If ye wish to do it, where can ye find the means? It is not in your power. Aha! aha! aha! we laugh you to scorn.

But you will quench it, will you? You will try it, do you say? And you hope you will accomplish your purpose? Yes. I know you will, when you have annihilated the sun; when you have quenched the moon with drops of your tears; when you have dried up the sea with your drinking. Then shall ye do it. And yet ye say ye will.

And next, I ask you, *suppose you did, what would become of the world then?* Ah! were I eloquent to-night, I might perhaps tell you. If I could borrow the language of a Robert Hall, I might hang the world in mourning; I might make the sea the great chief-mourner, with its dirge of howling winds, and its wild death-march of disordered waves; I might clothe all nature, not in words of green, but in garments of sombre blackness; I would bid hurricanes howl the solemn wailing—that death-shriek of a world—for what would become of us, if we should lose the gospel? As for me, I tell you fairly, I would cry, "Let me begone!" I would have no wish to be here without my Lord; and if the gospel be not true, I should bless God to annihilate me this instant; for I would not care to live if ye would destroy the name of Jesus Christ. But that would not be all, that one man should be miserable, for there are thousands and thousands who can speak as I do. Again, what would become of civilization if ye could take Christianity away? Where would be the hope of a perpetual peace? Where governments? Where your Sabbath-schools? Where all your societies? Where everything that ameliorates the condition of man, reforms his manners, and moralizes his character? Where? Let echo answer, "Where?" They would be gone, and not a scrap of them would be left. And where, O men, would be your hope of heaven? And where the knowledge of eternity? Where a help across the river death? Where a heaven? And where bliss everlasting? All were gone if his name did not endure forever. But we are sure of it, we know it, we affirm it, we declare it; we believe, and ever will, that "his name shall endure forever," — aye, forever! let who will try to stop it.

This is my first point; I shall have to speak with rather bated breath upon the second, although I feel so warm within as well as without, that I would to God I could speak with all my strength, as I might do.

II. But, secondly, as his religion, so *the honor of his name is to last forever.* Voltaire said he lived in the twilight of Christianity. He meant a lie; he spoke the truth. He did live in its twilight; but it was the twilight before the morning — not the twilight of the evening, as he meant to say; for the morning comes, when the light of the sun shall break upon us in its truest glory. The scorners have said that we should soon forget to honor Christ, and that one day no man should acknowledge him. Now, we assert again, ir the words of my text, "His name shall endure forever,' as to the honor of it. Yes, I will tell you how long i will endure. As long as on this earth there is a sinne who has been reclaimed by omnipotent grace, Christ's name shall endure; as long as there is a Mary ready to wash his feet with tears and wipe them with the hai of her head; as long as there breathes a chief of sin ners who has washed himself in the fountain openec for sin and for uncleanness; as long as there exists a Christian who has put his faith in Jesus, and found him his delight, his refuge, his stay, his shield, his song, and his joy, there will be no fear that Jesus' name will cease to be heard. We can never give up that name. We let the Unitarian take the gospel without a godhead in it; we let him deny Jesus Christ; but as long as Christians, true Christians, live, as long as we taste that the Lord is gracious, have manifestations of his love, sights of his face, whispers of his mercy, assurances of his affection, promises of his grace, hopes of his blessing, we cannot cease to honor his name. But if all these were gone — if *we* were to cease to sing his praise, would Jesus Christ's name be forgotten then? No; the stones would sing, the hills would be an orchestra, the mountains would skip like rams, and the little hills like lambs; for is he not their creator? And if these lips, and the lips of all mortals were dumb at once, there are creatures enough in this wide world besides. Why, the sun would lead the chorus; the moon would play upon her silver harp, and sweetly sing to her music; stars would dance in their measured courses; the shoreless depths of ether would become the home of songs; and the void immensity would burst out into one great shout, "Thou art the glorious Son of God; great is thy majesty, and infinite thy power." Can Christ's name be forgotten? No; it is painted on the skies; it is written on the floods; the winds whisper it; the tempests howl it; the seas chant it; the stars shine it; the beasts low it; the thunders proclaim it; earth shouts it; heaven echoes it. But if that were gone—if this great universe should all subside in God, just as a moment's foam subsides into the wave that bears it and is lost forever—would his name be forgotten then? No. Turn your eyes up yonder; see heaven's *terra firma.* "Who are these that are arrayed in white, and whence came they?" "These are they that came out of great tribulation; they have washed their robes, and made them white in the blood of the Lamb; therefore they are before the throne of God, and praise him day and night in his temple." And if these were gone; if the last harp of the glorified had been touched with the last fingers; if the last praise of the saints had ceased; if the last hallelujah had echoed through the then deserted vaults of heaven, for they would be gloomy then; if the last immortal had been buried in his grave, if graves there might be for immortals—would his praise cease then? No, by heaven! no; for yonder stand the angels; they too sing his glory; to him the cherubim and seraphim do cry without ceasing, when they mention his name, in that thrice holy chorus, "Holy, holy, holy, Lord God of armies." But if these were perished—if angels had been swept away, if the wing of seraph never flapped the ether, if the voice of the cherub never sung his flaming sonnet, if the living creatures ceased their everlasting chorus, if the measured symphonies of glory were extinct in silence, would his name then be lost? Ah! no; for as God upon the throne he sits, the everlasting One, the Father, Son, and Holy Ghost. And if the universe were all annihilated, still would his name be heard, for the Father would hear it, and the Spirit would hear it, and, deeply graven on immortal marble in the rocks of ages, it would stand—Jesus the Son of God, co-equal with his Father. "His name shall endure forever."

III. And so shall the *power of his name.* Do you inquire what this is? Let me tell you. Seest thou yonder thief hanging upon the cross? Behold the fiends at the foot thereof, with open mouths; charming themselves with the sweet thought, that another soul shall give them meat in hell. Behold the death-bird, fluttering his wings o'er the poor wretch's head; vengeance passes by and stamps him for her own; deep on his breast is written "a condemned sinner;" on his brow is the clammy sweat, expressed from him by agony and death. Look in his heart: it is filthy with the crust of years of sin; the smoke of lust is hanging within in black festoons of darkness; his whole heart is hell condensed. Now, look at him. He is dying. One foot seems to be in hell; the other hangs tottering in life—only kept by a nail. There is a power in Jesus' eye. That thief looks: he whispers, "Lord, remember me." Turn your eye again there. Do you see that thief? Where is the clammy sweat? It is there. Where is that horrid anguish? It is *not* there. Positively there is a smile upon his lips. The fiends of hell, where are they? There are none: but a bright seraph is present, with his wings outspread, and his hands ready to snatch that soul, now a precious jewel, and bear it aloft to the palace of the great King. Look within his heart; it is white with purity. Look at his breast; it is not written "condemned," but "justified." Look in the book of life: his name is graven there. Look on Jesus' heart: there on one of the precious stones he bears that poor thief's name. Yea, once more, look! seest thou that bright one amid the glorified, clearer than the sun, and fair as the moon? That is the thief! That is the power of Jesus; and that power shall endure forever. He who saved the thief can save the last man who shall ever live; for still

"There is a fountain filled with blood,
Drawn from Immanuel's veins;
And sinners plunged beneath that flood
Lose all their guilty stains.

The dying thief rejoic'd to see
The fountain in his day;
O may I there, tho' vile as he,
Wash all my sins away!

Dear dying Lamb! that precious blood
Shall never lose its power,
Till all the ransom'd church of God
Be saved to sin no more."

His powerful "name shall endure forever."

Nor is that all the power of his name. Let me take you to another scene, and ye shall witness somewhat else. There on that deathbed lies a saint; no gloom is on his brow, no terror on his face; weakly but placidly he smiles; he groans, perhaps, but yet he sings. He sighs now and then, but oftener he shouts. Stand by him. "My brother, what makes thee look in death's face with such joy?" "Jesus," he whispers. What makes thee so placid and calm? "The name of Jesus." See, he forgets everything! Ask him a question; he cannot answer it—he does not understand you. Still he smiles. His wife comes, inquiring, "Do you know my name?" He answers, "No." His dearest friend requests him to remember his intimacy. "I know you not," he says. Whisper in his ear, "Do you know the name of Jesus?" and his eyes flash glory, and his face beams heaven, and his lips speak sonnets, and his heart bursts with eternity; for he hears the name of Jesus, and that name shall endure forever. He who landed one in heaven will land me there. Come on, death. I will mention Christ's name there. O grave! this shall be my glory, the name of Jesus! Hell-dog! this shall be thy death—for the sting of death is extracted—Christ our Lord." "His name shall endure forever."

I had a hundred particulars to give you; but my voice fails, so I had better stop. You will not require more of me to-night; you perceive the difficulty I feel in speaking each word. May God send it home to your souls! I am not particularly anxious about my own name, whether that shall endure forever or not, provided it is recorded in my Master's book. George Whitfield, when asked whether he would found a denomination, said, "No; Brother John Wesley may do as he pleases, but let my name perish; let Christ's name last forever." Amen to that! Let my name perish; but let Christ's name last forever. I shall be quite contented for you to go away and forget me. I shall not see the faces of half of you again, I dare say; you may never be persuaded to step within the walls of a conventicle; you will think it perhaps not respectable enough to come to a Baptist meeting. Well, I do not say we are a very respectable people; we don't profess to be; but this one thing we do profess, we love our Bibles; and if it is not respectable to do so, we do not care to be had in esteem. But we do not know that we are so disreputable after all; for I believe, if I may state my own opinion, that if Protestant Christendom were counted out of that door — not merely every real Christian, but every professor — I believe the Pœdo-Baptists would have no very great majority to boast of. We are not, after all, such a very small, disreputable sect. Regard us in England, we may be; but take America, and Jamaica, and the West Indies, and include those who are Baptists in principle though not openly so, and we surrender to none, not even to the established church of this country, in numbers. That, however, we care very little about; for I say of the Baptist name, let it perish, but let Christ's name last forever. I look forward with pleasure to the day when there will not be a Baptist living. I hope they will soon be gone. You will say, Why? Because when everybody else sees baptism by immersion, we shall be immersed into all sects, and our sect will be gone. Once give us the predominance, and we are not a sect any longer. A man may be a Churchman, or a Wesleyan, or an Independent, and yet be a Baptist. So that I say, I hope the Baptist name will soon perish; but let Christ's name last forever. Yea, and yet again; much as I love dear Old England, I do not believe she will ever perish. No, Britain! thou shalt never perish, for the flag of Old England is nailed to the mast by the prayers of Christians, by the efforts of Sunday-schools and her pious men. But, I say, let even England's name perish; let her be merged in one great brotherhood; let us have no England, and no France, and no Russia, and no Turkey, but let us have Christendom; and I say, heartily from my soul, let nations and national distinctions perish, but let Christ's name last forever. Perhaps there is only one thing on earth that I love better than the last I have mentioned, and that is the pure doctrine of unadulterated Calvinism. But if that be wrong — if there be anything in that which is false — I, for one, say, let that perish too, and let Christ's name last forever. Jesus! Jesus! Jesus! Jesus! "Crown him Lord of all!" You will not hear me say anything else. These are my last words in Exeter Hall for this time. Jesus! Jesus! Jesus! Crown him Lord of all.

SERMON IX.

PAUL'S FIRST PRAYER.

"For behold he prayeth."—Acts ix. 11.

God has many methods of quenching persecution. He will not suffer his church to be injured by its enemies, or overwhelmed by its foes; and he is not short of means for turning aside the way of the wicked, or of turning it upside down. In two ways he usually accomplishes his end; sometimes by the confusion of the persecutor, and at others in a more blessed manner, by his conversion. Sometimes, he confuses and confounds his enemies; he makes the diviner mad; he lets the man who comes against him be utterly destroyed, suffers him to drive on to his own destruction, and then at last turns round in triumphant derision upon the man who hoped to have said aha! aha! to the church of God. But at other times, as in this case, he converts the persecutor. Thus, he transforms the foe into a friend; he makes the man who was a warrior against the gospel a soldier for it. Out of darkness he bringeth forth light; out of the eater he getteth honey; yea, out of stony hearts he raiseth up children unto Abraham.

Such was the case with Saul. A more furious bigot it is impossible to conceive. He had been bespattered with the blood of Stephen, when they stoned him to death; so officious was he in his cruelty, that the men left their clothes in the charge of a young man named Saul. Living at Jerusalem, in the college of Gamaliel, he constantly came in contact with the disciples of the Man of Nazareth; he laughed at them, he reviled them as they passed along the street; he procured enactments against them, and put them to death; and now, as a crowning point, this wehr-wolf, having tasted blood, becomes exceeding mad, determines to go to Damascus, that he may glut himself with the gore of men and women; that he may bind the Christians, and bring them to Jerusalem, there to suffer what he considered to be a just punishment for their heresy, and departure from their ancient religion. But oh, how marvellous was the power of God! Jesus stays this man in his mad career; just as with his lance in rest he was dashing against Christ. Christ met him, unhorsed him, threw him on the ground, and questioned him, "Saul, Saul, why persecutest thou me?" He then graciously removed his rebellious heart — gave him a new heart and a right spirit — turned his aim and object — led him to Damascus — laid him prostrate for three days and nights — spoke to him — made mystic sounds go murmuring through his ears — set his whole soul on fire; and when at last he started up from that three days' trance, and began to pray, then it was that Jesus from heaven descended, came in a vision to Ananias, and said, "Arise, and go into the street which is called Straight, and inquire in the house of Judas for *one* called Saul, of Tarsus; for, behold, he prayeth."

First, our text was an announcement; "Behold, he prayeth." Secondly, it was an argument; "For, behold, he prayeth." Then, to conclude, we will try to make an application of our text to your hearts. Though application is the work of God alone, we will trust that he will be pleased to make that application while the word is preached this morning.

I. First, here was *an announcement;* "Go to the house of Saul of Tarsus; for behold, he prayeth." Without any preface, let me say, that this was the announcement of a fact which was noticed in heaven; which was joyous to the angels; which was astonishing to Ananias, and which was a novelty to Saul himself.

It was the announcement of *an effect which was noticed in heaven.* Poor Saul had been led to cry for mercy, and the moment he began to pray, God began to hear. Do you not notice, in reading the chapter, what attention God paid to Saul? He knew the street where he lived; "Go to the street that is called *Straight.*" He knew the house where he resided; "Inquire at the *house of Judas.*" He knew his name; it was *Saul.* He knew the place where he came from; "Inquire for Saul of *Tarsus.*" And he knew that he had prayed. "Behold, *he prayeth.*" Oh! it is a glorious fact, tha prayers are noticed in heaven. The poor oroken-hearted sinner, climbing up to his chamber, bends his knee, but can only utter his wailing in the language of sighs and tears. Lo! that groan has made all the harps of heaven thrill with music; that tear has been caught by God, and put into the lachrymatory of heaven, to be perpetually preserved. The suppliant, whose fears prevent his words, will be well understood by the Most High.

He may only shed one hasty tear; but "prayer is the falling of a tear." Tears are the diamonds of heaven; sighs are a part of the music of Jehovah's throne; for though prayers be

> "The simplest form of speech
> That infant lips can try;"

so are they likewise the

> "Sublimest strains that reach
> The majesty on high."

Let me dilate on this thought a moment. Prayers are noticed in heaven. Oh! I know what is the case with many of you. You think, "If I turn to God, if I seek him, surely I am so inconsiderable a being, so guilty and vile, that it cannot be imagined he would take any notice of me." My friends, harbor no such heathenish ideas. Our God is no god who sits in one perpetual dream; nor doth he clothe himself in such thick darkness that he cannot see; he is not like Baal who heareth not. True, he may not regard battles; he cares not for the pomp and pageantry of kings; he listens not to the swell of martial music; he regards not the triumph and the pride of man; but whenever there is a heart big with sorrow, wherever there is an eye suffused with tears, wherever there is a lip quivering with agony, wherever there is a deep groan, or a penitential sigh, the ear of Jehovah is wide open; he marks it down in the registry of his memory; he puts our prayers, like rose leaves, between the pages of his book of remembrance, and when the volume is opened at last, there shall be a precious fragrance springing up therefrom. Oh! poor sinner, of the blackest and vilest character, thy prayers are heard, and even now God hath said of thee, "Behold, he prayeth." Where was it? In a barn? Where was it? In the closet? Was it at thy bedside this morning, or in this hall? Art thou now glancing thine eye to heaven? Speak, poor heart; did I hear thy lips just now mutter out, "God have mercy upon me, a sinner?" I tell thee, sinner, there is one thing which doth outstrip the telegraph. You know we can now send a message and receive an answer in a few moments; but I read of something in the Bible more swift than the electric fluid. "Before they call I will answer, and while they are speaking I will hear." So, then, poor sinner, thou art noticed; yea, thou art heard by him that sitteth on the throne.

Again, this was the announcement of *a fact joyous to heaven.* Our text is prefaced with "Behold," for doubtless, our Saviour himself regarded it with joy. Once only do we read of a smile resting upon the countenance of Jesus, when lifting up his eye to heaven, he exclaimed, "I thank thee, O Father, Lord of heaven and earth, because thou hast hid these things from the wise and prudent, and hast revealed them unto babes; even so, Father; for so it seemed good in thy sight." The Shepherd of our souls rejoices in the vision of his sheep securely folded, he triumphs in spirit when he brings a wanderer home. I conceive that when he spoke these words to Ananias, one of the smiles of Paradise must have shone from his eyes. "Behold," I have won the heart of my enemy, I have saved my persecutor, even now he is bending the knee at my footstool, "Behold, he prayeth." Jesus himself led the song, rejoicing over the new convert with singing. Jesus Christ was glad and rejoiced more over that lost sheep than over ninety and nine that went not astray. And angels rejoiced too. Why, when one of God's elect is born, angels stand around his cradle. He grows up, and runs into sin; angels follow him, tracking him all his way; they gaze with sorrow upon his many wanderings; the fair Peri drops a tear whene'er that loved one sins. Presently the man is brought under the sound of the gospel. The angel says, "Behold, he begins to hear." He waits a little while, the word sinks into his heart, a tear runs down his cheek, and at last he cries from his inmost soul, "God have mercy upon me!" See! the angel claps his wings, up he flies to heaven, and says, "Brethren angels, list to me, 'Behold, he prayeth.'" Then they set heaven's bells ringing; they have a jubilee in glory; again they shout with gladsome voices, for verily I tell you, "there is joy in heaven among the angels of God over one sinner that repenteth." They watch us till we pray, and when we pray, they say, "Behold, he prayeth."

Moreover, my dear friends, there may be other spirits in heaven that rejoice, besides the angels. Those persons are our friends who have gone before us. I have not many relations in heaven, but I have one whom I dearly love, who, I doubt not, often prayed for me, for she nursed me when I was a child and brought me up during part of my infancy, and now she sits before the throne in glory — suddenly snatched away. I fancy she looked upon her darling grandson, and as she saw him in the ways of sin, and vice, and folly, she could not look with sorrow, for there are no tears in the eyes of glorified ones; she could not look with regret, because they cannot know such a feeling before the throne of God; but ah! that moment when, by sovereign grace, I was constrained to pray, when all alone I bent my knee and wrestled, methinks I see her as she said, "Behold, he prayeth; behold he prayeth." Oh! I can picture her countenance. She seemed to have two heavens for a moment, a double bliss, a heaven in me as well as in herself — when she could say, "Behold, he prayeth." Ah! young man, there is your mother walking the golden streets. She is looking down upon you this hour. She nursed you; on her breast you lay when but a child, and she consecrated you to Jesus Christ. From heaven, she has been watching you with that intense anxiety which is compatible with happiness; this morning she is looking upon you. What sayest thou, young man? Does Christ by his Spirit say in thine heart, "Come unto me?" Dost thou drop the tear of repentance? Methinks I see thy mother as she cries, "Behold, he prayeth." Once more she bends before the throne of God and says, "I thank thee, O thou ever gracious One, that he who was my child on earth, has now become *thy* child in light."

But, if there is one in heaven who has more joy than another over the conversion of a sinner, it is a minister, one of God's true ministers. O, my hearers, ye little think how God's true ministers do love your souls. Perhaps ye think it is easy work to stand here and preach to you. God knows, if that were all, it were easy work; but when we think that when we speak to you, your salvation or damnation, in some measure, depends upon what we say — when we reflect that if we are unfaithful watchmen, your blood will God require at out hands — O, good God! when I reflect that I have preached to thousands in my lifetime, many thousands, and have perhaps said many things I ought not to have said, it startles me, it makes me shake and tremble." Luther said he could face his enemies, but could not go up his pulpit stairs without his knees knocking together. Preaching is not child's play; it is not a thing to be done without labor and anxiety; it is solemn work; it is awful work, if you view it in its relation to eternity. Ah! how God's minister prays for you! If you might have listened under the eaves of his chamber window, you would have heard him groaning every Sunday night over his sermons because he had not spoken with more effect; you would have heard him pleading with God, "Who hath believed our report? To whom is the arm of the Lord revealed?" Ah, when he observes you from his rest in heaven — when he sees you praying, how will he clap his hands and say, "Behold the child thou hast given me! behold, he prays." I am sure when we see one brought to know the Lord, we feel very much like one who has saved a fellow-creature from being drowned. There is a poor man in the flood; he is going down, he is sinking, he must be drowned; but I spring in, grasp him firmly, lift him on the shore, and lay him on the ground; the physician comes; he looks at him, he puts his hand upon him, and says, "I am afraid he is dead." We apply all the means in our power, we do what we can to restore life. I feel that I have been that man's deliverer, and oh, how I stoop down and put my ear beside his mouth! At last I say, "he breathes! he breathes!" What pleasure there is in that thought! He breathes; there is life still. So when we find a man praying, we shout — he breathes; he is not dead; he is alive; for while a man prays he is not dead in trespasses and sins, but is brought to life, is quickened by the power of the Spirit. "Behold he prayeth." This was joyful news in heaven, as well as being noticed by God.

Then, in the next place, this was *an event most astonishing to men.* Ananias lifted up both his hands in amazement. "O my Lord, I should have thought anybody would pray but that man! Is it possible?" I do not know how it is with other ministers, but sometimes I look upon such-and-such individuals in the congregation, and I say, "Well, they are very hopeful; I think I shall have them. I trust there is a work going on, and hope soon to hear them tell what the Lord has done for their souls." Soon, perhaps, I see nothing of them, and miss them altogether; but instead thereof, my good Master sends me one of whom I had no hope —an outcast, a drunkard, a reprobate, to the praise of the glory of his grace. Then I lift up my hands in astonishment, thinking "I should have thought of anybody rather than you." I remember a circumstance which occurred a little while ago. There was a poor man about sixty years old; he had been a rough sailor, one of the worst men in the village; it was his custom to drink, and he seemed to be delighted when he was cursing and swearing. He came into the chapel, however, one Sabbath day, when one nearly related to me was preaching from the text concerning Jesus weeping over Jerusalem. And the poor man thought, "What! did Jesus Christ ever weep over such a wretch as I am?" He thought he was too bad for Christ to care for him. At last he came to the minister, and said, "Sir, sixty years have I been sailing under the standard of the devil; it is time I should have a new owner; I want to scuttle the old ship and sink her altogether!

then I shall have a new one, and I shall sail under the colors of Prince Immanuel." Ever since that moment that man has been a praying character, walking before God in all sincerity. Yet, he was the very last man you would have thought of. Somehow God does choose the last men; he does not care for the diamond, but he picks up the pebble-stones, for he is able, out of "stones, to raise up children unto Abraham." God is more wise than the chemist: he not only refines gold, but he transmutes base metal into precious jewels; he takes the filthiest and the vilest, and fashions them into glorious beings, makes them saints, whereas they have been sinners, and sanctifies them, whereas they have been unholy.

The conversion of Saul was a strange thing; but, beloved, was it stranger than that you and I should have been Christians? Let me ask you if anybody had told you, a few years ago, that you would belong to a church and be numbered with the children of God, what would you have said? "Stuff and nonsense! I am not one of your canting Methodists; I am not going to have any religion; I love to think and do as I like." Did not you and I say so? and how on earth did we get here? When we look at the change that has passed over us, it appears like a dream. God has left many in our families who were better than we were, and why has he chosen us? Oh! is it not strange? Might we not lift up our hands in astonishment, as Ananias did, and say, "Behold, behold, behold: it is a miracle on earth, a wonder in heaven?"

The last thing I have to say here, is this — *this fact was a novelty to Saul himself.* "Behold he prayeth." What is there novel in that? Saul used to go up to the temple twice a day, at the hour of prayer. If you could have accompanied him, you would have heard him speak beautifully, in words like these: "Lord, I thank thee I am not as other men are; I am not an extortioner, nor a publican; I fast twice in the week, and give tithes of all I possess;" and so on. Oh! you might have found him pouring out a fine oration before the throne of God. And yet it saith, "Behold he prayeth." What! had he never prayed before? No, never. All he had ever done before went for nothing; it was not prayer. I have heard of an old gentleman, who was taught when a child to pray, "Pray God bless my father and mother," and he kept on praying the same thing for seventy years, when his parents were both dead. After that it pleased God, in his infinite mercy, to touch his heart, and he was led to see that notwithstanding his constancy to his forms, he had not been praying at all; he often said his prayers, but never prayed. So it was with Saul. He had pronounced his magniloquent orations, but they were all good-for-nothing. He had prayed his long prayers for a pretence; it had all been a failure. Now comes a true petition, and it is said, "Behold he prayeth." Do you see that man trying to obtain a hearing from his Maker? How he stands! He speaks Latin and blank verse before the Almighty's throne; but God sits in calm indifference, paying no attention. Then the man tries a different style; procures a book, and, bending his knee again, prays in a delightful form the best old prayer that could ever be put together; but the Most High disregards his empty formalities. At last the poor creature throws the book away, forgets his blank verse, and says, "O Lord, hear, for Christ's sake."

"Hear him," says God, "I have heard him." There is the mercy thou hast sought. One hearty prayer is better than ten thousand forms. One prayer coming from the soul is better than a myriad cold readings. As for prayers that spring from the mouth and head only, God abhors them; he loves those that come deep from the heart. Perhaps I should be impudent if I were to say that there are hundreds here this morning who never prayed once in their lives. There are some of you who never did. There is one young man over there, who told his parents when he left them, that he should always go through his form of prayer every morning and night. But he is ashamed, and he has left it off. Well, young man, what will you do when you come to die? Will you have "the watchword at the gates of death?" Will you "enter heaven by prayer?" No, you will not; you will be driven from his presence, and be cast away.

II. Secondly, we have here *an argument.* "*For*, behold he prayeth." It was an argument, first of all, *for Ananias' safety.* Poor Ananias was afraid to go to Saul; he thought it was very much like stepping into a lion's den. "If I go to his house," he thought, "the moment he sees me, he will take me to Jerusalem at once, for I am one of Christ's disciples; I dare not go." God says, "Behold he prayeth." "Well," says Ananias, "that is enough for me. If he is a praying man, he will not hurt me; if he is a man of real devotion, I am safe." Be sure you may always trust a praying man. I do not know how it is, but even ungodly men always pay a reverence to a sincere Christian. A master likes to have a praying servant after all; if he does not regard religion himself, he likes to have a pious servant, and he will trust him rather than any other. True, there are some of your professedly praying people that have not a bit of prayer in them. But whenever you find a really praying man, trust him with untold gold; for if he really prays, you need not be afraid of him. He who communes with God in secret, may be trusted in public. I always feel safe with a man who is a visitor at the mercy-seat. I have heard an anecdote of two gentlemen travelling together, somewhere in Switzerland. Presently they came into the midst of the forests; and you know the gloomy tales the people tell about the inns there, how dangerous it is to lodge in them. One of them, an Infidel, said to the other, who was a Christian, "I don't like stopping here at all; it is very dangerous indeed." "Well," said the other, "let us try." So they went into a house; but it looked so suspicious that neither of them liked it; and they thought they would prefer being at home in England. Presently the landlord said, "Gentlemen, I always read and pray with my family before going to bed; will you allow me to do so to-night?" "Yes," they said, "with the greatest pleasure." When they went up stairs, the Infidel said, "I am not at all afraid now. "Why?" said the Christian. "Because our host has prayed." "Oh!" said the other, "then it seems, after all, you think something of religion; because a man prays, you can go to sleep in his house." And it was marvellous how both of them did sleep. Sweet dreams they had for they felt that where the house had been roofed by prayer, and walled with devotion, there could not be found a man living that would commit an injury to them. This, then, was an argument to Ananias, that he might go with safety to Saul's house.

But more than this. Here was *an argument for Paul's sincerity.* Secret prayer is one of the best tests of sincere religion. If Jesus had said to Ananias, "Behold he preacheth," Ananias would have said, "that he may do, and yet be a deceiver." If he had said, "He has gone to a meeting of the church," Ananias would have said, "He may enter there as a wolf in sheep's clothing." But when he said, "Behold he prays," that was argument enough. A young person comes and tells me about what he has felt and what he has been doing. At last I say, "kneel down and pray." "I would much rather not." "Never mind, you shall." Down he falls on his knees, he has hardly a word to say; he begins groaning and crying, and there he stays on his knees till at last he stammers out, "Lord have mercy upon me a sinner; I am the greatest of sinners; have mercy upon me!" Then I am a little more satisfied, and I say, "I did not mind all your talk, I wanted your prayers." But oh! if I could trace him home; if I could see him go and pray alone, then I should feel sure; for he who prays in private is a real Christian. The mere reading of a book of daily devotion will not prove you a child of God; if you pray in private, then you have a sincere religion; a little religion, if sincere, is better than mountains of pretence. Home piety is the best piety. Praying will make you leave off sinning, or sinning will make you leave off praying. Prayer in the heart proves the reality of conversion. A man may be sincere, but sincerely wrong. Paul was sincerely right. "Behold he prayeth" was the best argument that his religion was right. If any one should ask me for an epitome of the Christian religion, I should say it is in that one word—"prayer." If I should be asked,

"What will take in the whole of Christian experience?" I should answer, "prayer." A man must have been convinced of sin before he could pray; he must have had some hope that there was mercy for him before he could pray. In fact, all the Christian virtues are locked up in that word, prayer. Do but tell me you are a man of prayer, and I will reply at once, "Sir, I have no doubt of the reality, as well as the sincerity, of your religion."

But one more thought, and I will leave this subject. *It was a proof of this man's election*, for you read directly afterwards, "Behold, he is a chosen vessel." I often find people troubling themselves about the doctrine of election. Every now and then I get a letter from somebody or other taking me to task for preaching election. All the answer I can give is, "There it is in the Bible; go and ask my Master why he put it there. I cannot help it. I am only a serving man, and I tell you the message from above. If I were a footman I should not alter my Master's message at the door. I happen to be an ambassador of heaven and I dare not alter the message I have received. If it is wrong, send up to head-quarters. There it is, and I cannot alter it." This much let me say in explanation. Some say, "How can I discover whether I am God's elect? I am afraid I am not God's elect." Do you pray? If it can be said, "Behold, he prayeth," it can also be said, "Behold he is a chosen vessel." Have you faith? If so, you are elect. Those are the marks of election. If you have none of these, you have no grounds for concluding that you belong to the peculiar people of God. Have you a desire to believe? Have you a wish to love Christ. Have you the millionth part of a desire to come to Christ? And is it a practical desire? Does it lead you to offer earnest, tearful supplication? If so, never be afraid of non-election; for whoever prays with sincerity, is ordained of God before the foundation of the world, that he should be holy and without blame before Christ in love.

III. Now for the application. A word or two with you, my dear friends, before I send you away this morning. I regret that I cannot better enter into the subject; but my glorious Master requires of each of us according to what we have, not according to what we have not. I am deeply conscious that I fail in urging home the truth so solemnly as I ought; nevertheless, "my work is with God and my judgment with my God," and the last day shall reveal that my error lay in judgment, but not in sincere affection for souls.

First, allow me to address the children of God. Do you not see, my dear brethren, that the best mark of our being sons of God is to be found in our devotion? "Behold he prayeth." Well, then, does it not follow, as a natural consequence, that the more we are found in prayer the brighter will our evidences be. Perhaps you have lost your evidence this morning; you do not know whether you are a child of God or not; I will tell you where you lost your confidence—you lost it in your closet. Whenever a Christian backslides, his wandering commences in his closet. I speak what I have felt. I have often gone back from God—never so as to fall finally, I know, but I have often lost that sweet savour of his love which I once enjoyed. I have had to cry,

"Those peaceful hours I once enjoyed,
How sweet their memory still!
But they have left an aching void,
The world can never fill."

I have gone up to God's house to preach, without either fire or energy; I have read the Bible, and there has been no light upon it; I have tried to have communion with God, but all has been a failure. Shall I tell where that commenced! It commenced in my closet. I had ceased, in a measure, to pray. Here I stand, and do confess my faults; I do acknowledge that whenever I depart from God it is there it doth begin. O Christians, would you be happy? Be much in prayer. Would ye be victorious? Be much in prayer.

> " Restraining prayer, we cease to fight,
> Prayer makes the Christians armor bright."

Mrs. Berry used to say, "I would not be hired out of my closet for a thousand worlds." Mr. Jay said, "If the twelve apostles were living near you, and you had access to them, if this intercourse drew you from the closet, they would prove a real injury to your souls." Prayer is the ship which bringeth home the richest freight. It is the soil which yields the most abundant harvest. Brother, when you rise in the morning your business so presses, that with a hurried word or two, down you go into the world, and at night, jaded and tired, you give God the fag end of the day. The consequence is, that you have no communion with him. The reason we have not more true religion now, is because we have not more prayer. Sirs, I have no opinion of the churches of the present day that do not pray. I go from chapel to chapel in this metropolis, and I see pretty good congregations; but I go to their prayer-meetings on a week evening, and I see a dozen persons. Can God bless us, can he pour out his Spirit upon us, while such things as these exist? He could, but it would not be according to the order of his dispensations, for he says, "When Zion travails she brings forth children." Go to your churches and chapels with this thought, that you want more prayer. Many of you have no business here this morning. You ought to be in your own places of worship. I do not want to steal away the people from other chapels; there are enough to hear me without them. But though you have sinned this morning, hear while you are here, as much to your profit as possible. Go home and say to your minister, "Sir, we must have more prayer." Urge the people to more prayer. Have a prayer-meeting, even if you have it all to yourself; and if you are asked how many were present, you can say, "Four." "Four! how so?" "Why, there was myself, and God the Father, God the Son, and God the Holy Ghost; and we have had a rich and real communion together." We must have an outpouring of real devotion, or else what is to become of many of our churches? O! may God awaken us all, and stir us up to pray, for when we pray we shall be victorious. I should like to take you, this morning, as Samson did the foxes, tie the firebrands of prayer to you, and send you in among the shocks of corn till you burn the whole up. I should like to make a conflagration by my words, and to set all the churches on fire, till the whole has smoked like a sacrifice to God's throne. If you pray, you have a proof that you are a Christian; the less you pray, the less reason have you to believe your Christianity; and if you have neglected to pray altogether, then you have ceased to breathe, and you may be afraid that you never did breathe at all.

And now, my last word is to the ungodly. O, sirs! I could fain wish myself anywhere but here; for if it be solemn work to address the godly, how much more when I come to deal with you. We fear lest, on the one hand, we should so speak to you as to make you trust in your own strength; while, on the other hand, we tremble lest we should lull you into the sleep of sloth and security. I believe most of us feel some difficulty as to the most fit manner to preach to you—not that we doubt but that the gospel is to be preached—but our desire is so to do it, that we may win your souls. I feel like a watchman, who, while guarding a city, is oppressed with sleep; how earnestly does he strive to arouse himself, while infirmity would overcome him. The remembrance of his responsibility bestirs him. His is no lack of *will*, but of power; and so I hope all the watchmen of the Lord are anxious to be faithful, while, at the same time, they know their imperfection. Truly the minister of Christ will feel like the old keeper of Eddystone lighthouse; life was failing fast, but summoning all his strength, he crept round once more to trim the lights before he died. O may the Holy Spirit enable us to keep the beacon-fire blazing, to warn you of the rocks, shoals, and quicksands, which surround you, and may we ever guide you to Jesus, and not to free-will or creature merit. If my friends knew how anxiously I have sought divine direction in the important matter of preaching to sinners, they would not feel as some of them do, when they fancy I address them wrongly. I want to do as God bids me, and if he tells me to speak to the dry bones and they shall live, I must do it, even if it does not please others; otherwise I should be condemned in my own conscience, and condemned of God. Now, with all the solemnity that man can summon, let me say that a prayerless soul is a Christless soul. As the Lord liveth, you who never prayed are without God, without hope, and strangers from the commonwealth of Israel. You who never know what a groan is, or a falling tear, are destitute of vital godliness. Let me ask you, sirs, whether you have ever thought in what an awful state you are? You are far from God, and therefore God is angry with you; for "God is angry with the wicked every day." O, sinner! lift thine eyes and behold the frowning countenance of God, for he is angry with you. And I beseech you, as you love yourselves, just for one moment contemplate what will become of you, if living as you are ye should at last die without prayer. Don't think that one prayer on your deathbed will save you. Deathbed prayer is a deathbed farce generally, and passes for nothing; it is a coin that will not ring in heaven, but is stamped by hypocrisy, and made of base metal. Take heed, sirs. Let me ask you, if you have never prayed, what will you do? It were a good thing for you, if death were an eternal sleep; but it is not. If you find yourself in hell, oh, the racks and pains! But I will not harrow up your feelings by attempting to describe them. May God grant you never may feel the torments of the lost. Only conceive that poor wretch in the flames who is saying, "O for one drop of water, to cool my parched tongue!" See how his tongue hangs from between his blistered lips! how it excoriates and burns the roof of his mouth, as if it were a firebrand. Behold him crying for a drop of water. I will not picture the scene. Suffice it for me to close up by saying, that the hell of hells will be to thee, poor sinner, the thought that it is to be forever. Thou wilt look up there on the throne of God, and it shall be written "forever!" When the damned jingle the burning irons of their torments, they shall say "forever!" When they howl, echo cries "forever!"

"'Forever' is written on their racks,
'Forever' on their chains;
'Forever' burneth in the fire,
'Forever' ever reigns."

Doleful thought! "If I could but get out, then I should be happy. If there were a hope of deliverance, then I might be peaceful; but I am here forever!" Sirs, if ye would escape eternal torments, if ye would be found amongst the numbers of the blessed, the road to heaven can only be found by prayer—by prayer to Jesus, by prayer for the Spirit, by supplication at his mercy seat. "Turn ye, turn ye, why will ye die, O house of Israel? As I live, saith the Lord, I have no pleasure in the death of him that dieth, but had rather that he should turn unto me and live." "The Lord is gracious and full of compassion." Let us go unto him and say, "He shall heal our backslidings, he shall love us freely and forgive us graciously, for his Son's name's sake." Oh! if I may but win one soul to-day, I will go home contented. If I may but gain twenty, then I will rejoice. The more I have, the more crowns I shall wear. Wear! No, I will take them all at once, and cast them at Jesus' feet, and say, "Not unto me, but unto thy name be all the glory, forever."

"Prayer was appointed to convey
The blessings God designs to give;
Long as they live, should Christians pray,
For only while they pray, they live.

"And wilt thou still in silence lie,
When Christ stands waiting for thy prayer?
My soul, thou hast a friend on high,
Arise, and try thine interest there.

'T is prayer supports the soul that's weak,
Though thought be broken, language lame;
Pray, if thou canst, or canst not speak,
But pray with faith in Jesu's name."

SERMON X.

JOSEPH ATTACKED BY THE ARCHERS.

"The archers have sorely grieved him, and shot *at him*, and hated him; but his bow abode in strength; and the arms of his hands were made strong by the hands of the mighty *God* of Jacob; from thence *is* the shepherd, the stone of Israel."— GENESIS xlix. 23, 24.

IT must have been a fine sight to see the hoary-headed Jacob sitting up in his bed whilst he bestowed his parting benediction upon his twelve sons. He had been noble in many instances during his life — at the sleeping place of Bethel, the brook of Jabbok, and the halting of Peniel. He had been a glorious old man; one before whom we might bow down with reverence, and truly say, " There were giants in those days." But his closing scene was the best. I think if ever he stood out more illustrious than at any other time, if his head was at any one season more than another, encircled with a halo of glory, it was when he came to die. Like the sun at setting, he seemed then to be the greater in brilliance, tinging the clouds of his weakness with the glory of grace within. Like good wine, which runs clear to the very bottom, unalloyed by dregs, so did Jacob till his dying hour continue to sing of love, of mercy, and of goodness, past and future. Like the swan, which (as old writers say) singeth not all its life until it comes to die, so the old patriarch remained silent as a songster for many years; but when he stretched himself on his last couch of rest, he stayed himself up in his bed, turned his burning eye from one to another, and although with a hoarse and faltering voice, he sang a sonnet upon each of his offspring, such as earthly poets, uninspired, cannot attempt to imitate. Looking upon his son Reuben, a tear was in his eye, for he recollected Reuben's sin; he passed over Simeon and Levi, giving some slight rebuke; upon the others he sung a verse of praise, as his eyes saw into the future history of the tribes. By-and-by his voice failed him, and the good old man, with long-drawn breath, with eyes pregnant with celestial fire, and heart big with heaven, lifted his voice to God, and said, "I have waited for thy salvation, O God," rested a moment on his pillow, and then again sitting up, recommenced the strain, passing briefly by the names of each. But oh! when he came to Joseph, his youngest son but one — when he looked on him, I picture that old man as the tears ran down his cheeks. There stood Joseph, with all his mother Rachel in his eyes — that dear-loved wife of his — there he stood, the boy for whom that mother had prayed with all the eagerness of an Eastern wife. For a long twenty years she had tarried a barren woman and kept no house, but then she was a joyful mother, and she called her son "Increase." Oh! how she loved the boy; and for that mother's sake, though she had been buried for some years, and hidden under the cold sod, old Jacob loved him too. But more than that, he loved him for his troubles. He was parted from him to be sold into Egypt. His father recollected

Joseph's trials in the round-house and the dungeon, and remembered his royal dignity as prince of Egypt; and now, with a full burst of harmony, as if the music of heaven had united with his own, as when the widened river meets the sea, and the tide coming up doth amalgamate with the stream that cometh down, and swelleth into a broad expanse, so did the glory of heaven meet the rapture of his earthly feelings, and giving vent to his soul, he sung, "Joseph is a fruitful bough, even a fruitful bough by a well; whose branches run over the wall; the archers have sorely grieved him, and shot *at him*, and hated him; but his bow abode in strength, and the arms of his hands were made strong by the hands of the mighty *God* of Jacob; (from thence *is* the shepherd, the stone of Israel;) *even* by the God of thy father, who shall help thee; and by the Almighty, who shall bless thee with blessings of heaven above, blessings of the deep that lieth under, blessings of the breasts, and of the womb; the blessings of thy father have prevailed above the blessings of my progenitors, unto the utmost bound of the everlasting hills; they shall be on the head of Joseph, and on the crown of the head of him that was separate from his brethren." What a splendid stanza with which to close! He has only one more blessing to give; but surely this was the richest which he conferred on Joseph.

Joseph is dead, but the Lord has his Josephs now. There are some still who understand by experience— and that is the best kind of understanding—the meaning of this passage, "The archers have sorely grieved him, and shot at him, and hated him; but his bow abode in strength, and the arms of his hands were made strong by the hands of the mighty *God* of Jacob."

There are four things for us to consider this morning. First of all, the cruel attack — "the archers have sorely grieved him, and shot at him, and hated him;" secondly, the shielded warrior — "but his bow abode in strength;" thirdly, his secret strength — "the arms of his hands were made strong by the mighty power of the God of Jacob;" and fourthly, the glorious parallel drawn between Joseph and Christ — "from thence is the shepherd, the stone of Israel."

I. First, then, we commence with *the cruel attack.* "The archers have sorely grieved him." Joseph's enemies were archers. The original has it, "masters of the arrows;" that is, men who were well skilled in the use of the arrow. Though all weapons are alike approved by the warrior in his thirst for blood, there seems something more cowardly in the attack of the archer than in that of the swordsman. The swordsman plants himself near you, foot to foot, and lets you defend yourself, and deal your blows against him; but the archer stands at a distance, hides himself in ambuscade, and, without your knowing it, the arrow comes whizzing through the air, and perhaps penetrates your heart. Just so are the enemies of God's people. They very seldom come foot to foot with us; they will not show their faces before us; they hate the light, they love darkness; they dare not come and openly accuse us to our face, for then we could reply; but they shoot the bow from a distance, so that we cannot answer them; cowardly and dastardly as they are, they forge their arrow-heads, and aim them, winged with hell-bird's feathers, at the hearts of God's people. The archers sorely grieved poor Joseph. Let us consider who are the archers who so cruelly shot at him. First, there were the archers of envy; secondly, the archers of temptation; and thirdly, the archers of slander and calumny.

1. First, *Joseph had to endure the archers of* ENVY. When he was a boy, his father loved him. The youth was fair and beautiful; in person he was to be admired; moreover, he had a mind that was gigantic, and an intellect that was lofty; but, best of all, in him dwelt the Spirit of the living God. He was one who talked with God; a youth of piety and prayerfulness; beloved of God, even more than he was by his earthly father. O! how his father loved him! for in his fond affection, he made him a princely coat of many colors, and treated him better than the others—a natural but foolish way of showing his fondness. Therefore his brethren hated him. Full often did they jeer at the youthful Joseph, when he retired to his prayers; when he was with them at a distance from his father's house, he was their drudge, their slave; the taunt, the jeer, did often wound his heart, and the young child endured much secret sorrow. On an ill day, as it happened, he was with them at a distance from home, and they thought to slay him; but upon the entreaty of Reuben, they put him into a pit, until, as Providence would have it, the Ishmaelites did pass that way. They then sold him for the price of a slave, stripped him of his coat, and sent him naked, they knew not, and they cared not, whither, so long as he might be out of their way, and no longer provoke their envy and their anger. Oh! the agonies he felt—parted from his father, losing his brethren, without a friend, dragged away by cruel man-sellers, chained upon a camel it may be, with fetters on his hands. Those who have borne the gyves

and fetters, those who have felt that they were not free men, that they had not liberty, might tell how sorely the archers grieved him when they shot at him the arrows of their envy. He became a slave, sold from his country, dragged from all he loved. Farewell to home and all its pleasures — farewell to a father's smiles and tender cares. He must be a slave, and toil where the slave's task-maker makes him; he must be stripped in the streets, he must be beaten, he must be scourged, he must be reduced from the man to the animal, from the free man to the slave. Truly the archers sorely shot at him. And, my brethren, do you hope, if you are the Lord's Josephs, that you shall escape envy? I tell you, nay; that green-eyed monster, envy, lives in London as well as elsewhere, and he creeps into God's church, moreover. Oh! it is hardest of all, to be envied by one's brethren. If the devil hates us, we can bear it; if the foes of God's truth speak ill of us, we buckle up our harness, and say, "Away, away, to the conflict." But when the friends within the house slander us; when brethren who should uphold us, turn our foes; and when they try to tread down their younger brethren; then, sirs, there is some meaning in the passage, "The archers have sorely grieved him, and shot at him, and hated him." But, blessed be God's name, it is sweet to be informed that "his bow abode in strength." None of you can be the people of God without provoking envy; and the better you are, the more you will be hated. The ripest fruit is most pecked by the birds, and the blossoms that have been longest on the tree, are the most easily blown down by the wind. But fear not; you have nought to do with what man shall say of you. If God loves you, man will hate you; if God honors you, man will dishonor you. But recollect, could ye wear chains of iron for Christ's sake, ye should wear chains of gold in heaven; could ye have rings of burning iron round your waists, ye should have your brow rimmed with gold in glory; for blessed are ye when men shall say all manner of evil against you falsely, for Christ's name's sake; for so persecuted they the prophets that were before you. The first archers were the archers of envy.

2. But a worse trial than this was to overtake him. *The archers of* TEMPTATION shot at him. Here I know not how to express myself. I would that some one more qualified to speak were here, that he might tell you the tale of Joseph's trial, and Joseph's triumph. Sold to a master who soon discovered his value, Joseph was made the bailiff of the house, and the manager of the household. His wanton mistress fixed her adulterous love on him; and he, being continually in her presence, was perpetually, day by day, solicited by her to evil deeds. Constantly did he refuse; still enduring a martyrdom at the slow fire of her enticements. On one eventful day she grasped him, seeking to compel him to crime; but he, like a true hero as he was, said to her, "How can I do this great wickedness and sin against God?" Like a wise warrior, he knew that in such a case fleeing was the better part of valor. He heard a voice in his ears: "Fly, Joseph, fly; there remains no way of victory but flight;" and out he fled, leaving his garment with his adulterous mistress. Oh, I say in all the annals of heroism there is not one that shall surpass this. You know it is *opportunity* that makes a man criminal; and he had abundant opportunity; but *importunity* will drive most men

astray. To be haunted day by day by solicitations of the softest kind — to be tempted hour by hour — oh! it needs a strength super-angelic, a might more than human, a strength which only God can grant, for a young man thus to cleanse his way, and take heed thereto according to God's word. He might have reasoned within himself, "Should I submit and yield, there lies before me a life of ease and pleasure; I shall be exalted, I shall be rich. She shall prevail over her husband, to cover me with honors; but should I still adhere to my integrity, I shall be cast into prison, I shall be thrown into the dungeon; there awaits me nothing but shame and disgrace." Oh! there was a power indeed within that heart of his; there was an inconceivable might, which made him turn away with unutterable disgust, with fear and trembling, while he said, "How can I? how can I — God's Joseph — how can I — other men might, but how can I do this great wickedness and sin against God." Truly the archers sorely grieved him and shot at him; but his bow abode in strength.

3. Then another host of archers assailed him; *these were the archers of* MALICIOUS CALUMNY. Seeing that he would not yield to temptation, his mistress falsely accused him to her husband, and his lord, believing the voice of his wife, cast him into prison. It was a marvellous providence that he did not put him to death; for Potiphar, his master, was the chief of the slaughtermen; he had only to call in a soldier, who would have cut him in pieces on the spot. But he cast him into prison. There was poor Joseph. His character ruined in the eyes of man, and very likely looked upon with scorn even in the prison-house; base crimi-

nals went away from him as if they thought him viler than themselves, as if they were angels in comparison with him. Oh! it is no easy thing to feel your character gone, to think that you are slandered, that things are said of you that are untrue. Many a man's heart has been broken by this, when nothing else could make him yield. The archers sorely grieved him when he was so maligned—so slandered. O child of God, dost thou expect to escape these archers? Wilt thou never be slandered? Shalt thou never be calumniated? It is the lot of God's servants, in proportion to their zeal, to be evil spoken of. Remember the noble Whitfield, how he stood and was the butt of all the jeers and scoffs of half an age; while his only answer was a blameless life.

> "And he who forged, and he who threw the dart,
> Had each a brother's interest in his heart."

They reviled him and imputed to him crimes that Sodom never knew. So shall it be always with those who preach God's truth, and all the followers of Christ—they must all expect it; but, blessed be God, they have not said worse things of us than they said of our Master. What have they laid to our charge? They may have said, "he is drunken and a wine-bibber;" but they have not said, "he hath a devil." They have accused us of being mad, so was it said of Paul. Oh, holy infatuation, heavenly furor, would that we could bite others until they had the same madness. We think, if to go to heaven be mad, we will not choose to be wise; we see no wisdom in preferring hell; we can see no great prudence in despising and hating God's truth. If to serve God be vile, we purpose to be viler still. Ah! friends, some now present know this verse by heart, "The archers have sorely grieved him, and shot at him, and hated him." Expect it; do not think it a strange thing; all God's people must have it. There are no royal roads to heaven — they are paths of trial and trouble; the archers will shoot at you as long as you are on this side the flood.

II. We have seen these archers shoot their flights of arrows; we will now go up the hill a little, behind a rock, to look at the shielded warrior, and see how his courage is while the archers have sorely grieved him. What is he doing? "His bow abideth in strength." Let us picture God's favorite. The archers are down below. There is a parapet of rock before him; now and then he looks over it to see what the archers are about, but generally he keeps behind. In heavenly security he is set upon a rock, careless of all below. Let us follow the track of the wild goat and behold the warrior in his fastness.

First, we notice that he has a bow himself, for we read that "*his bow* abode in strength." He could have retaliated if he pleased, but he was very quiet and would not combat with them. Had he pleased, he might have drawn his bow with all his strength, and sent his weapon to their hearts with far greater precision than they had ever done to him. But mark the warrior's quietness. There he rests, stretching his mighty limbs; his bow abode in strength; he seemed to say, "Rage on, aye, let your arrows spend themselves, empty your quivers on me, let your bow-strings be worn out, and let the wood be broken with its constant bending; here am I, stretching myself in safe repose; my bow abides in strength; I have other work to do besides shooting at you; my arrows are against you foes of God, the enemies of the Most High; I cannot waste an arrow on such pitiful sparrows as you are; ye are birds beneath my noble shot; I would not waste an arrow on you." Thus he remains behind the rock and despises them all. "His bow abideth in strength."

Mark well *his quietness.* His bow "abideth." It is not rattling, it is not always moving, but it abides, it is quite still; he takes no notice of the attack. The archers sorely grieved Joseph, but his bow was not turned against them, it abode in strength. He turned not his bow on them. He rested while they raged. Doth the moon stay herself to lecture every dog that bayeth at her? Doth the lion turn aside to rend each cur that barketh at him? Do the stars cease to shine because the nightingales reprove them for their dimness? Doth the sun stop in its course because of the officious cloud which veils it? Or doth the river stay because the willow dippeth its leaves into its waters? Ah! no; God's universe moves on, and if men will oppose it, it heeds them not. It is as God hath made it; it is working together for good, and it shall not be stayed by the censure nor moved on by the praise of man. Let your bows, my brethren, abide. Do not be in a hurry to set yourselves right. God will take care of you. Leave yourselves alone; only be very valiant for the Lord God of Israel; be steadfast in the truth of Jesus and your bow shall abide.

But we must not forget the next word. "His bow abode IN STRENGTH." Though his bow was quiet it was not because it was broken. Joseph's bow was like that of William the Conqueror; no man could bend it but Joseph himself; it abode in "strength." I see the warrior bending his bow—how with his mighty arms he pulls it down and draws the string to make it ready. His bow abode in strength; it did not snap, it did not start aside. His chastity was his bow, and he did not lose that; his faith was his bow, and that did not yield, it did not break; his courage was his bow, and that did not fail him; his character, his honesty was his bow, nor did he cast it away. Some men are so very particular about reputation. They think, "surely, surely, surely they shall lose their characters." Well, well, if we do not lose them through our own fault, we never need care about anybody else. You know there is not a man that stands at all prominent, but what any fool in the world can set afloat some bad tale against him. It is a great deal easier to set a story afloat than to stop it. If you want truth to go round the world you must hire an express train to pull it; but if you want a lie to go round the world, it will fly: it is as light as a feather, and a breath will carry it. It is well said in the old Proverb, "A lie will go round the world while truth is pulling its boots on." Nevertheless, it does not injure us; for if light as a feather it travels as fast, its effect is just about as tremendous as the effect of down, when it is blown against the walls of a castle; it produces no damage whatever, on account of its lightness and littleness. Fear not, Christian. Let slander fly, let envy send forth its forked tongue, let it hiss at you, your bow shall abide in strength. Oh! shielded warrior, remain quiet, fear no ill; but, like the eagle in its lofty eyrie, look thou down upon the fowlers in the plain; turn thy bold eye upon them and say, "Shoot ye may, but your shots will not reach half way to the pinnacle where I stand. Waste your powder upon me if ye will; I am beyond your reach." Then clap your wings, mount to heaven, and there laugh them to scorn, for ye have made your refuge God, and shall find a most secure abode.

III. The third thing in our text *is the secret strength.* "The arms of his hands were made strong by the hands of the mighty God of Jacob." First, notice, concerning his strength, that it was *real* strength. It says, "the arms of his hands," not his hands only. You know some people can do a great deal with their hands, but then it is often fictitious power; there is no might in the arm, there is no muscle; but of Joseph it is said "the *arms* of his hands were made strong." It was real potency, true muscle, real sinew, real nerve. It was not simply sleight of hand—the power of moving his fingers very swiftly—but the *arms* of his hands were made strong. Now that strength which God gives to his Josephs is real strength; it is not a boasted valor, a fiction, a thing of which men talk, an airy dream, an unsubstantial unreality, but it is real strength. I should not like to have a combat with one of God's Josephs. I should find their blows very heavy. I fear a Christian's strokes more than any other man's, for he has bone and sinew, and smites hard. Let the foes of the church expect a hard struggle if they attack an heir of life. Mightier than giants are men of the race of heaven; should they once arouse themselves to battle they could laugh at the spear and the habergeon. But they are a patient generation, enduring ills without resenting them, suffering scorn without reviling the scoffer. Their triumph is to come when their enemies shall receive the vengeance due; then shall it be seen by an assembled world that the "little flock" were men of high estate, and the "offscouring of all things" were verily men of real strength and dignity.

Even though the world perceive it not, the favored Joseph has real strength, not in his hands only, but in his arms—real might, real power. O ye foes of God, ye think God's people are despicable and powerless; but know that they have true strength from the omnipotence of their Father, a might substantial and divine. Your own shall melt away, and droop and die, like the snow upon the low mountain top, when the sun shines upon it, it melteth into water; but our vigor shall abide like the snow on the summit of the Alps, undiminished for ages. It is real strength.

Then observe that the strength of God's Joseph is *divine strength.* His arms were made strong by God. Why does one of God's ministers preach the gospel powerfully? Because God gives him assistance. Why does Joseph stand against temptation? Because God gives him aid. The strength of a Christian is divine strength. My brethren, I am more and more persuaded every day that the sinner has no power of himself, except that which is given him from above. I know that if I were to stand with my foot upon the golden threshold of heaven's portal, if I could put this thumb upon the latch, I could not open that door, after having gone so far towards heaven, unless I had still supernatural power communicated to me in that moment. If I had a stone to lift, to work my own salvation, without God's help to do that, I must be lost, even though it were so little. There is nought that we can do without the power of God. All true strength is divine. As the light cometh from the sun, as the shower from heaven; so doth spiritual strength come from the

Father of lights, with whom there is neither variableness nor shadow of a turning.

Again: I would have you notice in the text in what a *blessedly familiar way God* gives this strength to Joseph. It says, "the arms of his hands were made strong by the hands of the mighty God of Jacob." Thus it represents God as putting his hands on Joseph's hands, placing his arms on Joseph's arms. In old times, when every boy had to be trained up to archery, if his father were worth so many pounds a-year, you might see the father putting his hands on his boy's hands and pulling the bow for him, saying, "there, my son, in this manner draw the bow." So the text represents God as putting his hand on the hand of Joseph, and laying his broad arm along the arm of his chosen child, that he might be made strong. Like as a father teacheth his children; so the Lord teaches them that fear him. He puts his arms upon them. As Elijah laid with his mouth upon the child's mouth, with his hand upon the child's hand, with his foot upon the child's foot, so does God put his mouth to his children's mouth, his hand to his ministers' hand, his foot to his people's foot; and so he makes us strong. Marvellous condescension! Ye stars of glory, have ye ever witnessed such stoops of love? God Almighty, Eternal, Omnipotent, stoops from his throne and lays his hand upon the child's hand, stretching his arm upon the arm of Joseph, that he may be made strong!

One more thought, and I have done. The strength was *covenant strength*, for it is said, "The arms of his hands were made strong by the hands of the mighty *God of Jacob*." Now, wherever you read of the God of Jacob in the Bible, you may know that that respects

God's covenant with Jacob. Ah! I love to talk about God's everlasting covenant. Some of the Arminians cannot bear it, but I love a covenant salvation — a covenant not made with my fathers, not between me and God, but between Christ and God. Christ made the covenant to pay a price, and God made the covenant that he should have the people. Christ has paid the price and ratified the covenant; and I am quite sure that God will fulfil his part of it, by giving every elect vessel of mercy into the hands of Jesus. But, beloved, all the power, all the grace, all the blessings, all the mercies, all the comforts, all the things we have, we have through the covenant. If there were no covenant; if we could rend the everlasting charter up; if the king of hell could cut it with his knife, as the king of Israel did the roll of Baruck, then we should fail indeed: for we have no strength, except that which is promised in the covenant. Covenant mercies, covenant grace, covenant promises, covenant blessings, covenant help, covenant everything — the Christian must receive, if he would enter into heaven.

Now, Christian, the archers have sorely grieved you, and shot at you, and wounded you; but your bow abides in strength, and the arms of your hands are made strong. But do you know, O believer, that you are like your Master in this?

IV. That is our fourth point — *a glorious parallel.* "From thence is the shepherd, the stone of Israel." Jesus Christ was served just the same; the shepherd, the stone of Israel, passed through similar trials; he was shot at by the archers, he was grieved and wounded, but his bow abode in strength; his arms were made strong by the God of Jacob, and now every blessing rests "upon the crown of the head of him who was separated from his brethren." I shall not detain you long, but I have a few things to tell you: first about Christ as the shepherd, and then about Christ the stone.

Christ came into the world as a shepherd. As soon as he made his appearance, the Scribes and Pharisees said, "Ah! we have been the shepherds until this hour; now we shall be driven from our honors, we shall lose all our dignity, and our authority." Consequently, they always shot at him. As for the people, they were a fickle herd; I believe that many of them respected and admired Christ, though, doubtless, the vast majority hated him, for wherever he went he was a popular preacher; the multitude always thronged him and crowded round him, crying, "Hosannah." I think, if you had walked up to the top of that hill of Cavalry, and asked one of those men who cried out, "Crucify him, crucify him," "What do you say that for? Is he a bad man?" "No," he would have said, "he went about doing good." "Then why do you say 'crucify him?'" "Because Rabbi Simeon gave me a shekel to help the clamor." So the multitude were much won by the money and influence of the priests. But they were glad to hear Christ after all. It was the shepherds that hated him, because he took away their traffic, because he turned the buyers and sellers out of the temple, diminished their dignity and ignored their pretensions; therefore, they could not endure him. But the Shepherd of Israel mounted higher and higher; he gathered his sheep, carried the lambs in his bosom; and he now stands acknowledged as the great shepherd of the sheep, who shall gather them into one flock and lead them to heaven. Rowland Hill tells a curious tale, in his "Village Dialogues," about a certain Mr. Tiplash, a very fine intellectual preacher, who, in one of his flights of oratory, said, "O virtue, thou art so fair and lovely, if thou wert to come down upon earth, all men would love thee," with a few more pretty, beautiful things. Mr. Blunt, an honest preacher, who was in the neighborhood, was asked to preach in the afternoon, and he supplemented the worthy gentleman's remarks, by saying, "O virtue, thou didst come on earth, in all thy purity and loveliness; but instead of being beloved and admired, the archers sorely shot at thee and grieved thee; they took thee, virtue, and hung thy quivering limbs upon a cross; when thou didst hang there dying they hissed at thee, they mocked thee, they scorned thee; when thou didst ask for water they gave thee vinegar to drink, mingled with gall; yea, when thou diest thou hadst a tomb from charity, and that tomb, sealed by enmity and hatred." The Shepherd of Israel was despised, incarnate virtue was hated and abhorred; therefore fear not, Christians, take courage; for if your Master passed through it, surely you must.

To conclude: the text calls Christ the stone of Israel. I have heard a story — I cannot tell whether it is true or not — out of some of the Jewish rabbis; it is a tale concerning the text, "The stone which the builders refused, the same is become the headstone of the corner." It is said that when Solomon's temple was building, all the stones were brought from the quarry ready cut and fashioned, and there were marked on all the blocks the places where they were to be put. Amongst the stones was a very curious one; it seemed of no describable shape, it appeared unfit for any portion of the building. They tried it at this wall, but it would not fit; they tried it in another, but it could not be accommodated; so, vexed and angry, they threw it away. The temple was so many years building, that this stone became covered with moss, and grass grew around it. Everybody passing by laughed at the stone; they said Solomon was wise, and doubtless all the other stones were right; but as for that block, they might as well send it back to the quarry, for they were quite sure it was meant for nothing. Year after year rolled on, and the poor stone was still despised, the builders constantly refused it. The eventful day came when the temple was to be finished and opened, and the multitude was assembled to see the grand sight. The builders said, "Where is the top-stone? Where is the pinnacle?" They little thought where the crowning marble was, until some one said, "Perhaps that stone which the builders refused is meant to be the top-stone." They then took it, and hoisted it to the top of the house; and as it reached the summit they found it well adapted to the place. Loud hosannas made the welkin ring, as the stone which the builders refused, thus became the headstone of the corner. So is it with Christ Jesus. The builders cast him away. He was a plebeian; he was of poor extraction; he was a man acquainted with sinners, who walked in poverty and meanness; hence the worldly-wise despised him. But when God shall gather together, in one, all things that are in heaven and that are in earth, then Christ shall be the glorious consummation of all things.

> "Christ reigns in heaven the topmost stone,
> And well deserves the praise."

He shall be exalted; he shall be honored; his name shall endure as long as the sun, and all nations shall be blessed in him, yea, all generations shall call him blessed.

SERMON XI.

THE TOMB OF JESUS.

"Come see the place where the Lord lay."—MATT. xxviii. 6.

EVERY circumstance connected with the life of Christ is deeply interesting to the Christian mind. Wherever we behold our Saviour, he is well worthy of our notice.

"His cross, his manger, and his crown,
Are big with glories yet unknown."

All his weary pilgrimage, from Bethlehem's manger to Calvary's cross, is, in our eyes, paved with glory. Each spot upon which he trod is, to our souls, consecrated at once, simply because there the foot of earth's Saviour and our own Redeemer once was placed. When he comes to Calvary, the interest thickens; then our best thoughts are centered on him in the agonies of crucifixion, nor does our deep affection permit us to leave him, even when, the struggle being over, he yields up the ghost. His body, when it is taken down from the tree, still is lovely in our eyes—we fondly linger around the motionless clay. By faith we discern Joseph of Arimathea, and the timid Nicodemus, assisted by those holy woman, drawing out the nails and taking down the mangled body; we behold them wrapping him in clean, white linen, hastily girding him round with belts of spices; then putting him in his tomb, and departing for the Sabbath rest. We shall, on this occasion, go where Mary went on the morning of the first day of the week, when waking from her couch before the dawn, she aroused herself to be early at the sepulchre of Jesus. We will try, if it be possible, by the help of God's Spirit, to go as she did: not in body, but in soul: we will stand at that tomb; we will examine it, and we trust we shall hear some truth-speaking voice coming from its hollow bosom which will comfort and instruct us, so that we may say of the grave of Jesus when we go away, "It was none other than the gate of heaven"—a sacred place, deeply solemn, and sanctified by the slain body of our precious Saviour.

I. *An invitation given.* I shall commence my remarks this morning by inviting all Christians to come with me to the tomb of Jesus. "Come, see the place where the Lord lay." We will labor to render the place attractive, we will gently take your hand to guide you to it; and may it please our Master to make our hearts burn within us while we talk by the way.

Away ye profane, ye souls whose life is laughter, folly, and mirth! Away ye sordid and carnal minds who have no taste for the spiritual, no delight in the celestial. We ask not your company; we speak to God's beloved, to the heirs of heaven, to the sanctified, the redeemed, the pure in heart; and we say to them, "Come, see the place where the Lord lay." Surely ye need no argument to move your feet in the direction of the holy sepulchre; but still we will use the utmost power to draw your spirit thither. Come, then, for *'t is the shrine of greatness*, 't is the resting-place of *the man*, the Restorer of our race, the Conqueror of death and hell. Men will travel hundreds of miles to behold the place where a poet first breathed the air of earth; they will journey to the ancient tombs of mighty heroes, or the graves of men renowned by fame; but whither shall the Christian go to find the grave of one so famous as was Jesus? Ask me the greatest man who ever lived — I tell you the man Christ Jesus was "anointed with the oil of gladness above his fellows." If ye seek a chamber honored as the resting-place of genius, turn in hither; if ye would worship at the grave of holiness, come ye here; if ye would see the hallowed spot where the choicest bones that e'er were fashioned lay for awhile, come with me, Christian, to that quiet garden, hard by the walls of Jerusalem.

Come with me, moreover, *because it is the tomb of your best friend.* The Jews said of Mary, "she goeth unto his grave to weep there." Ye have lost your friends some of you, ye have planted flowers upon their tombs, ye go and sit at eventide upon the green sward, bedewing the grass with your tears, for there your mother lies, and there your father or your wife. Oh! in pensive sorrow come with me to this dark garden of our Saviour's burial; come to the grave of your best friend — your brother, yea, one who "sticketh closer than a brother." Come thou to the grave of thy dearest relative, O Christian, for Jesus is thy husband, "Thy maker is thy husband, the Lord of Hosts is his name." Doth not affection draw you? Do not the sweet lips of love woo you? Is not the place sanctified where one so well-beloved slept, although but for a moment? Surely ye need no eloquence; if it were needed I have none. I have but the power, in simple, but earnest accents, to repeat the words, "Come, see the place where the Lord lay." On this Easter morning pay a visit to his grave, for it is the grave of your best friend.

Yea, more, I will further urge you to this pious pilgrimage. *Come, for angels bid you.* Angels said, "Come, see the place where the Lord lay." The Syriac version reads, "Come, see the place where *our* Lord lay." Yes, angels put themselves with those poor women, and used one common pronoun—*our*. Jesus is the Lord of angels as well as of men. Ye feeble women—ye have called him Lord, ye have washed his feet, ye have provided for his wants, ye have hung upon his lips to catch his honeyed sentences, ye have sat entranced beneath his mighty eloquence; ye call him Master and Lord, and ye do well; "But," said the seraph, "he is my Lord too;" bowing his head, he sweetly said, "Come, see the place where *our* Lord lay." Dost fear then, Christian, to step into that tomb? Dost dread to enter there, when the angel pointeth with his finger and saith, "Come, we will go together, angels and men, and see the royal bedchamber?" Ye know that angels did go into his tomb, for they sat one at his head and the other at his foot in holy meditation. I picture to myself those bright cherubs sitting there talking to one another. One of them said, "It was there his feet lay;" and the other replied, "and there his hands, and there his head;" and in celestial language did they talk concerning the deep things of God; then they stooped and kissed the rocky floor, made sacred to the angels themselves, not because there they were redeemed, but because there their Master and their monarch, whose high behests they were obeying, did for awhile become the slave of death, and the captive of destruction. Come, Christian, then, for angels are the porters to unbar the door; come, for a cherub is thy messenger to usher thee into the death-place of death himself. Nay, start not from the entrance; let not the darkness affright thee; the vault is not damp with the vapors of death, nor doth the air contain aught of contagion. Come, for *it is a pure and healthy place.* Fear not to enter that tomb. I will admit that catacombs are not the places where we, who are full of joy, would love to go. There is something gloomy and noisome about a vault. There are noxious smells of corruption; oft-times pestilence is born where a dead body hath lain: but fear it not, Christian, for Christ was not left in hell, — in Hades, — neither did his body see corruption. Come, there is no scent, yea, rather a perfume. Step in here, and, if thou didst ever breathe the gales of Ceylon, or winds from the groves of Araby, thou shalt find them far excelled by that sweet holy fragrance left by the blessed body of Jesus; that alabaster vase which once held divinity, and was rendered sweet and precious thereby. Think not thou shalt find aught obnoxious to thy senses. Corruption Jesus never saw; no worms ever devoured his flesh; no rottenness ever entered into his bones; he saw no corruption. Three days he slumbered, but not long enough to putrify; he soon arose, perfect as when he entered, uninjured as when his limbs were composed for their slumber. Come then, Christian, summon up thy thoughts, gather all thy powers; here is a sweet invitation, let me press it again. Let me lead thee by the hand of meditation, my brother; let me take thee by the arm of thy fancy, and let me again say to thee, "Come, see the place where the Lord lay."

There is yet one reason more why I would have thee visit this royal sepulchre — *because it is a quiet spot.* Oh! I have longed for rest, for I have heard this world's rumors in my ears so long, that I have begged for

> "A lodge in some vast wilderness,
> Some boundless contiguity of shade,"

where I might hide myself forever. I am sick of this tiring and trying life; my frame is weary, my soul is mad to repose herself awhile. I would I could lie myself down a little by the edge of some pebbly brook, with no companion save the fair flowers or the nodding willows. I would I could recline in stillness, where the air brings balm to the tormented brain, where there is no murmur save the hum of the summer bee, no whisper save that of the zephyrs, and no song except the carolling of the lark. I wish I could be at ease for a moment. I have become a man of the world; my brain is racked, my soul is tired. Oh! wouldst thou be quiet, Christian? Merchant, wouldst thou rest from thy toils? wouldst thou be calm for once? Then come hither. It is in a pleasant garden, far from the hum of Jerusalem; the noise and din of business will not reach thee there: "Come, see the place where the Lord lay." It is a sweet resting spot, a withdrawing room for thy soul, where thou mayest brush thy garments from the dust of earth and muse awhile in peace.

II. *Attention requested.* Thus I have pressed the invitation; now we will enter the tomb. Let us examine it with deep attention, noticing every circumstance connected with it.

And, first, mark that it is a *costly tomb.* It is no common grave; it is not an excavation dug out by the spade for a pauper, in which to hide the last remains of his miserable and over-wearied bones. It is a princely tomb; it was made of marble, cut in the side of a hill. Stand here, believer, and ask why Jesus had such a costly sepulchre. He had no elegant garments; he wore a coat without seam, woven from the top throughout, without an atom of embroidery. He owned no sumptuous palace, for he had not where to lay his head. His sandals were not rich with gold, or studded with brilliants. He was poor. Why, then, does he lie in a noble grave? We answer, for this reason: Christ was unhonored till he had finished his sufferings; Christ's body suffered contumely, shame, spitting, buffeting, and reproach, until he had completed his great work; he was trampled under foot, he was "despised and rejected of men; a man of sorrows, and acquainted with grief;" but the moment he had finished his undertaking, God said, "No more shall that body be disgraced; if it is to sleep, let it slumber in an honorable grave; if it is to rest, let nobles bury it; let Joseph, the councillor, and Nicodemus, the man of Sanhedrim, be present at the funeral; let the body be embalmed with precious spices, let it have honor; it has had enough of contumely, and shame, and reproach, and buffeting; let it now be treated with respect." Christian, dost thou discern the meaning? Jesus, after he had finished his work, slept in a costly grave; for now his Father loved and honored him, since his work was done.

But, though it is a costly grave, *it is a borrowed one.* I see over the top of it, "Sacred to the memory of the family of Joseph of Arimathea;" yet Jesus slept there. Yes, he was buried in another's sepulchre. He who had no house of his own, and rested in the habitation of other men; who had no table, but lived upon the hospitality of his disciples; who borrowed boats in which to preach, and had not anything in the wide world, was obliged to have a tomb from charity. Oh! should not the poor take courage? They dread to be buried at the expense of their neighbors, but if their poverty be unavoidable, wherefore should they blush, since Jesus Christ himself was interred in another's grave? Ah! I wish I might have had Joseph's grave to let Jesus be buried in it. Good Joseph thought he had cut it out for himself, and that he should lay his bones there. He had it excavated as a family vault, and lo, the Son of David makes it one of the tombs of the kings. But he did not lose it by lending it to the Lord; rather, he had it back with precious interest. He only lent it three days; then Christ resigned it; he had not injured, but perfumed and sanctified it, and made it far more holy, so that it would be an honor in future to be buried there. It was a borrowed tomb; and why? I take it, not to dishonor Christ, but in order to show that, as his sins were borrowed sins, so his burial was in a borrowed grave. Christ had no transgressions of his own; he took ours upon his head; he never committed a wrong, but he took all my sin, and all yours, if ye are believers; concerning all his people, it is true, he bore their griefs and carried their sorrows in his own body on the tree; therefore, as they were others' sins, so he rested in another's grave; as they were sins imputed, so that grave was only imputedly his. It was not his sepulchre; it was the tomb of Joseph.

Let us not weary in this pious investigation, but with fixed attention observe everything connected with this holy spot. The grave, we observe, *was cut in a rock.* Why was this? The Rock of Ages was buried in a rock; a rock within a rock. But why? Most persons suggest that it was so ordained, that it might be clear that there was no covert way by which the disciples or others could enter and steal the body away. Very possibly it was the reason; but O! my soul, canst thou not find a spiritual reason? Christ's sepulchre was cut in a rock. It was not cut in mould that might be worn away by the water, or might crumble and fall into decay. The sepulchre stands, I believe, entire to this day; if it does not naturally, it does spiritually. The same sepulchre which took the sins of Paul shall take my iniquities into his bosom; for if I ever lose my guilt it must roll off my shoulders into the sepulchre. It was cut in a rock, so that if a sinner were saved a thousand years ago, I too can be delivered, for it is a rocky sepulchre where sin was buried—it was a rocky sepulchre of marble where my crimes were laid forever—buried never to have a resurrection.

You will mark, moreover, that tomb was *one wherin no other man had ever lain.* Christopher Ness says, when Christ was born he lay in a virgin's womb, and when he died he was placed in a virgin tomb; he slept where never man had slept before. The reason was that none might say that another person rose, for there never had been any other body there, thus a mistake of persons was impossible. Nor could it be said that some old prophet was interred in the place, and that Christ rose because he had touched his bones. You remember where Elisha was buried; and as they were burying a man, behold he touched the prophet's bones and arose. Christ touched no prophet's bones, for none had ever slept there; it was a new chamber where the monarch of the earth did take his rest for three days and three nights.

We have learned a little, then, with attention; but let us stoop down once more before we leave the grave, and notice something else. We see the grave, but do you *notice the grave-clothes*, all wrapped and laid in their places, the napkin being folded up by itself? Wherefore are the grave-clothes wrapped up? The Jews said robbers had abstracted the body; but if so, surely they would have stolen the clothes; they would never have thought of wrapping them up and laying them down so carefully; they would be too much in haste to think of it. Why was it then? To manifest to us that Christ did not come out in a hurried manner. He slept till the last moment; then he awoke; he came not in haste. They shall not come out in haste, neither by flight, but at the appointed moment shall his people come to him. So at the precise hour, the decreed instant, Jesus Christ leisurely awoke, took off his cerements, left them all behind him, and came forth in his pure and naked innocence, perhaps to show us that as clothes were the offspring of sin — when sin was atoned for by Christ, he left all raiment behind him, for garments are the badges of guilt — if we had not been guilty we should never have needed them.

Then the napkin, mark you, was laid by itself.

The grave-clothes were left behind for every departed Christian to wear. The bed of death is well sheeted with the garments of Jesus, but the napkin was laid by itself, because the Christian, when he dies, does not need that; it is used by the mourners, and the mourners only. We shall all wear grave-clothes, but we shall not need the napkin. When our friends die, the napkin is laid aside for us to use; but do our ascended brethren and sisters use it? No; the Lord God hath wiped away all tears from their eyes. We stand and view the corpses of the dear departed, we moisten their faces with our tears, letting whole showers of grief fall on their heads; but do *they* weep? Oh, no. Could they speak to us from the upper spheres they would say, "Weep not for me, for I am glorified. Sorrow not for me; I have left a bad world behind me and have entered into a far better." They have no napkin — they weep not. Strange it is that those who endure death weep not; but those who see them die, are weepers. When the child is born it weeps while others smile, (say the Arabs,) and when it dies it smiles while others weep. It is so with the Christian. O blessed thing! The napkin is laid by itself, because Christians will never want to use it when they die.

III. *Emotion excited.* We have thus surveyed the grave with deep attention, and, I hope, with some profit to ourselves. But that is not all. I love a religion which consists, in a great measure, of emotion. Now, if I had power, like a master, I would touch the strings of your hearts, and fetch a glorious tune of solemn music from them, for this is a deeply solemn place into which I have conducted you.

First, I would bid you stand and see the place where

the Lord lay with *emotions of deep sorrow.* Oh come, my beloved brother, thy Jesus once lay there. He was a murdered man, my soul, and thou the murderer.

"Ah, you my sins, my cruel sins,
His chief tormentors were,
Each of my crimes became a nail,
And unbelief the spear."

"Alas! and did my Saviour bleed?
And did my Sov'reign die?"

I slew him — this right hand struck the dagger to his heart. My deeds slew Christ. Alas! I slew my best beloved; I killed him who loved me with an everlasting love. Ye eyes, why do ye refuse to weep when ye see Jesus' body mangled and torn? Oh! give vent to your sorrow, Christians, for ye have good reason to do so. I believe in what Hart says, that there was a time in his experience when he could so sympathize with Christ, that he felt more grief at the death of Christ than he did joy. It seemed so sad a thing that Christ should have to die; and to me it often appears too great a price for Jesus Christ to purchase worms with his own blood. Methinks I love him so much, that if I had seen him about to suffer, I should have been as bad as Peter, and have said, "That be far from thee, Lord;" but then he would have said to me, "Get thee behind me, Satan;" for he does not approve of that love which would stop him from dying. "The cup which my Father hath given me, shall I not drink it?" But I think, had I seen him going up to his cross, I could fain have pressed him back, and said, "Oh! Jesus, thou shalt not die; I cannot have it. Wilt thou purchase my life with a price so dear?" It seems too costly for him who is the

Prince of Life and Glory to let his fair limbs be tortured in agony; that the hands which carried mercies should be pierced with accursed nails; that the temples that were always clothed with love should have cruel thorns driven through them. It appears too much. Oh! weep, Christian, and let our sorrow rise. Is not the price all but too great, that your beloved should for you resign *himself?* Oh! I should think, if a person were saved from death by another, he would always feel deep grief if his deliverer lost his life in the attempt. I had a friend, who, standing by the side of a piece of frozen water, saw a young lad in it, and sprang upon the ice in order to save him. After clutching the boy, he held him in his hands and cried out, "Here he is! Here he is! I have saved him." But, just as they caught hold of the boy, he sank himself, and his body was not found for some time afterwards, when he was quite dead. Oh! it is so with Jesus. My soul was drowning. From heaven's high portals he saw me sinking in the depths of hell; he plunged in:

"He SANK beneath his heavy woes,
To raise me to a crown;
There 's ne'er a gift his hand bestows,
But cost his heart a groan."

Ah! we may indeed regret our sin, since it slew Jesus.

Now, Christian, change thy note a moment. "Come, see the place where the Lord lay," *with joy and gladness.* He does not lie there now. Weep when ye see the tomb of Christ, but rejoice because it is empty. Thy sin slew him, but his divinity raised him up. Thy guilt hath murdered him, but his righteousness hath restored him. Oh! he hath burst the bonds of death, he hath ungirt the cerements of the tomb, and hath come out more than conqueror, crushing death beneath his feet. Rejoice, O Christian, for he is not there—he is risen. "Come, see the place where the Lord lay."

One more thought, and then I will speak a little concerning the doctrines we may learn from this grave. "Come, see the place where the Lord lay," *with solemn awe*, for you and I will have to lay there too.

"Hark! from the tomb a doleful sound,
Mine ears, attend the cry,
Ye ving men, come view the ground
Where ye must shortly lie.

"Princes, this clay must be your bed,
In spite of all your powers.
The tall, the wise, the reverend head,
Must lie as low as ours."

It is a fact we do not often think of, that we shall all be dead in a little while. I know that I am made of dust, and not of iron; my bones are not brass, nor my sinews steel; in a little while my body must crumble back to its native elements. But do you ever try to picture to yourself the moment of your dissolution? My friends, there are some of you who seldom realize how old you are, how near you are to death. One way of remembering our age, is to see how much remains. Think how old eighty is, and then see how few years there are before you will get there. We should remember our frailty. Sometimes I have tried to think of the time of my departure. I do not know whether I shall die a violent death or not; but I would to God that I might die suddenly; for sudden death is sudden glory. I would I might have such a blessed exit as Dr. Beaumont, and die in my pulpit, laying down my body with my charge, and ceasing at once to work and live. But it is not mine to choose. Suppose I lie lingering for weeks, in the midst of pains, and griefs, and agonies; when that moment comes, that moment which is too solemn for my lips to speak of, when the spirit leaves the clay — let the physician put it off for weeks, or years, as we say he does, though he does not — when that moment comes, O ye lips, be dumb, and profane not its solemnity. When death comes, how is the strong man bowed down! How doth the mighty man fall! They may say they will not die, but there is no hope for them; they must yield, the arrow has gone home. I knew a man who was a wicked wretch, and I remember seeing him pace the floor of his bedroom, saying, "O God, I will not die, I will not die." When I begged him to lie on his bed, for he was dying, he said he could not die while he could walk, and he would walk till he did die. Ah! he expired in the utmost torments, always shrieking, "O God, I will not die." Oh! that moment, that last moment. See how clammy is the sweat upon the brow, how dry the tongue, how parched the lips. The man shuts his eyes and slumbers, then opens them again; and if he be a Christian, I can fancy that he will say:

> "Hark! they whisper: angels say,
> Sister spirit, come away.
> What is this absorbs me quite —
> Steals my senses — shuts my sight —
> Drowns my spirit — draws my breath?
> Tell me, my soul, can this be death?"

We know not when he is dying. One gentle sigh, and

the spirit breaks away. We can scarcely say, "he is gone," before the ransomed spirit takes its mansion near the throne. Come to Christ's tomb, then, for the silent vault must soon be your habitation. Come to Christ's grave, for ye must slumber there. And even you, ye sinners, for one moment I will ask you to come also, because ye must die as well as the rest of us. Your sins cannot keep you from the jaws of death. I say, sinner, I want thee to look at Christ's sepulchre too, for when thou diest it may have done thee great good to think of it. You have heard of Queen Elizabeth, crying out that she would give an empire for a single hour. Or have you heard the despairing cry of the gentleman on board the "Arctic," when it was going down, who shouted to the boat, "Come back! I will give you £30,000 if you will come and take me in." Ah! poor man, it were but little if he had thirty thousand worlds, if he could thereby prolong his life: "Skin for skin, yea, all that a man hath, will he give for his life." Some of you who can laugh this morning, who came to spend a merry hour in this hall, will be dying, and then ye will pray and crave for life, and shriek for another Sabbath-day. Oh! how the Sabbaths ye have wasted will walk like ghosts before you! Oh! how they will shake their snaky hair in your eyes! How will ye be made to sorrow and weep, because ye wasted precious hours, which, when they are gone, are gone too far to be recalled. May God save you from the pangs of remorse.

IV. *Instruction imparted.* And now, Christian brethren, "Come, see the place where the Lord lay," to learn a doctrine or two. What did you see when you visited "the place where the Lord lay?" "He is not here: for he is risen." The first thing you perceive, if you stand by his empty tomb, *is his divinity.* The dead in Christ shall rise first at the resurrection; but he who rose first, their leader, rose in a different fashion. They rise by imparted power. He rose by his own. He could not slumber in the grave, because he was God. Death had no more dominion over him. There is no better proof of Christ's divinity than that startling resurrection of his, when he rose from the grave, by the glory of the Father. O Christian, thy Jesus is a God; his broad shoulders that hold thee up are indeed divine; and here thou hast the best proof of it—because he rose from the grave.

A second doctrine here taught well may charm thee, if the Holy Spirit apply it with power. Behold his empty tomb, O true believer: it is a sign of *thine acquittal*, and thy full discharge. If Jesus had not paid the debt, he ne'er had risen from the grave. He would have lain there till this moment if he had not cancelled the entire debt, by satisfying eternal vengeance. O beloved, is not that an overwhelming thought?

> "It is finished, it is finished,
> Hear the rising Saviour cry."

The heavenly turnkey came, a bright angel stepped from heaven and rolled away the stone; but he would not have done so if Christ had not done all: he would have kept him there, he would have said, "Nay, nay, thou art the sinner now; thou hast the sins of all thine elect upon thy shoulder, and I will not let thee go free till thou hast paid the uttermost farthing." In his going free I see my own discharge.

> "My Jesu's blood 's my full discharge."

As a justified man, I have not a sin now against me in God's book. If I were to turn over God's eternal book, I should see every debt of mine receipted and cancelled

> "Here 's pardon for transgressions past,
> It matters not how black their cast,
> And O my soul, with wonder view,
> For sins to come here 's pardon too.
> Fully discharged by Christ I am
> From Christ's tremendous curse and blame."

One more doctrine we learn, and with that we will conclude — *the doctrine of the resurrection.* Jesus rose, and as the Lord our Saviour rose, so all his followers must rise. Die I must — this body must be a carnival for worms; it must be eaten by those tiny cannibals; peradventure it shall be scattered from one portion of the earth to another; the constituent particles of this my frame will enter into plants, from plants pass into animals, and thus be carried into far distant realms; but, at the blast of the archangel's trumpet, every separate atom of my body shall find its fellow; like the bones lying in the valley of vision, though separated from one another, the moment God shall speak, the bone will creep to its bone; then the flesh shall come upon it; the four winds of heaven shall blow, and the breath shall return. So let me die, let beasts devour me, let fire turn this body into gas and vapor, all its particles shall yet again be restored; this very selfsame actual body shall start up from its grave, glorified and made like Christ's body, yet still the same body, for God hath said it. Christ's same body rose; so shall mine. O my soul, dost thou now dread to die? Thou wilt lose thy partner body a little while, but thou wilt be married again in heaven; soul and body shall again be united before the throne of God. The grave — what is it? It is the bath in which the Christian puts the clothes of his body to have them washed and cleansed. Death — what is it? It is the waiting-room where we robe ourselves for immortality; it is the place where the body, like Esther, bathes itself in spices that it may be fit for the embrace of its Lord. Death is the gate of life; I will not fear to die, then, but will say,

> "Shudder not to pass the stream;
> Venture all thy care on him;
> Him whose dying love and power
> Stilled its tossing, hushed its roar,
> Safe in the expanded wave;
> Gentle as a summer's eve.
> Not one object of his care
> Ever suffered shipwreck there."

Come, view the place then, with all hallowed meditation, where the Lord lay. Spend this afternoon, my beloved brethren, in meditating upon it, and very often go to Christ's grave, both to weep and to rejoice. Ye timid ones, do not be afraid to approach, for 't is no vain thing to remember that timidity buried Christ. Faith would not have given him a funeral at all; faith would have kept him above ground, and would never have let him be buried; for it would have said, it would be useless to bury Christ if he were to rise. Fear buried him. Nicodemus, the night disciple, and Joseph of Arimathea, secretly, for fear of the Jews, went and buried him. Therefore, ye timid ones, ye may go too. Ready-to-halt, poor Fearing, and thou, Mrs. Despondency, and Much-afraid, go often there; let it be your favorite haunt, there build a tabernacle, there abide. And often say to your heart, when you are in distress and sorrow, "Come, see the place where the Lord lay."

20

SERMON XII.

THE CARNAL MIND ENMITY AGAINST GOD.

"The carnal mind *is* enmity against God." — ROMANS viii. 7.

THIS is a very solemn indictment which the Apostle Paul here prefers against the carnal mind. He declares it to be enmity against God. When we consider what man once was, only second to the angels, the companion of God, who walked with him in the garden of Eden in the cool of the day; when we think of him as being made in the very image of his Creator, pure, spotless, and unblemished, we cannot but feel bitterly grieved to find such an accusation as this preferred against us as a *race*. We may well hang our harps upon the willows, while we listen to the voice of Jehovah solemnly speaking to his rebellious creature. "How art thou fallen from heaven, thou son of the morning!" "Thou sealest up the sum, full of wisdom, and perfect in beauty. Thou hast been in Eden, the garden of God; every precious stone was thy covering — the workmanship of thy tabrets and of thy pipes was prepared in thee in the day that thou wast created. Thou art the anointed cherub that covereth; and I have set thee so: thou wast upon the holy mountain of God; thou hast walked up and down in the midst of the stones of fire. Thou wast perfect in thy ways from the day that thou wast created, till iniquity was found in thee, and thou hast sinned; therefore, I will cast thee as profane out of the mountain of God: and I will destroy thee, O covering cherub, from the midst of the stones of fire."

There is much to sadden us in a view of the ruins of our race. As the Carthaginian, who might tread the desolate site of his much-loved city, would shed many tears when he saw it laid in heaps by the Romans; or as the Jew, wandering through the deserted streets of Jerusalem, would lament that the ploughshare had marred the beauty and the glory of that city which was the joy of the whole earth; so ought we to mourn for ourselves and our race, when we behold the ruins of that goodly structure which God had piled,— that creature, matchless in symmetry, second only to angelic intellect—that mighty being, man—when we behold how he is "fallen, fallen, fallen, from his high estate," and lies in a mass of destruction. A few years ago a star was seen blazing out with considerable brilliance, but soon disappeared; it has since been affirmed that it was a world on fire, thousands of millions of miles from us, and yet the rays of the conflagration reached us; the noiseless messenger of light gave to the distant dwellers on this globe the alarm of "A world on fire!" But what is the conflagration of a distant planet, what is the destruction of the mere material of the most ponderous orb, compared with this fall of humanity, this wreck of all that is holy and sacred in ourselves? To us, indeed, the things are scarcely comparable, since we are deeply interested in one, though not in the other. The fall of Adam was OUR fall; we fell in and with him; we were equal sufferers; it is the ruin of our own house that we lament, it is the destruction of our own city that we bemoan, when we stand and see written, in lines too plain for us to mistake their meaning, "The carnal mind"—that very selfsame mind which was once holiness, and has now become carnal—"is enmity against God." May God help me, this morning, solemnly to prefer this indictment against all! Oh! that the Holy Spirit may so convince us of sin, that we may unanimously plead "guilty" before God.

There is no difficulty in understanding my text: it needs scarcely any explanation. We all know that the word "carnal" here signifies fleshly. The old translators rendered the passage thus: "The mind of the flesh is enmity against God"—that is to say, the natural mind, that soul which we inherit from our fathers, that which was born within us when our bodies were fashioned by God. The fleshly mind, the *phronema sarkos*, the lusts, the passions of the soul; it is this which has gone astray from God, and become enmity against him.

But, before we enter upon a discussion of the doctrine of the text, observe how strongly the Apostle expresses it. "The carnal mind," he says, "IS ENMITY against God." He uses a noun, and not an adjective. He does not say it is opposed to God merely, but it is positive enmity. It is not black, but blackness; it is not *at* enmity, but *enmity* itself; it is not corrupt, but corruption; it is not rebellious, it is rebellion; it is not wicked, it is wickedness itself. The heart, though it be deceitful, is positively deceit; it is evil in the concrete, sin in the essence; it is the distillation, the quintessence of all things that are vile; it is not envious against God, it is envy; it is not at enmity, it is actual enmity.

Nor need we say a word to explain that it is "enmity *against God*." It does not charge manhood with an aversion merely to the dominion, laws, or doctrines of Jehovah; but it strikes a deeper and surer blow. It does not strike man upon the head; it penetrates into his heart; it lays the axe at the root of the tree, and pronounces him "enmity *against God*," against the person of the Godhead, against the Deity, against the mighty Maker of this world; not at enmity against his Bible or against his gospel, though that were true, but against God himself, against his essence, his existence, and his person. Let us, then, weigh the words of the text, for they are solemn words. They are well put together by that master of eloquence, Paul, and they were, moreover, dictated by the Holy Spirit, who telleth man how to speak aright. May he help us to expound, as he has already given us the passage to explain.

We shall be called upon to notice, this morning, first, *the truthfulness of this assertion;* secondly, *the universality of the evil here complained of;* thirdly, we will still further enter into the depths of the subject, and press it to your hearts, by showing *the enormity of the evil;* and after that, should we have time, we will deduce one or two doctrines from the general fact.

I. First, we are called upon to speak of *the truthfulness of this great statement.* "The carnal mind is enmity against God." It needs no proof, for since it is written in God's word, we, as Christian men, are bound to bow before it. The words of the Scriptures are words of infinite wisdom, and if reason cannot see the ground of a statement of revelation, it is bound, most reverently, to believe it, since we are well assured, even should it be above our reason, that it cannot be contrary thereunto. Here I find it written in the Scriptures, "The carnal mind is enmity against God;" and that of itself is enough for me. But, did I need witnesses, I would conjure up the nations of antiquity; I would unroll the volume of ancient history; I would tell you of the awful deeds of mankind. It may be I might move your souls to detestation, if I spake of the cruelty of this race to itself, if I showed you how it made the world an Aceldama, by its wars, and deluged it with blood by its fightings and murders; if I should recite the black list of vices in which whole nations have indulged, or even bring before you the characters of some of the most eminent philosophers, I should blush to speak of them, and you would refuse to hear; yea, it would be impossible for you, as refined inhabitants of a civilized country, to endure the mention of the crimes that were committed by those very men, who, now-a-days, are held up as being paragons of perfection. I fear, if all the truth were written, we should rise up from reading the lives of earth's mightiest heroes and proudest sages, and would say at once of all of them, "They are clean gone out of the way; they are altogether become unprofitable; there is none that doeth good; no, not one."

And, did not that suffice, I would point you to the delusions of the heathen; I would tell you of their priestcraft, by which their souls have been enthralled in superstition; I would drag their gods before you; I would let you witness the horrid obscenities, the diabolical rites which are to these besotted men most sacred things. Then after you had heard what the natural *religion* of man is, I would ask what must his *irreligion* be? If this is his devotion, what must be his impiety? If this be his ardent love of the Godhead, what must his hatred thereof be? Ye would, I am sure, at once confess, did ye know what the race is, that the indictment is proven, and that the world must unreservedly and truthfully exclaim, "guilty."

A further argument I might find in the fact, that the best of men have been always the readiest to confess their depravity. The holiest men, the most free from impurity, have always felt it most. He whose garments are the whitest, will best perceive the spots upon them. He whose crown shineth the brightest, will know when he hath lost a jewel. He who giveth the most light to the world, will always be able to discover his own darkness. The angels of heaven veil their faces; and the angels of God on earth, his chosen people, must always veil their faces with humility, when they think of what they were. Hear David: he was none of those who boast of a holy nature and a pure disposition. He says, "Behold, I was shapen in iniquity; and in sin did my mother conceive me." Hear all those holy men who have written in the inspired volume, and ye shall find them all confessing that they were not clean, no, not one; yea, one of them exclaimed, "O wretched man that I am; who shall deliver me from the body of this death?"

And more, I will summon one other witness to the truthfulness of this fact, who shall decide the question:

it shall be your conscience. Conscience, I will put thee in the witness-box, and cross-examine thee this morning! Conscience, truly answer! be not drugged with the laudanum of self-security! speak the truth! Didst thou never hear the heart say, "I wish there were no God?" Have not all men, at times, wished that our religion were not true? Though they could not entirely rid their souls of the idea of the Godhead, did they not wish that there might not be a God? Have they not had the desire that it might turn out that all these divine realities were a delusion, a farce, and an imposture? "Yea," saith every man; "that has crossed my mind sometimes. I have wished I might indulge in folly; I have wished there were no laws to restrain me; I have wished, as the fool, that there were no God." That passage in the Psalms, "The fool hath said in his heart, there is no God," is wrongly translated. It should be, "The fool hath said in his heart, *no God.*" The fool does not say in his heart *there is* no God, for he knows there is a God; but he says, "No God — I don't want any; I wish there were none." And who amongst us has not been so foolish as to desire that there were no God? Now, conscience, answer another question! Thou hast confessed that thou hast at times wished there were no God; now, suppose a man wished another dead, would not that show that he hated him? Yes, it would. And so, my friends, the wish that there were no God, proves that we dislike God. When I wish such a man dead and rotting in his grave; when I desire that he were *non est*, I must hate that man; otherwise I should not wish him to be extinct. So that wish — and I do not think there has been a man in this world who has not.

had it — proves that "the carnal mind is enmity against God."

But, conscience, I have another question! Has not thine heart ever desired, since there is a God, that he were a little less holy, a little less pure, so that those things which are now great crimes might be regarded as venial offences, as peccadillos? Has thy heart never said, "Would to God these sins were not forbidden! Would that he would be merciful and pass them by without an atonement! Would that he were not so severe, so rigorously just, so sternly strict to his integrity." Hast thou never said that, my heart? Conscience must reply, "Thou hast." Well, that wish to change God, proves that thou art not in love with the God that now is, the God of heaven and earth; and though thou mayest talk of natural religion, and boast that thou dost reverence the God of the green fields, the grassy meads, the swelling flood, the rolling thunder, the azure sky, the starry night, and the great universe — though thou lovest the poetic beau ideal of Deity, it is not the God of Scripture, for thou hast wished to change his nature, and in that hast thou proved that thou art at enmity with him. But wherefore, conscience, should I go thus round about? Thou canst bear faithful witness, if thou wouldst speak the truth, that each person here has so transgressed against God, so continually broken his laws, violated his Sabbath, trampled on his statutes, despised his gospel, that it is true, aye, most true, that "the carnal mind is enmity against God."

II. Now, secondly, we are called upon to notice the *universality of this evil.* What a broad assertion it is. It is not a single carnal mind, or a certain class of characters, but "*the* carnal mind." It is an unqualified statement, including every individual. Whatever mind may properly be called carnal, not having been spiritualized by the power of God's Holy Ghost, is "enmity against God."

Observe then, first of all, the universality of this as to *all persons.* Every carnal mind in the world is at enmity against God. This does not exclude even infants at the mother's breast. We call them innocent, and so they are of actual transgression, but as the poet says, "Within the youngest breast there lies a stone." There is in the carnal mind of an infant, enmity against God; it is not developed, but it lieth there. Some say that children learn sin by imitation. But no: take a child away, place it under the most pious influences, let the very air it breathes be purified by piety; let it constantly drink in draughts of holiness; let it hear nothing but the voice of prayer and praise; let its ear be always kept in tune by notes of sacred song; and that child, notwithstanding, may still become one of the grossest of transgressors; and though placed apparently on the very road to heaven, it shall, if not directed by divine grace, march downwards to the pit. Oh! how true it is that some who have had the best of parents, have been the worst of sons; that many who have been trained up under the most holy auspices, in the midst of the most favorable scenes for piety, have nevertheless, become loose and wanton! So it is not by imitation, but it is by nature, that the child is evil. Grant me that the child is carnal, and my text says, "The carnal mind is enmity against God." The young crocodile, I have heard, when broken from the shell, will in a moment begin to put itself in a posture of attack, opening its mouth as if it had been taught and trained. We know that young lions, when tamed and domesticated, still will have the wild nature of their fellows of the forest, and were liberty given them, would prey as fiercely as others. So with the child; you may bind him with the green withes of education, you may do what you will with him, since you cannot change his heart, that carnal mind shall still be at enmity against God; and notwithstanding intellect, talent, and all you may give to boot, it shall be of the same sinful complexion as every other child, if not as apparently evil; for "the carnal mind is enmity against God."

And if this applies to children, equally does it include every class of men. There be some men that are born into this world master-spirits, who walk about it as giants, wrapped in mantles of light and glory. I refer to the poets, men who stand aloft like Colossi, mightier than we, seeming to be descended from celestial spheres. There be others of acute intellect, who, searching into mysteries of science, discover things that have been hidden from the creation of the world; men of keen research, and mighty erudition; and yet of each of these—poet, philosopher, metaphysician, and great discoverer—it shall be said, "The carnal mind is enmity against God." Ye may train him up, ye may make his intellect almost angelic, ye may strengthen his soul until he shall take what are riddles to us, and unravel them with his fingers in a moment; ye may make him so mighty, that he can grasp the iron secrets of the eternal hills and grind them to atoms in his fist; ye may give him an eye so keen, that he can penetrate the arcana of rocks and mountains; ye may add a soul so potent, that he may slay the giant Sphinx, that had for ages troubled the mightiest men of learning; yet, when ye have done all, his mind shall be a depraved one, and his carnal heart shall still be in opposition to God. Yea, more, ye shall bring him to the house of prayer; ye shall make him sit constantly under the clearest preaching of the word, where he shall hear the doctrines of grace in all their purity, attended by a holy unction; but if that holy unction does not rest upon him, all shall be vain; he shall still come most regularly, but like the pious door of the chapel, that turneth in and out, he shall still be the same; having an outside superficial religion, and his carnal mind shall still be at enmity against God. Now, this is not my assertion, it is the declaration of God's word, and you must leave it if you do not believe it; but quarrel not with me, it is my Master's message; and it is true of every one of you — men, women, and children, and myself too — that if we have not been regenerated and converted, if we have not experienced a change of heart, our carnal mind is still at enmity against God.

Again, notice the universality of *this at all times.* The carnal mind is at all times enmity against God. "Oh," say some, "it may be true that we are at times opposed to God, but surely we are not always so." "There be moments," says one, "when I feel rebellious; at times my passions lead me astray; but surely there are other favorable seasons when I really am friendly to God, and offer true devotion. I have (continues the objector,) stood upon the mountain-top, until my whole soul has kindled with the scene below, and my lips have uttered the song of praise:

"'These are thy glorious works, parent of good,
Almighty, thine this universal frame,
Thus wondrous fair: thyself how wondrous then!'"

Yes, but mark, what is true one day is not false another; "the carnal mind is enmity against God" at all times. The wolf may sleep, but it is a wolf still. The snake with its azure hues, may slumber amid the flowers, and the child may stroke its slimy back, but it is a serpent still; it does not change its nature, though it is dormant. The sea is the house of storms, even when it is glassy as a lake; the thunder is still the mighty rolling thunder, when it is so much aloft that we hear it not. And the heart, when we perceive not its ebullitions, when it belches not forth its lava, and sendeth not forth the hot stones of its corruption, is still the same dread volcano. At all times, at all hours, at every moment, (I speak this as God speaketh it,) if ye are carnal, ye are each one of you enmity against God.

Another thought concerning the universality of this statement. *The whole of the mind* is enmity against God. The text says, "The carnal mind is enmity against God." That is, the entire man, every part of him—every power, every passion. It is a question often asked, "What part of man was injured by the fall?" Some think that the fall was only felt by the affections, and that the intellect was unimpaired; this they argue from the wisdom of man, and the mighty discoveries he has made, such as the law of gravitation, the steam-engine, and the sciences. Now, I consider these things as being a very mean display of wisdom, compared with what is to come in a hundred years, and very small compared with what might have been, if man's intellect had continued in its pristine condition.

I believe that the fall crushed man entirely; albeit, when it rolled like an avalanche upon the mighty temple of human nature, some shafts were still left undestroyed, and amidst the ruins you find here and there, a flute, a pedestal, a cornice, a column, not quite broken, yet the entire structure fell, and its most glorious relics are fallen ones, levelled in the dust. The whole of man is defaced. Look at *our memory;* is it not true that the memory is fallen? I can recollect evil things far better than those which savor of piety. I hear a ribald song, that music of hell shall jar in my ear when gray hairs shall be upon my head. I hear a note of holy praise: alas! it is forgotten! For memory graspeth with an iron hand ill things, but the good she holdeth with feeble fingers. She suffereth the glorious timbers from the forest of Lebanon to swim down the stream of oblivion, but she stoppeth all the draff that floateth from the foul city of Sodom. She will retain evil, she will lose good. Memory is fallen. So are the *affections.* We love everything earthly better than we ought; we soon fix our heart upon a creature, but very seldom on the Creator; and when the heart is given to Jesus, it is prone to wander. Look at the *imagination* too. Oh! how can the imagination revel, when the body is in an ill condition? Only give man something that shall well nigh intoxicate him; drug him with opium; and how will his imagination dance with joy! Like a bird uncaged, how will it mount with more than eagle's wings! He sees things he had not dreamed of even in the shades of night. Why did not his imagination work when his body was in a normal state — when it was healthy? Simply because it is depraved; and until he had entered a foul element — until the body had begun to quiver with a kind of intoxication—the fancy would not hold its carnival. We have some splendid specimens of what men could write, when they have been under the accursed influence of ardent spirits. It is because the mind is so depraved that it loves something which puts the body into an abnormal condition; and here we have a proof that the imagination itself has gone astray. So with *the judgment*—I might prove how ill it decides. So might I accuse the *conscience*, and tell you how blind it is, and how it winks at the greatest follies. I might review all our powers, and write upon the brow of each one, "Traitor against heaven! traitor against God!" The whole "carnal mind is enmity against God."

Now, my hearers, "the Bible alone is the religion of Protestants;" but whenever I find a certain book much held in reverence by our Episcopalian brethren, entirely on my side, I always feel the greatest delight in quoting from it. Do you know I am one of the best churchmen in the world; the very best, if you will judge me by the articles, and the very worst, if you measure me in any other way. Measure me by the articles of the Church of England, and I will not stand second to any man under heaven's blue sky in preaching the gospel contained in them; for if there be an excellent epitome of the gospel, it is to be found in the articles of the Church of England. Let me show you that you have not been hearing strange doctrine. Here is the 9th article, upon Original or Birth Sin: "Original Sin standeth not in the following of Adam; (as the Pelagians do vainly talk;) but it is the fault and corruption of the nature of every man, that naturally is engendered of the offspring of Adam; whereby man is very far gone from original righteousness, and is of his own nature inclined to evil, so that the flesh lusteth always contrary to the spirit; and, therefore, in every person born into this world, it deserveth God's wrath and damnation. And this infection of nature doth remain, yea, in them that are regenerated; whereby the lust of the flesh, called in the Greek, *phronema sarkos*, which some do expound the wisdom, some sensuality, some the affection, some the desire, of the flesh, is not subject to the Law of God. And although there is no condemnation for them that believe and are baptized, yet the apostle doth confess, that concupiscence and lust hath of itself the nature of sin." I want nothing more. Will any one who believes in the Prayer Book dissent from the doctrine that "the carnal mind is enmity against God?"

III. I have said that I would endeavor, in the third place, to show the great *enormity of this guilt*. I do fear, my brethren, that very often when we consider our state, we think not so much of the guilt as of the misery. I have sometimes read sermons upon the inclination of the sinner to evil, in which it has been very powerfully proved, and certainly the pride of human nature has been well humbled and brought low; but one thing always strikes me, if it is left out, as being a very great omission; viz., the doctrine that man is *guilty* in all these things. If his heart is against God, we ought to tell him it is his sin; and if he cannot repent, we ought to show him that sin is the sole cause of his disability—that all his alienation from God is sin—that as long as he keeps from God it is sin. I fear many of us here must acknowledge that we do not charge the sin of it to our own consciences. Yes, say we, we have many corruptions. Oh! yes. But we sit down very contented. My brethren, we ought not to do so. The having those corruptions is our crime which should be confessed as an enormous evil; and if I, as a minister of the gospel, do not press home the sin of the thing, I have missed what is the very virus of it. I have left out the very essence, if I have not shown that it is a crime. Now, "The carnal mind is enmity against God." What a sin it is! This will appear in two ways. Consider the relation in which we stand to God, and then remember what God is; and after I have spoken of these two things, I hope you will see, indeed, that it is a sin to be at enmity with God.

What is God to us? He is the Creator of the heavens and the earth; he bears up the pillars of the universe; his breath perfumes the flowers; his pencil paints them; he is the author of this fair creation; "we are the sheep of his pasture; he hath made us, and not we ourselves." He stands to us in the relationship of a Maker and Creator; and from that fact he claims to be our King. He is our legislator, our law-maker; and then, to make our crime still worse and worse, he is the ruler of providence; for it is he who keeps us from day to day. He supplies our wants; he keeps the breath within our nostrils; he bids the blood still pursue its course through the veins; he holdeth us in life, and preventeth us from death; he standeth before us, our creator, our king, our sustainer, our benefactor; and I ask, is it not a sin of enormous magnitude—is it not high treason against the emperor of heaven—is it not an awful sin, the depth of which we cannot fathom with the line of all our judgment—that we, his creatures, dependent upon him, should be at enmity with God?

But the crime may seem to be worse when we think of *what God is.* Let me appeal personally to you in an interrogatory style, for this has weight with it. Sinner! why art thou at enmity with God? God is the God of love; he is kind to his creatures; he regards you with his love of benevolence; for this very day his sun hath shone upon you, this day you have had food and raiment, and you have come up here in health and strength. Do you hate God because he loves you? Is that the reason? Consider how many mercies you have received at his hands all your life long! You are born with a body not deformed; you have had a tolerable share of health; you have been recovered many times from sickness; when lying at the gates of death, his arm has held back your soul from the last step to destruction. Do you hate God for all this? Do you hate him because he spared your life by his tender mercy? Behold his goodness that he hath spread before you! He might have sent you to hell; but you are here. Now, do you hate God for sparing you? Oh, wherefore art thou at enmity with him? My fellow creature, dost thou not know that God sent his Son from his bosom, hung him on the tree, and there suffered him to die for sinners, the just for the unjust? And dost thou hate God for that? Oh, sinner! is this the cause of thine enmity? Art thou so estranged that thou givest enmity for love? And when he surroundeth thee with favors, girdeth thee with mercies, encircleth thee with loving kindness, dost thou hate him for this? He might say, as Jesus did to the Jews, "For which of these works do ye stone me?" For which of these works do ye hate God? Did an earthly benefactor feed you, would you hate him? Did he clothe you, would you abuse him to his face? Did he give you talents, would you turn those powers against him? Oh, speak! Would you forge the iron and strike the dagger into the heart of your best friend? Do you hate your mother, who nursed you on her knee? Do you curse your father, who so wisely watched over you? Nay, ye say, we have some little gratitude towards earthly relatives. Where are your hearts, then? Where are your hearts, that ye can still despise God, and be at enmity with him? Oh! diabolical crime! Oh! satanic enormity! Oh! iniquity for which words fail in description! To hate the all-lovely — to despise the essentially good — to abhor the constantly merciful — to spurn the ever beneficent — to scorn the kind, the gracious one; above all, to hate the God who sent his son to die for man! Ah! in that thought, "The carnal mind is enmity against God:" there is something which may make us shake; for it is a terrible sin to be at enmity with God. I would I could speak more powerfully, but my Master alone can impress upon you the enormous evil of this horrid state of heart.

IV. But there are one or two doctrines which we will try to deduce from this. Is the carnal mind at enmity against God? Then *salvation cannot be by merit;* it must be by grace. If we are at enmity with God, what merit can we have? How can we deserve anything from the being we hate? Even if we were pure as Adam, we could not have any merit; for I do not think Adam had any desert before his Creator. When he had kept all his master's law he was but an unprofitable servant: he had done no more than he ought to have done; he had no surplus, no balance. But since we have become enemies, how much less can we hope to be saved by works! Oh! no; but the whole Bible tells us, from beginning to end, that salvation is not by the works of the law, but by the deeds of grace. Martin Luther declared that he constantly preached justification by faith alone, "because," said he, "the people would forget it; so that I was obliged almost to knock my Bible against their heads, to send it into their hearts." So it is true: we constantly forget that salvation is by grace alone. We always want to be putting in some little scrap of our own virtue; we want to be doing something. I remember a saying of old Matthew Wilkes: "Saved by your works! you might as well try to go to America in a paper boat!" Saved by your works! It is impossible! Oh! no, the poor legalist is like a blind horse going round and round the mill, or like the prisoner going up the treadwheel, and finding himself no higher after all he has done; he has no solid confidence, no firm ground to rest upon. He has not done enough — "never enough;" conscience always says, "this is not perfection; it ought to have been better." Salvation for enemies must be by an ambassador, — by an atonement, — yea, by Christ.

Another doctrine we gather from this is, *the necessity of an entire change of our nature.* It is true, that by birth we are at enmity with God. How necessary then it is that our nature should be changed! There are few people who sincerely believe this. They think that if they cry, "Lord, have mercy upon me," when they lay a-dying, they shall go to heaven directly. Let me suppose an impossible case for a moment. Let me imagine a man entering heaven without a change of heart. He comes within the gates. He hears a sonnet. He starts! It is to the praise of his *enemy.* He sees a throne, and on it sits one who is glorious; but it is his *enemy.* He walks streets of gold, but those streets belong to his *enemy.* He sees hosts of angels; but those hosts are the servants of his *enemy.* He is in an *enemy's* house: for he is at *enmity* with God. He could not join the song, for he would not know the tune. There he would stand, silent, motionless; till Christ would say, with a voice louder than ten thousand thunders, "What dost thou here? Enemies at a marriage banquet? Enemies in the children's house? Enemies in heaven? Get thee gone? 'Depart, ye cursed, into everlasting fire in hell!'" Oh! sirs, if the unregenerate man could enter heaven, I mention once more, the oft-repeated saying of Whitfield, he would be so unhappy in heaven, that he would ask God to let him run down to hell for shelter. There must be a change, if ye consider the future state; for how can enemies to God ever sit down at the banquet of the Lamb?

And to conclude, let me remind you—and it is in the text after all—that *this change must be worked by a power beyond your own.* An enemy may possibly make himself a friend; but *enmity* cannot. If it be but an adjunct of his nature to be an enemy, he may change himself into a friend; but if it is the very essence of his existence to be enmity, positive enmity, enmity cannot change itself. No, there must be something done more than we can accomplish. This is just what is forgotten in these days. We must have more preaching of the Holy Spirit, if we are to have more conversion work. I tell you, sirs, if you change yourselves, and make yourselves better, and better, and better, a thousand times, you will never be good enough for heaven, till God's Spirit has laid his hand upon you; till he has renewed the heart, till he has purified the soul, till he has changed the entire spirit and new-made the man, there can be no entering heaven. How seriously, then, should each stand and think. Here am I, a creature of a day, a mortal born to die, but yet an immortal! At present I am at enmity with God. What shall I do? Is it not my duty, as well as my happiness, to ask whether there be a way to be reconciled to God?

O, weary slaves of sin, are not your ways the paths of folly? Is it wisdom, O my fellow-creatures, is it wisdom to hate your Creator? Is it wisdom to stand in opposition against him? Is it prudent to despise the riches of his grace? If it be wisdom, it is hell's wisdom; if it be wisdom, it is a wisdom which is folly with God. Oh! may God grant that you may turn unto Jesus with full purpose of heart! He is the ambassador; he it is who can make peace through his blood; and though you came in here an enemy, it is possible you may go out through that door a friend yet, if you can but look to Jesus Christ, the brazen serpent which was lifted up.

And now, it may be, some of you are convinced of sin, by the Holy Spirit. I will now proclaim to you the way of salvation. "As Moses lifted up the serpent in the wilderness, even so must the Son of man be lifted up: that whosoever believeth in him should not perish, but have eternal life." Behold, O trembling penitent, the means of thy deliverance. Turn thy tearful eye to yonder Mount of Calvary! See the victim of justice — the sacrifice of atonement for your transgression. View the Saviour in his agonies, with streams of blood purchasing thy soul, and with intensest agonies enduring thy punishment. He died for *thee*, if now thou dost confess thy guilt. O come thou condemned one, self-condemned, and turn thine eye this way, for one look will save. Sinner! thou art bitten. Look! It is nought but "Look!" It is simply "Look!" If thou canst but look to Jesus thou art safe. Hear the voice of the Redeemer: "Look unto me, and be ye saved." Look! Look! Look! O guilty souls.

> "Venture on him, venture wholly,
> Let no other trust intrude;
> None but Jesus
> Can do helpless sinners good."

May my blessed Master help you to come to him, and draw you to his Son, for Jesu's sake. Amen and Amen.

SERMON XIII.

CHRIST'S PEOPLE—IMITATORS OF HIM.

"Now when they saw the boldness of Peter and John, and perceived that they were unlearned and ignorant men, they marvelled; and they took knowledge of them, that they had been with Jesus." — ACTS iv. 13.

BEHOLD! what a change divine grace will work in a man, and in how short a time. That same Peter, who so lately followed his master *afar off*, and with oaths and curses denied that he knew his name, is now to be found side by side with the loving John, boldly declaring that there is salvation in none other name save that of Jesus Christ, and preaching the resurrection of the dead, through the sacrifice of his dying Lord. The Scribes and Pharisees soon discover the reason of his boldness. Rightly did they guess that it rested not in his learning or his talents, for neither Peter nor John had been educated; they had been trained as fishermen; their education was a knowledge of the sea—of the fisherman's craft: none other had they: their boldness could not therefore spring from the self-sufficiency of knowledge, but from the Spirit of the living God. Nor did they acquire their courage from their station; for rank will confer a sort of dignity upon a man, and make him speak with a feigned authority, even when he has no talent or genius; but these men were, as it says in the original text, "ιδιωται," private men, who stood in no official capacity; men without rank or station. When they saw the boldness of Peter and John, and perceived that they were unlearned and private individuals, they marvelled, and they came to a right conclusion as to the source of their power — they had been dwelling with Jesus. Their conversation with the Prince of light and glory, backed up, as they might also have known, by the influence of the Holy Spirit, without which even that eminently holy example would have been in vain, had made them bold for their Master's cause. Oh! my brethren, it were well if this commendation, so forced from the lips of enemies, could also be compelled by our own example. If we could live like Peter and John; if our lives were "living epistles of God, known and read of all men;" if, whenever we were seen, men would take knowledge of us, that we had been with Jesus, it would be a happy thing for this world, and a blessed thing for us. It is concerning that I am to speak to you this morning; and as God gives me grace, I will endeavor to stir up your minds by way of remembrance, and urge you so to imitate Jesus Christ, our heavenly pattern, that men may perceive that you are disciples of the holy Son of God.

First, then, this morning, I will tell you *what a Christian should be;* secondly, I will tell you *when he should be so;* thirdly, *why he should be so;* and then, fourthly, *how he can be so.*

I. As God may help us then, first of all, we will speak of *what a believer should be.* A Christian should be a striking likeness of Jesus Christ. You have read lives of Christ, beautifully and eloquently written, and you have admired the talent of the persons who could write so well; but the best life of Christ is his living biography, written out in the words and actions of his people. If we, my brethren, were what we profess to be; if the Spirit of the Lord were in the heart of all his children, as we could desire; and if, instead of having abundance of formal professors, we were all possessors of that vital grace, I will tell you not only what we ought to be, but what we should be: we should be pictures of Christ, yea, such striking likenesses of him that the world would not have to hold us up by the hour together, and say, "Well, it seems somewhat of a likeness;" but they would, when they once beheld us, exclaim, "He has been with Jesus; he has been taught of him; he is like him; he has caught the very idea of the holy Man of Nazareth, and he expands it out into his very life and every day actions."

In enlarging upon this point, it will be necessary to premise, that when we here affirm that men should be such and such a thing, we refer to the people of God. We do not wish to speak to them in any legal way. We are not under the law, but under grace. Christian men hold themselves bound to keep all God's precepts; but the reason why they do so is, not because the *law* is binding upon them, but because the *gospel* constrains them: they believe, that having been redeemed by blood divine; having been purchased by Jesus Christ, they are more bound to keep his commands, than they would have been if they were under the law; they hold themselves to be ten thousand fold more debtors to God, than they could have been under the Mosaic dispensation. Not of force; not of compulsion; not through fear of the whip; not through legal bondage; but through pure, disinterested love and gratitude to God, they lay themselves out for his service, seeking to be Israelites indeed, in whom there is no guile. This much I have declared lest any man should think that I am preaching works as the way to salvation; I will yield to none in this, that I will ever maintain that by grace we are saved, and not by ourselves; but equally must I testify, that where the grace of God is, it will produce fitting deeds. To these I am ever bound to exhort you, while ye are ever expected to have good works for necessary purposes. Again, I do not, when I say that a believer should be a striking likeness of Jesus, suppose that any one Christian will perfectly exhibit all the features of our Lord and Saviour Jesus Christ; yet, my brethren, the fact that perfection is beyond our reach, should not diminish the ardor of our desire after it. The artist, when he paints, knows right well that he shall not be able to excel Apelles; but that does not discourage him; he uses his brush with all the greater pains, that he may at least in some humble measure resemble the great master. So the sculptor, though persuaded that he will not rival Praxiteles, will hew out the marble still, and seek to be as near the model as possible. Thus so the Christian man; though he feels he never can mount to the heights of complete excellence, and perceives that he never can on earth become the exact image of Christ, still holds it up before him, and measures his own deficiencies by the distance between himself and Jesus. This will he do; forgetting all he has attained, he will press forward, crying, *Excelsior!* going upwards still, desiring to be conformed more and more to the image of Christ Jesus.

First, then, a Christian should be like Christ in his *boldness*. This is a virtue now-a-days called impudence, but the grace is equally valuable by whatever name it may be called. I suppose if the Scribes had given a definition of Peter and John, they would have called them impudent fellows.

Jesus Christ and his disciples were noted for their courage. "When they saw the boldness of Peter and John, they took knowledge of them, that they had been with Jesus." Jesus Christ never fawned upon the rich; he stooped not to the great and noble; he stood erect, a man before men — the prophet of the people — speaking out boldly and freely what he thought. Have you never admired that mighty deed of his, when going to the city where he had lived and been brought up? Knowing that a prophet had no honor in his own country, the book was put into his hands (he had but then commenced his ministry), yet without tremor he unrolled the sacred volume, and what did he take for his text? Most men, coming to their own neighborhood, would have chosen a subject adapted to the taste, in order to earn fame. But what doctrine did Jesus preach that morning? One which in our age is scorned and hated — the doctrine of *election*. He opened the Scriptures, and began to read thus: "Many widows were in Israel in the days of Elias, when the heaven was shut up three years and six months, when great famine was throughout all the land; but unto none of them was Elias sent, save unto Sarepta, a city of Sidon, unto a woman that was a widow. And many lepers were in Israel in the time of

Eliseus, the prophet; and none of them was cleansed, saving Naaman, the Syrian." Then he began to tell, how God saveth whom he pleases, and rescues whom he chooses. Ah! how they gnashed their teeth upon him, dragged him out, and would have cast him from the brow of the hill. Do you not admire his intrepidity? He saw their teeth gnashing; he knew their hearts were hot with enmity while their mouths foamed with revenge and malice; still he stood like the angel who shut the lions' mouths; he feared them not; faithfully he proclaimed what he knew to be the truth of God, and still read on, despite them all. So, in his discourses. If he saw a Scribe or a Pharisee in the congregation, he did not keep back part of the price, but pointing his finger, he said, "Woe unto you, Scribes and Pharisees, hypocrites;" and when a lawyer came, saying, "Master, in speaking thus, thou condemnest us also;" he turned round and said, "Woe unto you, lawyers, for ye bind heavy burdens upon men, while ye yourselves will not touch them with so much as one of your fingers." He dealt out honest truth; he never knew the fear of man; he trembled at none; he stood out God's chosen, whom he had anointed above his fellows, careless of man's esteem. My friends, be like Christ in this. Have none of the time-serving religion of the present day, which is merely exhibited in evangelical drawing-rooms, — a religion which only flourishes in a hot-bed atmosphere, a religion which is only to be perceived in good company. No; if ye are the servants of God, be like Jesus Christ, bold for your master; never blush to own your religion; your profession will never disgrace you — take care you never disgrace *that*. Your love to Christ will never dishonor you; it may bring some temporary slight from your friends, or slanders from your enemies: but live on, and you shall live down their calumnies; live on, and ye shall stand amongst the glorified, honored even by those who hissed you, when *he* shall come to be glorified by his angels, and admired by them that love him. Be like Jesus, very valiant for your God, so that when they shall see your boldness, they may say, "He has been with Jesus."

But no one feature will give a portrait of a man; so the one virtue of boldness will never make you like Christ. There have been some who have been noble men, but have carried their courage to excess; they have thus been caricatures of Christ, and not portraits of him. We must amalgamate with our boldness the *loveliness* of Jesus' disposition. Let courage be the brass, let love be the gold. Let us mix the two together, so shall we produce a rich Corinthian metal, fit to be manufactured into the beautiful gate of the temple. Let your love and courage be mingled together. The man who is bold may indeed accomplish wonders. John Knox did much, but he might perhaps have done more if he had had a little love. Luther was a conqueror—peace to his ashes, and honor to his name!—still, we who look upon him at a distance, think that if he had sometimes mixed a little mildness with it—if, while he had the *fortiter in re*, he had been also *suaviter in modo*, and spoken somewhat more gently, he might have done even more good than he did. So, brethren, while we too are bold, let us ever imitate the loving Jesus. The child comes to him; he takes it on his knee, saying, "Suffer little children to come unto me, and forbid them not." A widow has just lost her only son: he weeps at the bier, and with a word restores life to the dead man. He sees a paralytic, a leper, or a man long confined to his bed; he speaks, they rise, and are healed. He lived for others, not for himself. His constant labors were without any motive, except the good of those who lived in the world. And to crown all, ye know the mighty sacrifice he made, when he condescended to lay down his life for man — when on the tree, quivering with agony, and hanging in the utmost extremity of suffering, he submitted to die for our sakes, that we might be saved. Behold in Christ love consolidated! He was one mighty pillar of benevolence. As God is love, so Christ is love. Oh, ye Christians, be ye loving also. Let your love and your beneficence beam out on all men. Say not, "Be ye warmed, and be ye filled," but "give a portion to seven, and also to eight." If ye cannot imitate Howard, and unlock the prison doors — if ye cannot visit the sad house of misery, yet each in your proper sphere speak kind words, do kind actions; live out Christ again in the kindness of your life. If there is one virtue which most commends Christians, it is that of kindness: it is to love the people of God, to love the church, to love the world, to love all. But how many have we in our churches of crab-tree Christians, who have mixed such a vast amount of vinegar and such a tremendous quantity of gall in their constitutions, that they can scarcely speak one good word to you; they imagine it impossible to defend religion except by passionate ebullitions; they cannot speak for their dishonored Master without being angry with their opponent; and if anything is awry, whether it be in the house, the church, or anywhere else, they conceive it to be their duty to set their faces like flint, and to defy everybody. They are like isolated icebergs, no one cares to go near them. They float about on the sea of forgetfulness, until at last they are melted and gone; and though, good souls, we shall be happy enough to meet them in heaven, we are precious glad to get rid of them from the earth. They were always so unamiable in disposition, that we would rather live an eternity with them in heaven than five minutes on earth. Be ye not thus, my brethren. Imitate Christ in your loving spirits; speak kindly, act kindly, and do kindly, that men may say of you, "He has been with Jesus."

Another great feature in the life of Christ was his deep and *sincere humility;* in which let us imitate him. While we will not cringe or bow—(far from it; we are the freemen whom the truth makes free; we walk through this world equal to all, inferior to none)—yet we would endeavor to be like Christ, continually humble. Oh, thou proud Christian, (for though it be a paradox there must be some, I think; I would not be so uncharitable as to say that there are not some such persons) if thou art a Christian, I bid thee look at thy Master, talking to the children, bending from the majesty of his divinity to speak to mankind on earth, tabernacling with the peasants of Galilee, and then—aye, depth of condescension unparalleled—washing his disciples' feet, and wiping them with the towel after supper. This is your Master, whom ye profess to worship; this is your Lord, whom ye adore. And ye, some of you who count yourselves Christians, cannot speak to a person who is not dressed in the same kind of clothing as yourselves, who have not exactly as much money per year as you have. In England, it is true that a sovereign will not speak to a shilling, and a shilling will not notice a sixpence, and a sixpence will sneer at a penny. But it should not be so with Christians. We ought to forget caste, degree, and rank, when we come into Christ's church. Recollect, Christian, who your Master was — a man of the poor. He lived with them; he ate with them. And will ye walk with lofty heads and stiff necks, looking with insufferable contempt upon your meaner fellow-worms? What are ye? The meanest of all, because your trickeries and adornments make you proud. Pitiful, despicable souls ye are! How small ye look in God's sight! Christ was humble; he stooped to do anything which might serve others. He had no pride; he was an humble man, a friend of publicans and sinners, living and walking with them. So, Christian, be thou like thy Master — one who can stoop; yea, be thou one who thinks it no stooping, but rather esteems others better than himself, counts it his honor to sit with the poorest of Christ's people, and says, "If my name may be but written in the obscurest part of the book of life, it is enough for me, so unworthy am I of his notice!" Be like Christ in his humility.

So might I continue, dear brethren, speaking of the various characteristics of Christ Jesus; but as you can think of them as well as I can, I shall not do so. It is easy for you to sit down and paint Jesus Christ, for you have him drawn out here in his word. I find that time would fail me if I were to give you an entire likeness of Jesus; but let me say, imitate him in his *holiness*. Was he zealous for his master? So be you. Ever go about doing good. Let not time be wasted. It is too precious. Was he self-denying, never looking to his own interest? So be you. Was he devout? So be you fervent in your prayers. Had he deference to his Father's will? So submit yourselves to him. Was he patient? So learn to endure. And best of all, as the highest portraiture of Jesus, try to forgive your enemies as he did; and let those sublime words of your Master, "Father, forgive them, for they know not what they do," always ring in your ears. When you are prompted to revenge; when hot anger starts, bridle the steed at once, and let it not dash forward with you headlong. Remember, anger is temporary insanity. Forgive as you hope to be forgiven. Heap coals of fire on the head of your foe by your kindness to him. Good for evil, recollect, is god-like. Be god-like, then; and in all ways, and by all means, so live that your enemies may say, "He has been with Jesus."

II. Now, *when should Christians be this?* For there is an idea in the world that persons ought to be very religious on a Sunday, but that it does not matter what they are on a Monday. How many pious preachers are there on a Sabbath-day, who are very impious preachers during the rest of the week! How many are there who come up to the house of God with a solemn countenance, who join the song and profess to pray, yet have neither part nor lot in the matter, but are "in the gall of bitterness and in the bonds of iniquity!" This is true of some of you who are present here. When should a Christian, then, be like Jesus Christ? Is there a time when he may strip off his regimentals — when the warrior may unbuckle his armor, and become like other men? Oh! no; at all times and in every place let the Christian be what he professes to be. I remember talking some time ago with a person who said, "I do not like visitors who come to my house and introduce religion; I think we ought to have religion on the Sabbath-day, when we go to the house of God, but not in the drawing-room." I suggested to the individual that there would be a great deal of work for the upholsterers, if there should be no religion except in the house of God. "How is that?" was the question. "Why," I replied, "we should need to have beds fitted up in all our places of worship, for surely we need religion to die with, and consequently, every one would want to die there." Aye, we all need the consolations of God at last; but how can we expect to enjoy them unless we obey the precepts of religion during life? My brethren, let me say, be ye like Christ at all times. Imitate him in *public*. Most of us live in some sort of publicity; many of us are called to work before our fellow-men every day. We are watched; our words are caught; our lives are examined, taken to pieces. The eagle-eyed, argus-eyed world observes everything we do, and sharp critics are upon us. Let us live the life of Christ in public. Let us take care that we exhibit our Master, and not ourselves — so that we can say, "It is no longer I that live, but Christ that liveth in me." Take heed that you carry this into the *church* too, you who are church members. Be like Christ in the church. How many there are of you like Diotrephes, seeking pre-eminence? How many are trying to have some dignity and power over their fellow Christians, instead of remembering that it is the fundamental rule of all our churches, that there all men are equal — alike brethren, alike to be received as such. Carry out the spirit of Christ, then, in your churches, wherever ye are; let your fellow members say of you, "He has been with Jesus."

But, most of all, take care to have religion in your *houses*. A religious house is the best proof of true piety. It is not my chapel, it is my house — it is not my minister, it is my home-companion who can best judge me; it is the servant, the child, the wife, the friend, that can discern most of my real character. A good man will improve his household. Rowland Hill once said, he would not believe a man to be a true Christian if his wife, his children, the servants, and even the dog and cat, were not the better for it. That is being religious. If your household is not the better for your Christianity — if men cannot say, "This is a better house than others," then be not deceived — ye have nothing of the grace of God. Let not your servant, on leaving your employ, say, "Well, this is a queer sort of a religious family, there was no prayer in the morning; I began the day with my drudgery; there was no prayer at night; I was kept at home all the Sabbath-day. Once a fortnight, perhaps, I was allowed to go out in the afternoon, when there was nowhere to go to where I could hear a gospel sermon. My master and mistress went to a place where of course they heard the blessed gospel of God, — that was all for them; as for me, I might have the dregs and leavings of some overworked curate in the afternoon." Surely, Christian men will not act in that way. No! Carry out your godliness in your family. Let every one say that you have practical religion. Let it be known and read in the house, as well as in the world. Take care of your character there; for what we are there, we really are. Our life abroad is often but a borrowed part, the actor's part of a great scene, but at home the vizard is removed, and men are what they seem. Take care of your home duties.

Yet again, my brethren, before I leave this point, imitate Jesus in *secret.* When no eye seeth you except the eye of God, when darkness covers you, when you are shut up from the observation of mortals, even then be ye like Jesus Christ. Remember his ardent piety, his secret devotion — how, after laboriously preaching the whole day, he stole away in the midnight shades to cry for help from his God. Recollect how his entire life was constantly sustained by fresh inspirations of the Holy Spirit, derived by prayer. Take care of your secret life: let it be such that you will not be ashamed to read at the last great day. Your inner life is written in the book of God, and it shall one day be open before you. If the entire life of some of you were known, it would be no life at all: it would be a death Yea, even of some true Christians we may say, it is scarce a *life.* It is a dragging on of an existence — one hasty prayer a day — one breathing, just enough to save their souls alive, but no more. O my brethren strive to be more like Jesus Christ. These are times when we want more secret prayer. I have had much fear all this week. I know not whether it is true; but when I feel such a thing I like to tell it to those of you who belong to my own church and congregation. I have trembled lest, by being away from our own place, you have ceased to pray as earnestly as you once did. I remember your earnest groans and petitions — how you would assemble together in the house of prayer in multitudes, and cry out to God to help his servant.

23

We cannot meet in such style at present; but do you still pray in private? Have you forgotten me? Have you ceased to cry out to God? Oh! my friends, with all the entreaties that a man can use, let me appeal to you. Recollect who I am, and what I am — a child, having little education, little learning, ability, or talent; and here am I called upon, week after week, to preach to this crowd of people. Will ye not, my beloved, still plead for me? Has not God been pleased to hear your prayers ten thousand times? And will ye now cease, when a mighty revival is taking place in many churches? Will ye now stop your petitions? Oh! no; go to your houses, fall upon your knees, cry aloud to God to enable you still to hold up your hands like Moses on the hill, that Joshua below may fight and overcome the Amalekites. Now is the time for victory: shall we lose it? This is the high tide that will float us over the bar; now let us put out the oars; let us pull by earnest prayer, crying for God the spirit to fill the sails! Ye who love God, of every place and every denomination, wrestle for your ministers; pray for them; for why should not God even now put out his Spirit? What is the reason why we are to be denied Pentecostal seasons? Why not this hour, as one mighty band, fall down before him and entreat him, for his Son's sake, to revive his drooping church? Then would all men discern that we are verily the disciples of Christ.

III. But now, thirdly, *why should Christians imitate Christ?* The answer comes very naturally and easily, Christians should be like Christ, first, *for their own sakes.* For their honesty's sake, and for their credit's sake, let them not be found liars before God and men.

For their own healthful state, if they wish to be kept from sin and preserved from going astray, let them imitate Jesus. For their own happiness' sake, if they would drink wine on the lees well refined; if they would enjoy holy and happy communion with Jesus; if they would be lifted up above the cares and troubles of this world, let them imitate Jesus Christ. Oh! my brethren, there is nothing that can so advantage you, nothing can so prosper you, so assist you, so make you walk towards heaven rapidly, so keep your head upwards towards the sky, and your eyes radiant with glory, like the imitation of Jesus Christ. It is when, by the power of the Holy Spirit, you are enabled to walk with Jesus in his very footsteps, and tread in his ways, you are most happy and you are most known to be the sons of God. For your own sake, my brethren, I say, be like Christ.

Next, for *religion's sake*, strive to imitate Jesus. Ah! poor religion, thou hast been sorely shot at by cruel foes, but thou hast not been wounded one half so much by them as by thy friends. None have hurt thee, O Christianity, so much as those who profess to be thy followers. Who have made these wounds in this fair hand of godliness? I say, the professor has done this, who has not lived up to his profession; the man who with pretences enters the fold, being nought but a wolf in sheep's clothing. Such men, sirs, injure the gospel more than others: more than the laughing Infidel, more than the sneering critic, doth the man hurt our cause who professes to love it, but in his actions doth belie his love. Christian, lovest thou that cause? Is the name of the dear Redeemer precious to thee? Wouldst thou see the kingdoms of the world become the kingdoms of our Lord and his Christ? Dost thou wish to see the proud man humbled and the mighty abased? Dost thou long for the souls of perishing sinners, and art thou desirous to win them, and save their souls from the everlasting burning? Wouldst thou prevent their fall into the regions of the damned? Is it thy desire that Christ should see the travail of his soul, and be abundantly satisfied? Doth thy heart yearn over thy fellow-immortals? Dost thou long to see them forgiven? Then be consistent with thy religion. Walk *before God* in the land of the living. Behave as an elect man should do. Recollect what manner of people we ought to be in all holy conversation and godliness. This is the best way to convert the world; yea, such conduct would do more than even the efforts of missionary societies, excellent as they are. Let but men see that our conduct is superior to others, then they will believe there is something in our religion; but, if they see us quite the contrary to what we avow, what will they say? "These religious people are no better than others! Why should we go amongst them?" And they say quite rightly. It is but common-sense judgment. Ah! my friends, if ye love religion for her own sake, be consistent, and walk in the love of God. Follow Christ Jesus.

Then, to put it in the strongest form I can, let me say, *for Christ's sake*, endeavor to be like him. Oh! could I fetch the dying Jesus here, and let him speak to you! My own tongue is tied this morning, but I would make his blood, his scars, and his wounds speak. Poor dumb mouths, I bid each of them plead in his behalf. How would Jesus, standing here, show you his hands this morning! "My friends," he would say, "behold me!

these hands were pierced for you; and look ye here at this my side. It was opened as the fountain of your salvation. See my feet; there entered the cruel nails. Each of these bones were dislocated for your sake. These eyes gushed with torrents of tears. This head was crowned with thorns. These cheeks were smitten; this hair was plucked; my body became the centre and focus of agony. I hung quivering in the burning sun; and all for you, my people. And will ye not love me now? I bid you be like me. Is there any fault in me? Oh! no. Ye believe that I am fairer than ten thousand fairs, and lovelier than ten thousand loves. Have I injured you? Have I not rather done all for your salvation? And do I not sit at my Father's throne, and e'en now intercede on your behalf? If ye love me,"— Christian, hear that word; let the sweet syllables ring for ever in your ears, like the prolonged sounding of silver-toned bells;—"if ye love me, if ye love me, keep my commandments." O Christian, let that "if" be put to thee this morning. "If ye love me." Glorious Redeemer! is it an "if" at all? Thou precious, bleeding Lamb, can there be an "if"? What, when I see thy blood gushing from thee; is it an "if"? Yes, I weep to say it is an "if." Oft my thoughts make it "if," and oft my words make it "if." But yet methinks my soul feels it is not "if," either.

> "Not to mine eyes is light so dear,
> Nor friendship half so sweet."

"Yes, I love thee, I know that I love thee. Lord, thou knowest all things, thou knowest that I love thee," can the Christian say. "Well, then," says Jesus, looking down with a glance of affectionate approbation, "*since* thou lovest me, keep my commandments." O beloved, what mightier reason can I give than this? It is the argument of love and affection. Be like Christ, since gratitude demands obedience; so shall the world know that ye have been with Jesus.

IV. Ah! then ye wept; and I perceive ye felt the force of pity, and some of you are inquiring, "How can I imitate him?" It is my business, then, before you depart, to tell you how you can become transformed into the image of Christ.

In the first place, then, my beloved friends, in answer to your inquiry, let me say, you must know Christ as your Redeemer before you can follow him as your Exemplar. Much is said about the example of Jesus, and we scarcely find a man now who does not believe that our Lord was an excellent and holy man, much to be admired. But excellent as his example, it would be impossible to imitate it, had he not also been our sacrifice. Do ye this morning know that his blood was shed for you? Can ye join with me in this verse?—

"O the sweet wonders of that cross,
Where God the Saviour lov'd and died;
Her noblest life my spirit draws
From his dear wounds and bleeding side."

If so, you are on a fair way to imitate Christ. But do not seek to copy him until you are bathed in the fountain filled with blood drawn from his veins. It is not possible for you to do so; your passions will be too strong and corrupt, and you will be building without a foundation, a structure, which will be about as stable as a dream. You cannot mould your life to his pattern until you have had his spirit, till you have been clothed in his righteousness. "Well," say some, "we have proceeded so far, what next shall we do? We know we have an interest in him, but we are still sensible of manifold deficiencies." Next, then, let me entreat you to study Christ's character. This poor Bible is become an almost obsolete book, even with some Christians. There are so many magazines, periodicals, and such like ephemeral productions, that we are in danger of neglecting to search the Scriptures. Christian, wouldst thou know thy master? Look at him. There is a wondrous power about the character of Christ, for the more you regard it the more you will be conformed to it. I view myself in the glass, I go away, and forget what I was. I behold Christ, and I become like Christ. Look at him, then; study him in the evangelists, studiously examine his character. "But," say you, "we have done that, and we have proceeded but little farther." Then, in the next place, correct your poor copy every day. At night, try and recount all the actions of the twenty-four hours, scrupulously putting them under review. When I have proof-sheets sent to me of any of my writings, I have to make the corrections in the margin. I might read them over fifty times, and the printers would still put in the errors if I did not mark them. So must you do, if you find anything faulty, at night make a mark in the margin, that you may know where the fault is, and to-morrow may amend it. Do this day after day, continually, noting your faults one by one, so that you may better avoid them. It was a maxim of the old philosophers, that, three times in the day, we should go over our actions. So let us do; let us not be forgetful; let us rather examine ourselves each night, and see wherein we have done amiss, that we may reform our lives.

Lastly, as the best advice I can give, seek more of the Spirit of God; for this is the way to become Christ-like. Vain are all your attempts to be like him till you have sought his spirit. Take the cold iron, and attempt to weld it if you can into a certain shape. How fruitless the effort! Lay it on the anvil, seize the blacksmith's hammer with all your might, let blow after blow fall upon it, and you shall have done nothing. Twist it, turn it, use all your implements, but you shall not be able to fashion it as you would. But put it in the fire, let it be softened and made made malleable, then lay it on the anvil, and each stroke shall have a mighty effect, so that you may fashion it into any form you may desire. So take your heart, not cold as it is, not stony as it is by nature, but put it into the furnace; there let it be molten, and after that it can be turned like wax to the seal, and fashioned into the image of Jesus Christ.

Oh, my brethren, what can I say now to enforce my text, but that, if ye are like Christ on earth, ye shall be like him in heaven? If by the power of the Spirit ye become followers of Jesus, ye shall enter glory. For at heaven's gate there sits an angel, who admits no one who has not the same features as our adorable Lord. There comes a man with a crown upon his head. "Yes," he says, "thou hast a crown, it is true, but crowns are not the medium of access here." Another approaches, dressed in robes of state and the gown of learning. "Yes," says the angel, "it may be good, but gowns and learning are not the marks that shall admit you here." Another advances, fair, beautiful, and comely. "Yes," saith the angel, "that might please on earth, but beauty is not wanted here." There cometh up another, who is heralded by fame, and prefaced by the blast of the clamor of mankind; but the angel saith, "It is well with man, but thou hast no right to enter here." Then there appears another; poor he may have been; illiterate he may have been; but the angel, as he looks at him, smiles and says, "It is Christ again; a second edition of Jesus Christ is there. Come in, come in. Eternal glory thou shalt win. Thou art like Christ; in heaven thou shalt sit, because thou art like him." Oh! to be like Christ is to enter heaven; but to be unlike Christ is to descend to hell. Likes shall be gathered together at last, tares with tares, wheat with wheat. If ye have sinned with Adam and have died, ye shall lie with the spiritually dead forever, unless ye rise in Christ to newness of life; then shall we live with him throughout eternity. Wheat with wheat, tares with tares. "Be not deceived; God is not mocked: whatsoever a man soweth, that shall he also reap." Go away with this one thought, then, my brethren, that you can test yourselves by Christ. If you are like Christ, you are of Christ, and shall be with Christ. If you are unlike him, you have no portion in the great inheritance. May my poor discourse help to fan the floor and reveal the chaff; yea, may it lead many of you to seek to be partakers of the inheritance of the saints in light, to the praise of his grace. To him be all honor given! Amen.

SERMON XIV.

THOUGHTS ON THE LAST BATTLE.

"The sting of death is sin; and the strength of sin is the law. But, thanks be unto God, which giveth us the victory through our Lord Jesus Christ."—1 Cor. xv. 56, 57.

While the Bible is one of the most poetical of books, though its language is unutterably sublime, yet we must remark how constantly it is true to nature. There is no straining of a fact, no glossing over a truth. However dark may be the subject, while it lights it up with brilliance, yet it does not deny the gloom connected with it. If you will read this chapter of Paul's epistle, so justly celebrated as a master-piece of language, you will find him speaking of that which is to come after death with such exultation and glory that you feel, "If this be to die, then it were well to depart at once." Who has not rejoiced, and whose heart has not been lifted up or filled with a holy fire, while he has read such sentences as these: "In a moment, in the twinkling of an eye, at the last trump: for the trumpet shall sound, and the dead shall be raised incorruptible, and we shall be changed. For this corruptible must put on incorruption, and this mortal must put on immortality. So, when this corruptible shall have put on incorruption, and this mortal shall have put on immortality, then shall be brought to pass the saying that is written, Death is swallowed up in victory. O death, where is thy sting? O grave, where is thy victory?" Yet, with all that majestic language, with all that bold flight of eloquence, he does not deny that death is a gloomy thing. Even his very figures imply it. He does not laugh at it; he does not say, "Oh, it is nothing to die;" he describes death as a monster, he speaks of it as having a sting; he tells us wherein the strength of that sting lies; and even in the exclamation of triumph, he imputes that victory not to unaided flesh, but he says, "Thanks be to God, who giveth us the victory through our Lord Jesus Christ."

When I select such a text as this, I feel that I cannot preach from it. The thought o'ermasters me; my words do stagger; there are no utterances that are great enough to convey the mighty meaning of this wondrous text. If I had the eloquence of all men united in one, if I could speak as never man spake, (with the exception of that one godlike man of Nazareth) I could not compass so vast a subject as this. I will not therefore pretend to do so, but offer you such thoughts as my mind is capable of producing.

To night we shall speak of three things: first, *the sting of death;* secondly, *the strength of sin;* and thirdly, *the victory of faith.*

I. First, *the sting of death.* The apostle pictures death as a terrible dragon, or monster, which, coming upon all men, must be fought with by each one for himself. He gives us no hopes whatever that any of us can avoid it. He tells us of no bridge across the river Death; he does not give us the faintest hope that it is possible to emerge from this state of existence into another without dying: he describes the monster as being exactly in our path, and with it we must fight, each man personally, separately, and alone; each man must die; we all must cross the black stream; each one of us must go through the iron gate. There is no passage from this world into another without death. Having told us, then, that there is no hope of our escape, he braces up our nerves for the combat; but he gives us no hope that we shall be able to slay the monster; he does not tell us that we can strike our sword into his heart, and so overturn and overwhelm death; but pointing to the dragon, he seems to say, "Thou canst not slay it, man; there is no hope that thou shouldst ever put thy foot upon its neck and crush its head; but one thing can be done—it has a sting which thou mayest extract; thou canst not crush death under foot, but thou mayest pull out the sting which is deadly; and then thou need not fear the monster, for monster it shall be no longer, but rather it shall be a swift winged angel to waft thee aloft to heaven." Where, then, is the sting of this dragon? Where must I strike? What is the sting? The apostle tells us, "that the sting of death is sin." Once let me cut off that, and then, though death may be dreary and solemn, I shall not dread it; but, holding up the monster's sting, I shall exclaim, "O death, where is thy sting? O grave, where is thy victory?" Let us now dwell upon the fact, that "the sting of death is sin."

1. First, sin puts a sting into death, from the fact that *sin brought death into the world.* Men could be more content to die if they did not know it was a punish-

ment. I suppose if we had never sinned, there would have been some means for us to go from this world to another. It cannot be supposed that so huge a population would have existed, that all the myriads who have lived from Adam down till now could ever have inhabited so small a globe as this; there would not have been space enough for them. But there might have been provided some means for taking us off when the proper time should come, and bearing us safely to heaven. God might have furnished horses and chariots of fire for each of his Elijahs; or, as it was said of Enoch, so it might have been declared of each of us, "He *is* not, for God hath taken him." Thus to die, if we may call it death to depart from this body and to be with God, would have been no disgrace; in fact, it would have been the highest honor: fitting the loftiest aspiration of the soul, to live quickly its little time in this world, then to mount and be with its God; and in the prayers of the most pious and devout man, one of his sublimest petitions would be, "O God, hasten the time of my departure, when I shall be with thee." When such sinless beings thought of their departure, they would not tremble, for the gate would be one of ivory and pearl — not as now, of iron — the stream would be as nectar, far different from the present "bitterness of death." But alas! how different! Death is now the punishment of sin. "In the day thou eatest thereof thou shalt surely die." "*In Adam* all die." By his sin every one of us become subject to the penalty of death, and thus, being a punishment, death has its sting. To the best man, the holiest Christian, the most sanctified intellect, the soul that has the nearest and dearest intercourse with God, death must appear to have a sting, because sin was its mother. O fatal offspring of sin, I only dread thee because of thy parentage! If thou didst come to me as an honor, I could wade through Jordan even now, and, when its chilling billows were around me, I would smile amidst its surges; and in the swellings of Jordan, my song should swell too, and the liquid music of my voice should join with the liquid swellings of the floods, "Hallelujah! It is blessed to cross to the land of the glorified." This is one reason why the sting of sin is death.

2. But I must take it in another sense. "The sting of death is sin:"—that is to say, *that which shall make death most terrible to man will be sin, if it is not forgiven.* If that be not the exact meaning of the apostle, still it is a great truth, and I may find it here. If sin lay heavy on me and were not forgiven—if my transgressions were unpardoned—if such were the fact, (though I rejoice to know it is not so) it would be the very sting of death to me. Let us consider a man dying, and looking back on his past life: he will find in death a sting, and that sting will be his past sin. Imagine a conqueror's deathbed. He has been a man of blood from his youth up. Bred in the camp, his lips were early set to the bugle, and his hand, even in infancy, struck the drum. He had a martial spirit; he delighted in the fame and applause of men; he loved the dust of battle and the garment rolled in blood. He has lived a life of what men call glory. He has stormed cities, conquered countries, ravaged continents, overrun the world. See his banners hanging in the hall, and the marks of glory on his escutcheon. He is one of earth's proudest warriors. But now he comes to die; and when he lies down to expire, what shall

invest his death with horror? It shall be his sin. Methinks I see the monarch dying; he lies in state; around him are his nobles and his councillors; but there is somewhat else there. Hard by his side there stands a spirit from Hades; it is a soul of a departed woman. She looks on him and says, "Monster! my husband was slain in battle through thy ambition: I was made a widow, and my helpless orphans and myself were starved." And she passes by. Her husband comes, and opening wide his bloody wounds, he cries, "Once I called thee monarch; but, by thy vile covetousness, thou didst provoke an unjust war. See here these wounds — I gained them in the siege. For thy sake I mounted first the scaling ladder; this foot stood upon the top of the wall, and I waved my sword in triumph, but in hell I lifted up my eyes in torment. Base wretch, thine ambition hurried me thither!" Turning his horrid eyes upon him, he passes by. Then up comes another, and another, and another yet: waking from their tombs, they stalk around his bed and haunt him; the dreary procession still marches on, looking at the dying tyrant. He shuts his eyes, but he feels the cold and bony hand upon his forehead; he quivers, for the sting of death is in his heart. "O Death!" says he; "to leave this large estate, this mighty realm, this pomp and power — this were somewhat; but to meet those men, those women, and those orphan children, face to face; to hear them saying, 'Art thou become like one of us?' while kings whom I have dethroned, and monarchs whom I have cast down shall rattle their chains in my ears, and say, 'Thou wast our destroyer, but how art thou fallen from heaven, O Lucifer, son of the morning! How art thou brought down as in a moment from thy glory and thy pride!'" There, you see, the sting of death would be the man's sin. It would not sting him that he had to die, but that he had sinned, that he had been a bloody man, that his hands were red with wholesale murder — this would plague him indeed, for "the sting of death is sin."

Or, suppose another character — a minister. He has stood before the world, proclaiming something which he called the gospel. He has been a noted preacher; the multitude have been hanging on his lips; they have listened to his words; before his eloquence a nation stood amazed, and thousands trembled at his voice. But his preaching is over; the time when he can mount the pulpit is gone; another standing-place awaits him, another congregation, and he must hear another and a better preacher than himself. There he lies. He has been unfaithful to his charge. He preached philosophy to charm his people, instead of preaching truth and aiming at their hearts. And, as he pants upon his bed, that worst and most accursed of men — for surely none can be worse than he — there comes up one, a soul from the pit, and looking him in the face, says, "I came to thee once, trembling on account of sin; I asked thee the road to heaven, and thou didst say, 'Do such and such good works,' and I did them, and am damned. Thou didst tell me an untruth; thou didst not declare plainly the word of God." He vanishes only to be followed by another; he has been an irreligious character, and as he sees the minister upon his deathbed, he says, "Ah! and art thou here? Once I strolled into thy house of prayer, but thou hadst such a sermon that I could not understand. I listened; I wanted to hear something from thy lips, some truth that might burn my soul and make me repent; but I knew not what thou saidst; and here I am." The ghost stamps his foot, and the man quivers like an aspen leaf, because he knows it is all true. Then the whole congregation arise before him as he lies upon his bed; he looks upon the motley group; he beholds the snowy heads of the old, and the glittering eyes of the young; and lying there upon his pillow, he pictures all the sins of his past life, and he hears it said, "Go thou! unfaithful to thy charge; thou didst not divest thyself of thy love of pomp and dignity; thou didst not speak

> 'As though thou ne'er might'st speak again,
> A dying man to dying men.'"

Oh! it may be something for that minister to leave his charge, somewhat for him to die; but worst of all, the sting of death will be his sin: to hear his parish come howling after him to hell; to see his congregation following behind him in one mingled herd, he having led them astray, having been a false prophet instead of a true one, speaking peace, peace, where there was no peace, deluding them with lies, charming them with music, when he ought rather to have told them in rough and rugged accents the Word of God. Verily, it is true, it is true, the sting of death to such a man shall be his great, his enormous, his heinous sin of having deluded others.

Thus, then, having painted two full-length pictures, I might give each one of you miniatures of yourselves. I might picture thee, O drunkard, when thy cups are drained, and when thy liquor shall no longer be sweet to thy taste, when worse than gall shall be the dainties that thou drinkest, when, within an hour, the worms shall make a carnival upon thy flesh; I might picture thee as thou lookest back upon thy misspent life. And thou, O swearer, methinks I see thee there, with thine oaths echoed back by memory to thine own dismay. And thou, man of lust and wickedness, thou who hast debauched and seduced others, I see thee there; and the sting of death to thee, how horrible, how dreadful! It shall not be that thou art groaning with pain, it shall not be that thou art racked with agony, it shall not be that thy heart and flesh faileth, but the sting, the sting, shall be thy sin. How many in this place can spell the word "remorse?" I pray you may never know its awful meaning. Remorse, remorse! You know its derivation; it signifies to bite. Ah! now we dance with our sins — it is a merry life with us — we take their hands, and, sporting in the noontide sun, we dance, we dance, and live in joy. But then those sins shall bite us. The young lions we have stroked and played with shall bite; the young adder, the serpent, whose azure hues have well delighted us, shall bite, shall sting, when remorse shall occupy our souls. I might, but I will not, tell you a few stories of the awful power of remorse; it is the first pang of hell; it is the ante-chamber of the pit. To have remorse is to feel the sparks that blaze upwards from the fire of the bottomless Gehennam; to feel remorse is to have eternal torment commenced within the soul. The sting of death shall be unforgiven, unrepented sin.

3. But if sin in the retrospect be the sting of death, what must *sin in the prospect be?* My friends, we do not often enough look at what sin is to be. We see what it is; first the seed, then the blade, then the ear,

and then the full corn in the ear. It is the wish, the imagination, the desire, the sight, the taste, the deed; but what is sin in its next development? We have observed sin as it grows; we have seen it, at first, a very little thing, but expanding itself until it has swelled into a mountain. We have seen it like "a little cloud, the size of a man's hand," but we have beheld it gather until it covered the skies with blackness, and sent down drops of bitter rain. But what is sin to be in the next state? We have gone so far, but sin is a thing that cannot stop. We have seen whereunto it *has* grown, but whereunto *will* it grow? for it is not ripe when we die; it has to go on still; it is set going, but it has to unfold itself forever. The moment we die, the voice of justice cries, "Seal up the fountain of blood; stop the stream of forgiveness; he that is holy let him be holy still; he that is filthy let him be filthy still." And after that, the man goes on growing filthier and filthier still; his lust developes itself, his vice increases; all those evil passions blaze with tenfold more fury, and, amidst the companionship of others like himself, without the restraints of grace, without the preached word, the man becomes worse and worse; and who can tell whereunto his sin may grow? I have sometimes likened the hour of our death to that celebrated picture, which I think you have seen in the National Gallery, of Perseus holding up the head of Medusa. That head turned all persons into stone who looked upon it. There is a warrior there with a dart in his hand; he stands stiffened, turned into stone, with the javelin even in his fist. There is another, with a poniard beneath his robe, about to stab; he is now the statue of an assassin, motionless and cold. Another is creeping along stealthily, like a man in ambuscade, and there he stands a consolidated rock; he has looked only upon that head, and he is frozen into stone. Well, such is death. What I am when death is held before me, that I must be forever. When my spirit goes, if God finds me hymning his praise, I shall hymn it in heaven; doth he find me breathing out oaths, I shall follow up those oaths in hell. Where death leaves me judgment finds me. As I die, so shall I live eternally.

> "There are no acts of pardon passed
> In the cold grave to which we haste."

It is forever, forever, forever! Ah! there are a set of heretics in these days who talk of short punishment, and preach about God's transporting souls for a term of years, and then letting them die. Where did such men learn their doctrine, I wonder? I read in God's word that the angel shall plant one foot upon the earth, and the other upon the sea, and shall swear by him that liveth and was dead, that *time* shall be no longer. But, if a soul could die in a thousand years, it would die in *time;* if a million of years could elapse, and then the soul could be extinguished, there would be such a thing as *time;* for, talk to me of years, and there is *time.* But, sirs, when that angel has spoken the word, "*Time* shall be no longer," things will then be eternal; the spirit shall proceed in its ceaseless revolution of weal or woe, never to be stayed, for there is no time to stop it; the fact of its stopping would imply time; but everything shall be eternal, for time shall cease to be. It well becomes you, then, to consider where ye are and what ye are. Oh! stand and tremble on the narrow neck of land 'twixt the two unbounded seas, for God in heaven alone can tell how soon thou mayest be launched upon the eternal future. May God grant that, when that last hour may come, we may be prepared for it! Like the thief, unheard, unseen, it steals through night's dark shade. Perhaps, as here I stand, and rudely speak of these dark, hidden things, soon may the hand be stretched, and dumb the mouth that lisps the faltering strain. Oh! thou that dwellest in heaven, thou power supreme, thou everlasting King, let not that hour intrude upon me in an ill-spent season; but may it find me rapt in meditation high, hymning my great Creator. So, in the last moment of my life, I will hasten beyond the azure, to bathe the wings of this my spirit in their native element, and then to dwell with thee forever,

> "Far from a world of grief and sin,
> With God eternally shut in."

II. "The strength of sin is the law."

I have attempted to show how to fight this monster —it is by extracting and destroying its sting. I prepare myself for the battle. It is true I have sinned, and therefore I have put a sting into death, but I will endeavor to take it away. I attempt it, but the monster laughs me in the face, and cries, "The strength of sin is the law. Before thou canst destroy sin thou must in some way satisfy the law. Sin cannot be removed by thy tears or by thy deeds, for the law is its strength; and until thou hast satisfied the vengeance of the law, until thou hast paid the uttermost farthing of its demands, my sting cannot be taken away, for the very strength of sin is the law." Now, I must try and explain this doctrine that the strength of sin is the law.

Most men think that sin has no strength at all. "Oh," say many, "we may have sinned very much, but we will repent, and we will be better for the rest of our lives; no doubt God is merciful, and he will forgive us." And we hear many divines often speak of sin as if it were a very venial thing. Inquire of them what is a man to do? There is no deep repentance required, no real inward workings of divine grace, no casting himself upon the blood of Christ. They never tell us about a complete atonement having been made. They have, indeed, some shadowy idea of an atonement, that Christ died just as a matter of form to satisfy justice; but as to any literal taking away of our sins, and suffering the actual penalty for us, they do not consider that God's law requires any such thing. I suppose they do not, for I never hear them assert the positive satisfaction and substitution of our Lord Jesus Christ. But without that, how can we take away the strength of sin?

1. The strength of sin is in the law, first, in this respect, that *the law being spiritual, it is quite impossible for us to live without sin.* If the law were merely carnal, and referred to the flesh; if it simply related to open and overt actions, I question, even then, whether we could live without sin; but when I turn over the ten commandments and read, "Thou shalt not covet," I know it refers even to the wish of my heart. It is said, "Thou shalt not commit adultery;" but it is said, also, that whosoever looketh on a woman to lust after her hath already committed that sin. So that it is not merely the act, it is the thought; it is not the deed simply, it is the very imagination, that is a sin. Oh now sinner, how canst thou get rid of sin? Thy very thoughts, the inward workings of thy mind, these

are crimes — this is guilt and desperate wickedness. Is there not, now, strength in sin? Hath not the law put a potency in it? Has it not nerved sin with such a power that all thy strength cannot hope to wipe away the black enormity of thy transgression?

2. Then, again, the law puts strength into sin in this respect — that *it will not abate one tittle of its stern demands.* It says to every man who breaks it, "I will not forgive you." You hear persons talk about God's mercy. Now, if they do not believe in the gospel they must be under the law; but where in the law do we read of mercy? If you will read the commandments through, there is a curse after them, but there is no provision made for pardon. The law itself speaks not of that; it thunders out without the slightest mitigation, "The soul that sinneth it shall die." If any of you desire to be saved by works, remember one sin will spoil your righteousness; one dust of this earth's dross will spoil the beauty of that perfect righteousness which God requires at your hands. If ye would be saved by works, men and brethren, ye must be as holy as the angels, ye must be as pure and as immaculate as Jesus; for the law requires perfection, and nothing short of it; and God, with unflinching vengeance, will smite every man low who cannot bring him a perfect obedience. If I cannot, when I come before his throne, plead a perfect righteousness as being mine, God will say, "you have not fulfilled the demands of my law; depart, accursed one! You have sinned, and you must die." "Ah," says one, "can we ever have a perfect righteousness, then?" Yes, I will tell you of that in the third point; thanks be unto Christ, who giveth us the victory through his blood and through his

righteousness, who adorns us as a bride in her jewels, as a husband arrays his wife with ornaments.

3. Yet again; the law gives strength to sin from the fact that, *for every transgression, it will exact a punishment.* The law never remits a farthing of debt: it says, "Sin — punishment." They are linked together with adamantine chains; they are tied, and cannot be severed. The law speaks not of sin and mercy; mercy comes in the gospel. The law says, "Sin — die; transgress — be chastised; sin — hell." Thus are they linked together. Once let me sin, and I may go to the foot of stern Justice, and as, with blind eyes, she holds the scales, I may say, "O Justice, remember, I was holy once; remember that on such and such an occasion I did keep the law." "Yes," saith Justice, "all I owe thee thou shalt have; I will not punish thee for what thou hast not done; but remember you *this* crime, O sinner?" and she puts in the heavy weight. The sinner trembles, and he cries, "But canst thou not forget that? Wilt thou not cast it away?" "Nay," saith Justice, and she puts in another weight. "Sinner, dost thou recollect *this* crime?" "Oh!" says the sinner, "wilt thou not for mercy's sake —?" "I will not have mercy," says Justice; "Mercy has its own palace, but I have nought to do with forgiveness here; mercy belongs to Christ. If you will be saved by Justice, you shall have your full of it. If you come to me for salvation, I will not have mercy brought in to help me; she is not my vicegerent; I stand here alone without her." And again, as she holds the scales, she puts in another iniquity, another crime, another enormous transgression; and each time the man begs and prays that he may have that passed by. Says Justice, "Nay,

I must exact the penalty; I have sworn I will, and I will. Canst thou find a substitute for thyself? If thou canst, there is the only room I have for mercy. I will exact it of that substitute, but even at his hands I will have the utmost jot and tittle; I will abate nothing; I am God's Justice, stern and unflinching, I will not alter, I will not mitigate the penalty." She still holds the scales. The plea is in vain. "Never will I change!" she cries; "bring me the blood, bring me the price to its utmost; count it down, or else, sinner, thou shalt die.

Now, my friends, I ask you, if ye consider the spirituality of the law, the perfection it requires, and its unflinching severity, are you prepared to take away the sting of death in your own persons? Can you hope to overcome sin yourselves? Can you trust that, by some righteous works, you may yet cancel your guilt? If you think so, go, O foolish one, go! O madman, go! work out thine own salvation with fear and trembling, without the God that worketh in thee; go, twist thy rope of sand; go, build a pyramid of air; go, prepare a house with bubbles, and think it is to last forever; but know it will be a dream with an awful awakening, for as a dream when one awaketh will he despise alike your image and your righteousness. "The strength of sin is the law."

III. But now, in the last place, we have before us *the victory of faith*. The Christian is the only champion who can smite the dragon of death, and even *he* cannot do it of himself; but when he has done it, he shall cry, "Thanks be to God who giveth us the victory through our Lord Jesus Christ." One moment, and I will show you how the Christian can look upon death with complacency, through the merits of Jesus Christ.

First, Christ has taken away the strength of sin in this respect, *that he has removed the law.* We are not under bondage, but under grace. Law is not our directing principle, grace is. Do not misunderstand me. The principle that I *must* do a thing — that is to say, the principle of law, "do, or be punished; do, or be rewarded," is not the motive of the Christian's life; his principle is grace: "God has done so much for me, what ought I to do for him?" We are not under the law in that sense, but under grace.

Then Christ has removed the law in this sense, that *he has completely satisfied it.* The law demands a perfect righteousness; Christ says, "Law, thou hast it; find fault with me; I am the sinner's substitute; have I not kept thy commandments? Wherein have I violated thy statutes?" "Come here, my beloved," he says, and then he cries to Justice, "Find a fault in this man; I have put my robe upon him; I have washed him in my blood; I have cleansed him from his sin. All the past is gone; as for the future, I have secured it by sanctification; as for the penalty, I have borne it myself; at one tremendous draught of love I have drunk that man's destruction dry; I have borne what he should have suffered; I have endured the agonies he ought to have endured. Justice, have I not satisfied thee? Did I not say upon the tree, and didst thou not coincide with it, 'It is finished; it is finished?' Have I not made so complete an atonement that there is now no need for that man to die and expiate his guilt? Do I not complete the perfect righteousness of this poor once condemned, but now justified spirit?" "Yes," saith Justice, "I am well satisfied, and even more content, if possible, than if the sinner had brought a spotless righteousness of his own." And now, what saith the Christian after this? Boldly he comes to the realms of death, and entering the gates there, he cries, "Who shall lay anything to the charge of God's elect?" And when he had said it, the dragon drops his sting. He descends into the grave; he passes by the place where fiends lie down in fetters of iron; he sees their chains, and looks into the dungeon where they dwell, and as he passes by the prison door, he shouts, "Who shall lay anything to the charge of God's elect?" They growl and bite their iron bonds, and hiss in secret, but they cannot lay aught to his charge. Now see him mount aloft. He approaches God's heaven, he comes against the gates, and Faith still triumphantly shouts, "Who shall lay anything to the charge of God's elect?" And a voice comes from within: "Not Christ, for he hath died; not God, for he hath justified." Received by Jesus, Faith enters heaven, and again she cries, "Who even here amongst the spotless and ransomed, shall lay anything to the charge of God's elect?" Now the law is satified, sin is gone; and now surely we need not fear the sting of the dragon, but we may say, as Paul did, when he rose into the majesty of poetry — such beautiful poetry that Pope himself borrowed his words, only transposing the sentences, "O grave, where is thy victory? O death, where is thy sting?"

If it were necessary to night, I might speak to you concerning the *resurrection*, and I might tell you how much that takes away the sting of death, but I will confine myself to the simple fact, that the sting of death is sin, that the strength of sin is the law, and that Christ gives us the victory by taking the sting away, and removing the strength of sin by his perfect obedience.

And now, sirs, how many are there here who have any hope that for them Christ Jesus died? Am I coming too close home, when most solemnly I put the question to each one of you, as I stand in God's presence this night, to free my head of your blood; as I stand and appeal with all the earnestness this heart is capable of, "Are you prepared to die? Is sin pardoned? is the law satisfied? Can you view the flowing

> "Of Christ's soul-redeeming blood,
> With Divine assurance knowing,
> That he hath made your peace with God?"

O! can ye now put one hand upon your heart, and the other upon the Bible, and say, "God's word and I agree; the witness of the Spirit here and the witness there are one. I have renounced my sins, I have given up my evil practices; I have abhorred my own righteousness; I trust in nought but Jesus' doings; simply do I depend on him.

> 'Nothing in my hands I bring,
> Simply to thy cross I cling.'"

If so, should you die where you are — sudden death were sudden glory.

But, my hearers, shall I be faithful with you? or shall I belie my soul? Which shall it be? Are there not many here who, each time the bell tolls the departure of a soul, might well ask the question, "Am I prepared?" and they must say, "No." I shall not turn prophet to-night; but were it right for me to say so, I fear not one half of you are prepared to die. Is that true? Yea, let the speaker ask himself the question,

"Am I prepared to meet my Maker face to face?" Oh, sit in your seat and catechise your souls with that solemn question. Let each one ask himself, "Am I prepared, should I be called, to die?" Methinks I hear one say with confidence, "I know that my Redeemer liveth." "Let him that thinketh he standeth take heed lest he fall." I hear another say with trembling accents,

> "Ah! guilty, weak, and helpless worm,
> On Christ's kind arms I fall;
> He is my strength and righteousness,
> My Jesus and my all."

Yes, sweet words! I would rather have written that one verse than Milton's "Paradise Lost." It is such a matchless picture of the true condition of the believing soul. But I hear another say, "I shall not answer such a question as that. I am not going to be dull to-day. It may be gloomy weather outside to-day, but I do not want to be made melancholy." Young man, young man, go thy way. Let thine heart cheer thee in the days of thy youth; but for all this the Lord shall bring thee to judgment. What wilt thou do, careless spirit, when thy friends have forsaken thee, when thou art alone with God? Thou dost not like to be alone, young man, now, dost thou? A falling leaf will startle thee. To be alone an hour will bring on an insufferable feeling of melancholy. But thou wilt be alone — and a dreary alone it will be — with God an enemy! How wilt thou do in the swellings of Jordan? What wilt thou do when he taketh thee by the hand at eventide, and asketh thee for an account; when he says, "What didst thou do in the beginning of thy days? how didst thou spend thy life?" When he asks thee, "Where are the years of thy manhood?" When he questions thee about thy wasted Sabbaths, and inquires how thy latter years were spent, what wilt thou say then? Speechless, without an answer, thou wilt stand. Oh, I beseech you, as ye love yourselves, take care! Even now, begin to weigh the solemn matters of eternal life. Oh! say not, "Why so earnest? why in such haste?" Sirs, if I saw you lying in your bed, and your house was on fire, the fire might be at the bottom of the house, and you might slumber safely for the next five minutes; but with all my might I would pull you from your bed, or I would shout, "Awake! awake! the flame is under thee." So, with some of you who are sleeping over hell's mouth, slumbering over the pit of perdition, may I not awake you? may I not depart a little from clerical rules, and speak to you as one speaketh to his fellow whom he loves? Ah! if I loved you not, I need not be here. It is because I wish to win your souls, and, if it be possible, to win for my Master some honor, that I would thus pour out my heart before you. As the Lord liveth, sinner, thou standest on a single plank over the mouth of hell, and that plank is rotten. Thou hangest over the pit by a solitary rope, and the strands of that rope are breaking. Thou art like that man of old, whom Dionysius placed at the head of the table; before him was a dainty feast, but the man ate not, for directly over his head was a sword suspended by a hair. So art thou, sinner. Let thy cup be full, let thy pleasures be high, let thy soul be elevated, seest thou that sword? The next time thou sittest in the theatre, look up and see that sword; the next time thou art in a tavern, look at that sword; when next in thy business thou scornest the rules of God's gospel, look at that sword. Though thou seest it not it is there. Even now, ye may hear God saying to Gabriel, "Gabriel, that man is sitting in his seat in the Hall; he is hearing, but is as though he heard not; unsheathe thy blade; let the glittering sword cut through that hair; let the weapon fall upon him and divide his soul and body." *Stop, thou Gabriel, stop!* Save the man a little while. Give him yet an hour, that he may repent. Oh, let him not die. True, he has been here these ten or a dozen nights, and he has listened without a tear; but stop, and peradventure he may repent yet. Jesus backs up my entreaty, and he cries, "Spare him yet another year, till I dig about him and dung him, and though he now cumbers the ground, he may yet bring forth fruit, that he may not be hewn down and cast into the fire." I thank thee, O God; thou wilt not cut him down to-night; but to-morrow may be his last day. Ye may never see the sun rise, though you have seen it set. Take heed. Hear the word of God's gospel, and depart with God's blessing. "Whosoever believeth on the name of the Lord Jesus Christ shall be saved." "He that believeth and is baptized shall be saved." "He is able to save to the uttermost, all that come unto him." "Whosoever cometh unto him, he will in no wise cast out." Let every one that heareth say, "Come; whosoever is athirst, let him come and take of the water of life, freely."

SERMON XV.

HEAVEN AND HELL.*

"And I say unto you, that many shall come from the east and west, and shall sit down with Abraham, and Isaac, and Jacob, in the kingdom of heaven. But the children of the kingdom shall be cast out into outer darkness: there shall be weeping and gnashing of teeth.—MATTHEW viii. 11, 12.

THIS is a land where plain speaking is allowed, and where the people are willing to afford a fair hearing to any one who can tell them that which is worth their attention. To-night I am quite certain of an attentive audience, for I know you too well to suppose otherwise. This field, as you are all aware, is private property; and I would just give a suggestion to those who go out in the open air to preach—that it is far better to get into a field, or a plot of unoccupied building-ground, than to block up the roads and stop business; it is moreover far better to be somewhat under protection, so that we can at once prevent disturbance.

To-night, I shall, I hope, encourage you to seek the road to heaven. I shall also have to utter some very sharp things concerning the end of the lost in the pit

---

* Delivered in open air, at Hackney, to an audience of twelve thousand persons.

of hell. Upon both these subjects I will try and speak, as God helps me. But, I beseech you, as you love your souls, weigh right and wrong this night; see whether what I say be the truth of God. If it be not, reject it utterly, and cast it away; but if it is, at your peril disregard it; for, as you shall answer before God, the great Judge of heaven and earth, it will go ill with you if the words of his servant and of his Scripture be despised.

My text has two parts. The first is very agreeable to my mind, and gives me pleasure; the second is terrible in the extreme; but, since they are both the truth, they must be preached. The first part of my text is, "I say unto you, that many shall come from the east and west, and shall sit down with Abraham, and Isaac, and Jacob, in the kingdom of heaven." The sentence which I call the black, dark, and threatening part is this: "But the children of the kingdom shall be cast out into outer darkness: there shall be weeping and gnashing of teeth."

I. Let us take the first part. Here is a *most glorious promise.* I will read it again: "Many shall come from the east and west, and shall sit down with Abraham, and Isaac, and Jacob, in the kingdom of heaven." I like that text, because it tells me what heaven is, and gives me a beautiful picture of it. It says, it is a place where I shall sit down with Abraham, and Isaac, and Jacob. O what a sweet thought that is for the working man! He often wipes the hot sweat from his face, and he wonders whether there is a land where he shall have to toil no longer. He scarcely ever eats a mouthful of bread that is not moistened with the sweat of his brow. Often he comes home weary, and flings himself upon his couch, perhaps too tired to sleep. He says, "Oh! is there no land where I can rest? Is there no place where I can sit, and for once let these weary limbs be still? Is there no land where I can be quiet? Yes, thou son of toil and labor,

"There is a happy land
Far, far, away —"

where toil and labor are unknown. Beyond yon blue welkin there is a city fair and bright, it walls are jasper, and its light is brighter than the sun. There "the weary are at rest, and the wicked cease from troubling." Immortal spirits are yonder, who never wipe sweat from their brow, for "they sow not, neither do they reap;" they have not to toil and labor.

"There, on a green and flowery mount,
Their weary souls shall sit;
And with transporting joys recount
The labors of their feet."

To my mind, one of the best views of heaven is, that *it is a land of rest* — especially to the working man. Those who have not to work hard, think they will love heaven as a place of service. That is very true. But to the working man, to the man who toils with his brain or with his hands, it must ever be a sweet thought that there is a land where we shall rest. Soon, this voice will never be strained again; soon, these lungs will never have to exert themselves beyond their power; soon, this brain shall not be racked for thought; but I shall sit at the banquet-table of God; yea, I shall recline on the bosom of Abraham, and be at ease forever. Oh! weary sons and daughters of Adam, you will not have to drive the ploughshare into the unthankful soil in heaven, you will not need to rise to daily toils before the sun hath risen, and labor still when the sun hath long ago gone to his rest; but ye shall be still, ye shall be quiet, ye shall rest yourselves, for all are rich in heaven, all are happy there, all are peaceful. Toil, trouble, travail, and labor, are words that cannot be spelled in heaven; they have no such things there, for they always rest.

And mark the *good company they sit with.* They are to "sit down with Abraham, and Isaac, and Jacob." Some people think that in heaven we shall know nobody. But our text declares here, that we "shall sit down with Abraham, and Isaac, and Jacob." Then I am sure that we shall be aware that they are Abraham, and Isaac, and Jacob. I have heard of a good woman, who asked her husband, when she was dying, "My dear, do you think you will know me when you and I get to heaven?" "Shall I know you?" he said, "why, I have always known you while I have been here, and do you think I shall be a greater fool when I get to heaven?" I think it was a very good answer. If we have known one another here, we shall know one another there. I have dear departed friends up there, and it is always a sweet thought to me, that when I shall put my foot, as I hope I may, upon the threshhold of heaven, there will come my sisters and brothers to clasp me by the hand and say, "Yes, thou loved one, and thou art here." Dear relatives that have been separated, you will meet again in heaven. One of you has lost a mother — she is gone above; and if you follow the track of Jesus, you shall meet here there. Methinks I see yet another coming to meet you at the door of Paradise; and though the ties of natural affection may be in a measure forgotten, — I may be allowed to use a figure — how blessed would she be as she turned to God, and said, "Here am I, and the children that thou hast given me." We shall recognize our friends: — husband, you will know your wife again. Mother, you will know those dear babes of yours — you marked their features when they lay panting and gasping for breath. You know how ye hung over their graves when the cold sod was sprinkled over them, and it was said, "Earth to earth, dust to dust, and ashes to ashes." But ye shall hear those loved voices again: ye shall hear those sweet voices once more; ye shall yet know that those whom ye loved have been loved by God. Would not that be a dreary heaven for us to inhabit, where we should be alike unknowing and unknown? I would not care to go to such a heaven as that. I believe that heaven is a fellowship of the saints, and that we shall know one another there. I have often thought I should love to see Isaiah; and, as soon as I get to heaven, methinks, I would ask for him, because he spoke more of Jesus Christ than all the rest. I am sure I should want to find out good George Whitfield — he who so continually preached to the people, and wore himself out with a more than seraphic zeal. O yes! we shall have choice company in heaven when we get there. There will be no distinction of learned and unlearned, clergy and laity, but we shall walk freely one among another; we shall feel that we are brethren; we shall "sit down with Abraham, and Isaac, and Jacob." I have heard of a lady who was visited by a minister on her deathbed, and she said to him, "I want to ask you one question, now I am about to die." "Well," said the minister, "what is it?" "Oh!" said she, in a very affected way, "I want to know if there are two places in heaven, because I could not bear that Betsey in the kitchen should be in heaven along with me, she is so unrefined?" The minister turned round and said, "O don't trouble yourself about that, madam. There is no fear of that; for, until you get rid of your accursed pride, you will never enter heaven at all." We must all get rid of our pride. We must come down and stand on an equality in the sight of God, and see in every man a brother, before we can hope to be found in glory. Aye, we bless God, we thank him that there will be no separate table for one and for another. The Jew and the Gentile will sit down together. The great and the small shall feed in the same pasture, and we shall "sit down with Abraham, and Isaac, and Jacob, in the kingdom of heaven."

But my text hath a yet greater depth of sweetness, for it says, that "*many* shall come and shall sit down." Some narrow-minded bigots think that heaven will be a very small place, where there will be a very few people, who went to their chapel or their church. I confess, I have no wish for a very small heaven, and love to read in the Scriptures that there are many mansions in my Father's house. How often do I hear people say, "Ah! straight is the gate and narrow is the way, and few there be that find it. There will be very few in heaven; there will be most lost." My friend, I differ from you. Do you think that Christ will let the devil beat him? that he will let the devil have more in hell than there will be in heaven? No: it is impossible. For then Satan would laugh at Christ. There will be more in heaven than there are among the lost. God says, that "there will be a number that no man can number who will be saved;" but he never says, that there will be a number that no man can number that will be lost. There will be a host beyond all count who will get into heaven. What glad tidings for you and for me! for, if there are so many to be saved, why should not I be saved? why should not you? why should not yon man, over there in the crowd, say, "Cannot I be one among the multitude?" And may not that poor woman there take heart, and say, "Well, if there were but half-a-dozen saved, I might fear that I should not be one; but, since many are to come, why should not I also be saved?" Cheer up, disconsolate! Cheer up, son of mourning, child of sorrow, there is hope for thee still! I can never know that any man is past God's grace. There be a few that have sinned that sin that is unto death, and God gives them up; but the vast host of mankind are yet within the reach of sovereign mercy — "and many of them shall come from the east and from the west, and shall sit down in the kingdom of heaven."

Look at my text again, and you will see where these people come from. They are to "come from the east and west." The Jews said that they would all come from Palestine, every one of them, every man, woman, and child; that there would not be one in heaven that was not a Jew. And the Pharisees thought that, if they were not all Pharisees, they could not be saved. But Jesus Christ said, there will be many that will come from the east and from the west. There will be a multitude from that far off land of China, for God is doing a great work there, and we hope that the gospel will yet be victorious in that land. There will be a multitude from this western land of England, from the western country beyond the sea in America, and from the south in Australia, and from the north in Canada, Siberia, and Russia. From the uttermost parts of the earth there shall come many to sit down in the kingdom of God. But I do not think this text is to be understood so much geographically as spiritually. When it says that they "shall come from the east and west," I think it does not refer to nations particularly, but to different kinds of people. Now, "the east and the west" signify those who are the very furthest off from religion; yet many of them will be saved and get to heaven. There is a class of persons who will always be looked upon as hopeless. Many a time have I heard a man or woman say of such a one, "He cannot be saved: he is too abandoned. What is *he* good for? Ask *him* to go to a place of worship — he was drunk on Saturday night. What would be the use of reasoning with *him?* There is no hope for him. He is a hardened fellow. See what he has done these many years. What good will it be to speak to him? Now, hear this, ye who think your fellows worse than yourselves — ye who condemn others, whereas ye are often just as guilty: Jesus Christ says, "many shall come from the east and west." There will be many in heaven that were drunkards once. I believe, among that blood-bought throng, there are many who reeled in and out the tavern half their lifetime. But, by the power of divine grace, they were able to dash the liquor-cup to the ground. They renounced the riot of intoxication — fled away from it — and served God. Yes! Ther will be many in heaven who were drunkards on eartl

There will be many harlots: some of the most abandoned will be found there. You remember the story of Whitfield's once saying, that there would be some in heaven who were "the devil's castaways;" some that the devil would hardly think good enough for him, and yet whom Christ would save. Lady Huntingdon once gently hinted that such language was not quite proper. But, just at the time, there happened to be heard come a ring at the bell, and Whitfield went down stairs. Afterwards he came up and said, "Your ladyship, what do you think a poor woman had to say to me just now? She was a sad profligate, and she said, 'O, Mr. Whitfield, when you were preaching, you told us that Christ would take in the devil's castaways, and I am one of them,'" and that was the means of her salvation. Shall anybody ever check us from preaching to the lowest of the low? I have been accused of getting all the rabble of London around me. God bless the rabble! God save the rabble! then, say I. But, suppose they are "the rabble," who need the gospel more than they do? Who require to have Christ preached to them more than they do? We have lots of those who preach to ladies and gentlemen, and we want some one to preach to the rabble in these degenerate days. Oh! here is comfort for me, for many of the rabble are to come from the east and from the west. Oh! what would you think if you were to see the difference between some that are in heaven and some that shall be there? There might be found one whose hair hangs across his eyes, his locks are matted, he looks horrible, his bloated eyes start from his face, he grins almost like an idiot, he has drunk away his very brain until life seems to have departed, so far as sense and being are concerned; yet I would tell to you, "that man is capable of salvation"—and in a few years I might say "look up yonder;" see you that bright star? discern you that man with a crown of pure gold upon his head? do you notice that being clad in robes of sapphire and in garments of light? That is the selfsame man who sat there a poor benighted, almost idiotic being; yet sovereign grace and mercy have saved him! There are none, except those, as I have said before, who have sinned the unpardonable sin, who are beyond God's mercy. Fetch me out the worst, and still I would preach the gospel to them; fetch me out the vilest, still I would preach to them, because I recollect my Master said, "Go ye out into the highways and hedges and compel them to come in that my house may be filled." "Many shall come from the east and west, and shall sit down with Abraham, and Isaac, and Jacob, in the kingdom of heaven."

There is one more word I must notice before I have done with this sweet portion—that is the word "*shall.*" Oh! I love God's "shalls" and "wills." There is nothing comparable to them. Let a man say "shall," what is it good for? "I will," says man, and he never performs; "I shall," says he, and he breaks his promise. But it is never so with God's "shalls." If he says "shall" it shall be; when he says "will" it will be. Now he has said here, "many *shall* come." The devil says "they shall not come;" but "they shall come." Their sins say "you can't come;" God says you "shall come." You, yourselves, say, "you won't come;" God says "you shall come." Yes! there are some here who are laughing at salvation, who can scoff at Christ and mock at the gospel; but I tell you some of you shall come yet. "What!" you say, "can God make me become a Christian?" I tell you yes, for herein rests the power of the gospel. It does not ask your consent; but it gets it. It does not say, Will you have it? but it makes you willing in the day of God's power. Not against your will, but it makes you willing. It shows you its value, and then you fall in love with it; and straightway you run after it and have it. Many people have said, "we will not have anything to do with religion," yet they have been converted. I have heard of a man who once went to chapel to hear the singing, and as soon as the minister began to preach, he put his fingers in his ears and would not listen. But by-and-by some tiny insect settled on his face, so that he was obliged to take one finger out of his ears to brush it away. Just then the minister said, "he that hath ears to hear let him hear." The man listened; and God met with him at that moment to his soul's conversion. He went out a new man, a changed character. He who came in to laugh retired to pray; he who came in to mock went out to bend his knee in penitence; he who entered to spend an idle hour went home to spend an hour in devotion with his God. The sinner became a saint; the profligate became a penitent. Who knows that there may not be some like that here? The gospel wants not your consent, it gets it. It knocks the enmity out of your heart. You say, "I do not want to be saved;" Christ says you shall be. He makes your will turn round, and then you cry, "Lord, save, or I perish." Ah, might Heaven exclaim, "I knew I would make you say that;" and then he rejoices over you because he has changed your will and made you willing in the day of his power. If Jesus Christ were to stand on this platform to-night, what would many people do with him? "O!" say some, "we would make him a King." I do not believe it. They would crucify him again, if they had the opportunity. If he were to come and say, "Here I am, I love you, will you be saved by me?" not one of you would consent if you were left to your will. If he should look upon you with those eyes, before whose power the lion would have crouched; if he spoke with that voice which poured forth a cataract of eloquence like a stream of nectar rolling down from the cliffs above, not a single person would come to be his disciple. No; it wants the power of the Spirit to make men come to Jesus Christ. He himself said, "No man can come to me except the Father who hath sent me draw him." Ah! we want that; and here we have it. They shall come! they shall come! ye may laugh, ye may despise us; but Jesus Christ shall not die for nothing. If some of you reject him there are some that will not. If there are some that are not saved, others *shall* be. Christ *shall* see his seed, he *shall* prolong his days, and the pleasure of the Lord *shall* prosper in his hands. Some think that Christ died, and yet, that some for whom he died will be lost. I never could understand that doctrine. If Jesus, my surety, bore my griefs and carried my sorrows, I believe myself to be as secure as the angels in heaven. God cannot ask payment twice. If Christ paid my debt, shall I have to pay it again? No.

> "Free from sin I walk at large,
> The Saviour's blood 's my full discharge;
> At his dear feet content I lay,
> A sinner saved, and homage pay."

They shall come! They shall come! And nought in

heaven, nor on earth, nor in hell, can stop them from coming.

And now, thou chief of sinners, list one moment, while I call thee to Jesus. There is one person here to-night, who thinks himself the worst soul that ever lived. There is one who says to himself, "I do not deserve to be called to Christ, I am sure!" Soul! I call thee! thou lost, most wretched outcast, this night, by authority given me of God, I call thee to come to my Saviour. Sometime ago, when I went into the County Court to see what they were doing, I heard a man's name called out, and immediately the man said, "Make way! make way! they call me!" And up he came. Now, I call the chief of sinners to-night, and let him say, "Make way! make way doubts! make way fears! make way sins! Christ calls me! And if Christ calls me, that is enough!"

"I'll to his gracious feet approach
Whose sceptre mercy gives.
Perhaps he may command me "Touch!"
And then the suppliant lives.

"I can but perish if I go;
I am resolved to try,
For if I stay away, I know
I must forever die.

"But, should I die with mercies sought,
When I the king have tried,
That were to die, delightful thought!
As sinner never died."

Go and try my Saviour! Go and try my Saviour! If he casts you away after you have sought him, tell it in the pit, that Christ would not hear you. But *that* you shall never be allowed to do. It would dishonor the mercy of the covenant for God to cast away one penitent sinner; and it never shall be while it is written, "Many shall come from the east and west, and shall sit down with Abraham, and Isaac, and Jacob, in the kingdom of heaven."

II. The second part of my text is heart-breaking. I could preach with great delight to myself from the first part; but here is a dreary task to my soul, because there are gloomy words here. But, as I have told you, what is written in the Bible must be preached, whether it be gloomy or cheerful. There are some ministers who never mention anything about hell. I heard of a minister, who once said to his congregation, "If you do not love the Lord Jesus Christ, you will be sent to that place which it is not polite to mention." He ought not to have been allowed to preach again, I am sure, if he could not use plain words. Now, if I saw that house on fire over there, do you think I would stand and say, "I believe the operation of combustion is proceeding yonder?" No; I would call out "Fire! Fire!" and then everybody would know what I meant. So, if the Bible says, "The children of the kingdom shall be cast out into outer darkness," am I to stand here and mince the matter at all? God forbid! We must speak the truth as it is written. It is a terrible truth, for it says, "*the children of the kingdom* shall be cast out!" Now, who are those children? I will tell you. "The children of the kingdom" are those people who are noted for the externals of piety, but who have nothing of the internals of it. People whom you will see, with their Bibles and Hymn Books, marching off to chapel as religiously as possible, or going to church as devoutly and demurely as they can, looking as sombre and serious as parish beadles, and fancying that they are quite sure to be saved, though their heart is not in the matter; nothing but their bodies. These are the persons who are "the children of the kingdom." They have no grace, no life, no Christ, and they shall be cast into utter darkness.

Again, these people are *the children of pious fathers and mothers.* There is nothing touches a man's heart, mark you, like talking about his mother. I have heard of a swearing sailor, whom nobody could manage, not even the police, who was always making some disturbance wherever he went. Once he went into a place of worship, and no one could keep him still; but a gentleman went up and said to him, "Jack, you had a mother once." With that the tears ran down his cheeks. He said, "Ha! bless you, sir, I had; and I brought her gray hairs with sorrow to the grave, and a pretty fellow I am to be here to-night." He then sat down, quite sobered and subdued by the very mention of his mother. Ah! and there are some of you, "children of the kingdom," who can remember your mothers. Your mother took you on her knee and taught you early to pray; your father tutored you in the ways of godliness. And yet you are here to-night, without grace in your heart — without hope of heaven. You are going downwards towards hell as fast as your feet can carry you. There are some of you who have broken your poor mother's heart. Oh! if I could tell you what she has suffered for you when you have at night been indulging in your sin. Do you know what your guilt will be, ye "children of the kingdom," if ye perish after a pious mother's prayers and tears have fallen upon you? I can conceive of no one entering hell with a worse grace than the man who goes there with drops of his mother's tears on his head, and with his father's prayers following him at his heels. Some of you will inevitably endure this doom; some of you, young men and women, shall wake up one day and find yourselves in utter darkness, while your parents shall be up there in heaven, looking down upon you with upbraiding eyes, seeming to say, "What! after all we did for you, all we said, are ye come to this?" "Children of the kingdom!" do not think that a pious mother can save you. Do not think, because your father was a member of such-and-such a church, that his godliness will save you. I can suppose some one standing at heaven's gate, and demanding, "Let me in! Let me in!" What for? "Because my mother is in there." Your mother had nothing to do with you. If she was holy, she was holy for herself; if she was evil, she was evil for herself. "But my grandfather prayed for me?" That is no use: did you pray for yourself? "No; I did not." Then grandfather's prayers, and grandmother's prayers, and father's and mother's prayers may be piled on the top of one another till they reach the stars, but they never can make a ladder for you to go to heaven by. You must seek God for yourself; or rather God must seek you. You must have vital experience of godliness in your heart, or else you are lost, even though all your friends were in heaven. That was a dreadful dream which a pious mother once had, and told to her children. She thought the judgment-day was come. The great books were opened. They all stood before God. And Jesus Christ said, "Separate the chaff from the wheat; put the goats on the left hand, and the sheep on the right." The mother dreamed that she and her children were standing just in the middle of the great assembly. And the angel came, and said, "I must take the mother, she is a sheep: she must go to the right hand. The children are goats: they must go on the left." She thought as she went, her children clutched her, and said, "Mother, can we part? Must we be separated?" She then put her arms around them, and seemed to say, "My children, I would, if possible, take you with me." But in a moment the angel touched her: her cheeks were dried, and now, overcoming natural affection, being rendered supernatural and sublime, resigned to God's will, she said, "My children, I taught you well, I trained you up, and you forsook the ways of God; and now all I have to say is, Amen to your condemnation." Thereupon they were snatched away, and she saw them in perpetual torment, while she was in heaven. Young man, what will you think, when the last day comes, to hear Christ say, "Depart, ye cursed?" And there will be a voice just behind him, saying, Amen. And, as you inquire whence came the voice, you will find it was your mother. Or, young woman, when thou art cast away into utter darkness, what will you think to hear a voice saying, Amen. And as you look, there sits your father, his lips still moving with the solemn curse. Ah! "children of the kingdom," the penitent reprobates will enter heaven, many of them; publicans and sinners will get there; repenting drunkards and swearers will be saved; but many of the "children of the kingdom" will be cast out. Oh! to think that you who have been so well trained should be lost, while many of the worse will be saved. It will be the hell of hells for you to look up and see there "poor Jack," the drunkard, lying in Abraham's bosom, while you, who have had a pious mother, are cast into hell, simply because you would not believe on the Lord Jesus Christ, but put his gospel from you, and lived and died without it! That were the very sting of all, to see ourselves cast away, when the chief of sinners finds salvation.

Now list to me a little while — I will not detain you long — whilst I undertake the doleful task of telling you what is to become of these "children of the kingdom." Jesus Christ says they are to be "cast into utter darkness, where there is weeping and gnashing of teeth."

First, notice, they are to be *cast out.* They are not said to *go;* but, when they come to heaven's gates, they are to be *cast* out. As soon as hypocrites arrive at the gates of heaven, Justice will say, "There he comes! there he comes! He spurned a father's prayers, and mocked a mother's tears. He has forced his way downward against all the advantages mercy has supplied. And now, there he comes. Gabriel, take the man." The angel, binding you hand and foot, holds you one single moment over the mouth of the chasm. He bids you look down — down — down. There is no bottom; and you hear coming up from the abyss, sullen moans, and hollow groans, and screams of tortured ghosts. You quiver, your bones melt like wax, and your marrow quakes within you. Where is now thy might? and where thy boasting and bragging? Ye shriek and cry, ye beg for mercy; but the angel, with one tremendous grasp, seizes you fast, and then hurls you down, with the cry, "Away, away!" And down you go to the pit that is bottomless, and roll forever downward —

downward—downward—ne'er to find a resting-place for the sole of your feet. Ye shall be cast out.

And *where are you to be cast to?* Ye are to be cast "into outer darkness;" ye are to be put in the place where there will be no hope. For, by "light," in Scripture, we understand "hope;" and you are to be put "into outer darkness," where there is no light—no hope. Is there a man here who has no hope? I cannot suppose such a person. One of you, perhaps, says, "I am thirty pounds in debt, and shall be sold up by-and-by; but I have a hope that I may get a loan, and so escape my difficulty." Says another, "My business is ruined, but things may take a turn yet—I have a hope." Says another, "I am in great distress, but I hope that God will provide for me." Another says, "I am fifty pounds in debt; I am sorry for it; but I will set these strong hands to work, and do my best to get out of it." One of you thinks a friend is dying, but you have a hope that, perhaps, the fever may take a turn—that he may yet live. But, in hell, there is no hope. They have not even the hope of dying—the hope of being annihilated. They are forever—forever—forever—lost! On every chain in hell, there is written "forever." In the fires, there blazes out the words, "forever." Up above their heads, they read "forever." Their eyes are galled, and their hearts are pained with the thought that it is "forever." Oh! if I could tell you to-night that hell would one day be burned out, and that those who were lost might be saved, there would be a jubilee in hell at the very thought of it. But it cannot be—it is "*forever*" they are "cast into utter darkness."

But I want to get over this as quickly as I can; for

who can bear to talk thus to his fellow creatures? What is it that the lost are doing? They are "weeping and gnashing their teeth." Do you gnash your teeth now? You would not do it except you were in pain and agony. Well, in hell there is always gnashing of teeth. And do you know why? There is one gnashing his teeth at his companion, and mutters, "I was led into hell by you; you led me astray, you taught me to drink the first time." And the other gnashes his teeth and says, "What if I did? you made me worse than I should have been in after times." There is a child who looks at her mother, and says, "Mother, you trained me up to vice." And the mother gnashes her teeth again at the child, and says, "I have no pity for you, for you excelled me in it, and led me into deeper sin." Fathers gnash their teeth at their sons, and sons at their fathers. And, methinks, if there are any who will have to gnash their teeth more than others, it will be seducers, when they see those whom they have led from the paths of virtue, and hear them saying, "Ah! we are glad you are in hell with us, you deserve it, for you led us here." Have any of you, to-night, upon your consciences the fact that you have led others to the pit? O may sovereign grace forgive you. "We have gone astray like lost sheep." said David. Now, a lost sheep never goes astray alone, if it is one of a flock. I lately read of a sheep that leaped over the parapet of a bridge, and was followed by every one of the flock. So, if one man goes astray, he leads others with him. Some of you will have to account for others' sins when you get to hell, as well as your own. Oh, what "weeeping and gnashing of teeth" there will be in that pit!

Now shut the black book. Who wants to say any more about it? I have warned you solemnly. I have told you of the wrath to come? The evening darkens and the sun is setting. Ah! and the evenings darken with some of you. I can see gray-headed men here. Are your gray hairs a crown of glory, or a fool's cap to you? Are you on the very verge of heaven, or are you tottering on the brink of your grave, and sinking down to perdition?

Let me warn you, gray-headed men; your evening is coming. O, poor tottering gray-head, wilt thou take the last step into the pit? Let a young child step before thee, and beg thee to consider. There is thy staff — it has nothing of earth to rest upon: and now, ere thou diest, bethink thyself this night; let seventy years of sin start up; let the ghosts of thy forgotten transgressions march before thine eyes. What wilt thou do with seventy wasted years to answer for—with seventy years of criminality to bring before God? God give thee grace this night to repent and to put thy trust in Jesus.

And you middle-aged men are not safe; the evening lowers with you, too; you may soon die. A few mornings ago, I was roused early from my bed, by the request that I would hasten to see a dying man. I hurried off with all speed to see the poor creature; but, when I reached the house, he was dead — a corpse. As I stood in the room, I thought, "Ah! that man little thought he should die so soon." There were his wife and children, and friends — they little thought he should die; for he was hale, strong, and hearty but a few days before. None of you have a lease of your lives. If you have, where is it? Go and see if you have it anywhere in your chest at home. No! ye may die to-morrow. Let me therefore warn you by the mercy of God; let me speak to you as a brother may speak; for I love you, you know I do, and would press the matter home to your hearts. Oh, to be amongst the many who shall be accepted in Christ — how blessed that will be! and God has said that whosoever shall call on his name shall be saved: he casts out none that come unto him through Christ.

And now, ye youths and maidens, one word with you. Perhaps ye think that religion is not for you. "Let us be happy," say you: "let us be merry and joyous." How long, young man, how long? "Till I am twenty-one." Are you sure that you will live till then? Let me tell you one thing. If you do live till that time, if you have no heart for God now, you will have none then. Men do not get better if left alone. It is with them as with a garden: if you let it alone, and permit weeds to grow, you will not expect to find it better in six months — but worse. Ah! men talk as if they could repent when they like. It is the work of God to give us repentance. Some even say, "I shall turn to God on such-and-such a day. Ah! if you felt aright, you would say, "I must run to God, and ask him to give me repentance now, lest I should die before I have found Jesus Christ, my Saviour."

Now, one word in conclusion. I have told you of heaven and hell; what is the way, then, to escape from hell and to be found in heaven? I will not tell you my old tale again to-night. I recollect when I told it you before, a good friend in the crowd said, "Tell us something fresh, old fellow." Now really, in preaching ten times a week, we cannot always say things fresh. You have heard John Gough, and you know he tells his tales over again. I have nothing but the old gospel. "He that believeth and is baptized shall be saved." There is nothing here of works. It does not say, "He who is a good man shall be saved," but "he who believes and is baptized." Well, what is it to believe? It is to put your trust entirely upon Jesus. Poor Peter once believed, and Jesus Christ said to him, "Come on, Peter, walk to me on the water." Peter went stepping along on the tops of the waves without sinking; but when he looked at the waves, he began to tremble, and down he went. Now, poor sinner, Christ says, "Come on; walk on your sins; come to me;" and if you do, he will give you power. If you believe on Christ, you will be able to walk over your sins — to tread upon them and overcome them. I can remember the time when my sins first stared me in the face. I thought myself the most accursed of all men. I had not committed any very great open transgressions against God; but I recollected that I had been well trained and tutored, and I thought my sins were thus greater than other people's. I cried to God to have mercy; but I feared that he would not pardon me. Month after month, I cried to God, but he did not hear me, and I knew not what it was to be saved. Sometimes I was so weary of the world that I desired to die; but then I recollected that there was a worse world after this, and that it would be an ill matter to rush before my Maker unprepared. At times I wickedly thought God a most heartless tyrant, because he did not answer my prayer; and then, at others, I thought, "I deserve his displeasure; if he sends me to hell, he will be just." But I remember the hour when I stepped into a little place of worship, and saw a tall, thin man step into the pulpit: I have never seen him from that day, and probably never shall, till we meet in heaven. He opened the Bible and read, with a feeble voice, "Look unto me, and be ye saved all the ends of the earth; for I am God, and beside me there is none else." Ah! thought I, I am one of the ends of the earth; and then turning round, and fixing his gaze on me, as if he knew me, the minister said, "Look, look, look." Why, I thought I had a great deal to *do*, but I found it was only to *look*. I thought I had a garment to spin out for myself; but I found that if I looked, Christ would give me a garment. Look, sinner, that is to be saved. Look unto him, all ye ends of the earth, and be saved. That is what the Jews did, when Moses held up the brazen serpent. He said, "Look!" and they looked. The serpent might be twisting round them, and they might be nearly dead; but they simply looked, and the moment they looked, the serpent dropped off, and they were healed. Look to Jesus, sinner. "None but Jesus can do helpless sinners good." There is a hymn we often sing, but which I do not think is quite right. It says,

> "Venture on him, venture wholly;
> Let no other trust intrude."

Now, it is no venture to trust in Christ, not in the least; he who trusts in Christ is quite secure. I recollect that, when dear John Hyatt was dying, Matthew Wilks said to him, in his usual tone, "Well, John, could you trust your soul in the hands of Jesus Christ now?" "Yes," said he, "a million! a million souls!" I am sure that every Christian that has ever trusted in Christ can say

Amen to that. Trust in him; he will never deceive you My blessed Master will never cast you away.

I cannot speak much longer, and I have only to thank you for your kindness. I never saw so large a number so still and quiet. I do really think, after all the hard things that have been said, that the English people know who loves them, and that they will stand by the man who stands by them. I thank every one of you; and above all, I beg you, if there be reason or sense in what I have said, bethink yourselves of what you are, and may the Blessed Spirit reveal to you your state! May he show you that you are dead, that your are lost, ruined. May he make you feel what a dreadful thing it would be to sink into hell! May he point you to heaven! May he take you as the angel did of old, and put his hand upon you, and say, "Flee! flee! flee! Look to the mountain; look not behind thee; stay not in all the plain." And may we all meet in heaven at last; and there we shall be happy forever.

P. S. This sermon was watered by many prayers of the faithful in Zion. The preacher did not intend it for publication; but seeing that it is now in print, he will not apologize for its faulty composition or rambling style; but instead thereof, he would beg the prayers of his readers, that this feeble sermon may all the more exalt the honor of God, by the salvation of many who shall read it. "The excellency of the power is of God, and not of man."

www.ingramcontent.com/pod-product-compliance
Lightning Source LLC
LaVergne TN
LVHW010155110826
845151LV00002B/526

* 9 7 8 1 4 2 5 5 3 8 0 6 4 *